GYM SHOES AND IRISES

(PERSONALIZED TZEDAKAH)

BOOK TWO

CAROLINA AGENCY FOR
JEWISH EDUCATION
P.O. BOX 13574
CHARLOTTE, N.C. 28270

BOOKS BY DANNY SIEGEL

Essays

1980 -   ANGELS (out of print)

1982 -   GYM SHOES AND IRISES
          (Personalized Tzedakah)

1987 -   GYM SHOES AND IRISES - BOOK TWO

Poetry

1969 -   SOULSTONED (out of print)

1976 -   AND GOD BRAIDED EVE'S HAIR (out of print)

1978 -   BETWEEN DUST AND DANCE (out of print)

1980 -   NINE ENTERED PARADISE ALIVE (out of print)

1983 -   UNLOCKED DOORS
          (An Anthology)

1985 -   THE GARDEN:
          Where Wolves and Lions Do No Harm
          to the Sheep and the Deer

1985 -   THE LORD IS A WHISPER AT MIDNIGHT
          (Psalms and Prayers)

1986 -   BEFORE OUR VERY EYES
          Readings for a Journey Through Israel

Midrash and Halachah

1983 -   WHERE HEAVEN AND EARTH TOUCH
          (Book One)

1984 -   WHERE HEAVEN AND EARTH TOUCH
          (Book Two)

1985 -   WHERE HEAVEN AND EARTH TOUCH
          (Book Three)

1985 -   WHERE HEAVEN AND EARTH TOUCH
          SOURCE BOOK
          (Selected Hebrew and Aramaic Sources)

Humor

1982 -   THE UNORTHODOX BOOK OF JEWISH
          RECORDS AND LISTS
          (With Allan Gould)

Gym Shoes and Irises
(PERSONALIZED TZEDAKAH)

BOOK TWO
WITH A LISTING OF OVER 100 TZEDAKAH PEOPLE AND PROJECTS

Danny Siegel

THE TOWN HOUSE PRESS
Spring Valley, New York

Author's Note: The photograph on the front cover has been
retouched. No destruction nor desecration of United States
currency is intended.

Library of Congress Catalogue Card Number: 86-105737
International Standard Book Number: 0-940653-03-6

First Printing, 1987

Cover by Jay Wolke

For Ordering:
The Town House Press
28 Midway Road, Spring Valley NY 10977

For all the people—
The Mitzvah Heroes,
The Good People,
The Tzedakah Geniuses
and Righteous Ones—
who do their glorious work
so quietly
they are known only to those
whose lives they touch.

ACKNOWLEDGMENTS

I am grateful to all of the following people who have helped me complete this book. I hope I have included all of them:

Phyllis Greene, Howard Wasserman, Louise Cohen, Stacy Bunnage, Dr. Abraham Gittelson, Shulamit Gittelson, Nina Bunin, Melanie Berman, Dr. Diane Jacobstein, David Shneyer, Garth Potts, Dr. Leora Weinstein, Jules Gutin, Rabbi Joseph Braver, Marci Fox, Judy Kupchan, Aileen Zarin, David Bell, Marc Sternfeld, Dr. Mark Mannis, Judy Mannis, Dr. Jay Masserman, Rabbi Marc Wilson, the students of Temple Beth Ami, Rockville, MD, Arnold and Anita Bogus, Jacob Kabb, Rabbi Sylvan Kamens, Sandy Silverstein, Trude Holzmann, Jane Berkey, Harriet Hoffman, David Morris, Glenn Easton, Barbara Bermack, Rabbi Mordecai Kieffer, Rabbi Moshe Edelman, Rabbi Barry Dov Lerner, Reuven Lerner, Bruce Greenfield, Diane Schilit, Rabbi Steven M. Glazer, Dr. J. Steven Kahan, Bena Siegel, Rabbi Michael Katz, Rabbi Michael Zedek, Suzanne Gladney, Rabbi Abraham Morhaim, Rabbi Jack Moline, Rich Moline, Brenda Rosenbaum, Erica Raphael, Dr. Tobie Bresloff, Dr. M.J. Willard, Sue Strong, Rabbi Ron Hoffberg, Allan and Joyce Sugarman, Rabbi Gary Greene, Kate Kinser, Reverend Harold Wilke, Jack and Sandy Gruenberg, Gloria Eisman, Rabbi Leon Waldman, Allan and Merle Gould, Gloria Eiseman, and Hanan Alexander.

The author expresses his gratitude to the Jewish Publication Society of America for permission to use quotes from their translations of *The Torah* (1962), *The Prophets,* (1978), and *The Writings* (1982).

Various articles have appeared in the following publications: *New Traditions, Moment Magazine, United Synagogue Youth, Tikkun Olam Publications, The Reconstructionist, Jewish Education Quarterly, Canadian Forum* (Toronto), *California Magazine.*

I am grateful to following people who provided photographs for this book: Louise Cohen, Joel Grishaver of Torah Aura Productions, Rabbi Mordecai Kieffer, Barbara Bermack, North American Jewish Students Network, Dr. Tobie Bresloff, Dr. M.J. Willard, Sue Strong, Rabbi Michael Zedek, Rita Nannini, and The Council on Jewish Life of the Jewish Federation Council of Greater Los Angeles.

TABLE OF CONTENTS

SYLVIA ORZOFF'S MITZVAH

LOS ANGELES: In 23 years of collecting money in a blue-and-white tin can in front of Canter's Deli on Fairfax Avenue, Sylvia Orzoff, 76, has netted more than $2 million for the Jewish National Fund.

California Magazine
November 1986

116 PRACTICAL MITZVAH SUGGESTIONS

(In No Particular Order of Importance)

1. Pick some immediately-solvable Tzedakah situation and solve it: shoes, holiday meal, table and chairs for recently-arrived immigrant family, space heater, large print prayerbook for synagogues. Get to know the feeling that you have done something easy that makes a difference. Flex your Mitzvah muscles.

2. Put a booksale rack for Jewish books in your synagogue or JCC lobby. Overcharge for the books and give the difference to Tzedakah.

3. Learn some magic, clowning, and balloon-animal making and use these skills in local institutions and for agencies such as Big Brother and Big Sister programs. It is a great way to do the Mitzvah of Bikkur Cholim —Visiting the Sick — in pediatrics wards of hospitals. (Debra Friedmann, alias Panda the Clown, is willing to offer help in this area: 4615 Verplanck Place, NW, Washington, DC 20016, 202-364-1505.)

4. Establish a Flower Committee to take leftover flowers from synagogue and other Jewish communal events to shelters, hospitals, or residences for the elderly.

5. Plant trees in Israel in honor of friends for specific occasions (or in memory of friends who have passed away).

6. Plant trees in Israel for others for no particular reason at all.

7. Open a separate checking account for Tzedakah and deposit a portion of your income as soon as it arrives.

8. Contribute to your local UJA-Federation campaign.

9. Take a tour of your local Tzedakah agencies, Federation-sponsored and other, private-organizations. (Some communities, like San Francisco, take contributors on a day-long bus tour.) Ask questions, learn about the workings of the agency, and get involved.

10. Seek out the local Mitzvah heroes. Meet them, talk to them, invite them to speak to community groups (particularly the religious schools). Apprentice yourself to one of them.

11. Install a food barrel in your local synagogue or other Jewish communal building. Collect food and distribute to individuals in need, either through local agencies or individual contacts. Have children and adults decorate the food barrel together.

12. Purchase a Soviet Jewry bracelet through your local Soviet Jewry organization. Wear the bracelet until that specific Refusenik is free, then replace it with another. (Nationally — contact: National Conference on Soviet Jewry, 10 E. 40th St., #907, NY, NY 10016, 212-679-6122. It goes without saying that letter writing to American, Canadian, and Soviet officials are appropriate aspects of this project.)

13. Seek out unused Yiddish books in your library, in your friends' libraries, and community libraries and send them to the National Yiddish Book Center. (POB 969, Old East Street School, Amherst, MA 01004, 413-256-1241.) They have people around the United States and Canada ("Zamlers") who will help with the shipping. (By consulting local Sefardi Jews, you might want to help set up a similar project for books in Ladino.)

14. Make a home-made Tzedakah box (Pushka) for your home. When it is full, have the entire family decide where the money should go.

15. Have your synagogue give a Tzedakah box to every bar and bat mitzvah kid. Ideal synagogue gift for weddings, Chanukat HaBayit (moving into a new home), conversion, and other occasions. Get residents of the local residence for the elderly to make the Tzedakah boxes. (This is a most successful program at The Temple - Congregation B'nai Jehudah, Kansas City. Contact Rabbi Michael Zedek, 712 E. 69th St., Kansas City, MO 64131, 816-363-1050.)

16. Have the synagogue provide a Tzedakah box for every family unit. A good time to distribute them is when people come to pick up their High Holiday tickets.

17. At organizational programs and meetings, have each member give $1.00 to a specific member. That person will become the Shaliach/Shelichah-Messenger to distribute the money. At the next meeting, he or she reports on the allocation, unless there is a need for secrecy about the recipient.

18. Call your Rabbi and ask about his or her private Tzedakah discretionary fund. Indicate that your are willing to be "on call" if emergencies arise and extra assistance is needed. Rabbis know of an incredibly wide range of Tzedakah situations where secrecy is an absolute must. This is a great way to be an anonymous miracle worker.

19. Pick one night of Channukah when you will want relief from the burden and craziness of giving gifts, and donate the money you would have used for a gift to Tzedakah. Buy extra gifts and give them to those who would not otherwise have Channukah presents.

20. Ask the finder of the Afikoman on Passover if he or she would be willing to have the cost of the gift given to Tzedakah instead. Contribute to that individual's favorite Tzedakah.

21. Contribute the money you would have used for food on Yom Kippur or other fast days to MAZON or other organizations helping to feed the hungry. (MAZON: 2288 Westwood Blvd., #200, Los Angeles, CA 90064, 213-470-7769, Irving Cramer, Director.)

22. Tie in all kinds of personal celebrations with Tzedakah — birthdays, promotions, graduations, anniversaries, etc. — by asking relatives and friends to contribute to Tzedakah in your honor. Specify which are your favorite Tzedakah projects.

23. At various celebrations, instead of floral centerpieces, have a card

noting that the cost of the flowers was contributed to Tzedakah. Or:

  (a) Have a centerpiece made of books, to be contributed to a local synagogue or Jewish communal library.
  (b) Have trees planted in honor of the guests, with their certificates on the tables.
  (c) Have cans of food, to be donated after the celebration to a local agency that will channel the food to hungry people.
  (d) All of the above.

24. Encourage the synagogue to sell a Torah, prayerbooks, or other items they may have more than enough of, and use the money from the sale for Tzedakah. (Jewish Law support this practice. "We may sell a synagogue, and, similarly all holy objects — even a Sefer Torah — in order to provide for Torah students or to marry off orphans with the money from-the sales." [Shulchan Aruch, Orach Chaim 153:6.]) There is always a need for Jewish education scholarships, and we may easily extend the meaning of "orphans" to include some community members who may feel disadvantaged, lonely, alienated, or in some way feel distanced from the community. Some Mitzvah people I know would include latchkey kids, the elderly, single-parent families, singles, widows and widowers, people with disabilities — any one of a number people — in this group.

25. Adopt "The Tzedakah Habit" of buying an extra item of food whenever you go grocery shopping — for distribution to hungry people.

26. Label one shelf of your food pantry "Tzedakah Food" so you, family, and friends will remember which items have been set aside for Tzedakah.

27. Encourage your local bakeries and grocery stores to channel day-old and leftover foods for local pantries, soup kitchens, and shelters for the homeless.

28. Go "Dumpster Dipping" — take friends to dumpsters at local supermarkets to salvage still-edible and usable foods. Distribute to local pantries, soup kitchens, and shelters.

29. At organizational meetings and programs, have people bring in a can of food for the organization's food barrel.

30. After checking the Health Code, find ways to take leftover food from Jewish communal affairs to appropriate recipients. Encourage local Jewish caterers to get involved. (Call City Harvest, 212-349-4004 for details.)

31. Have your synagogue ask each member to bring a non-perishable food item for the food barrel before Kol Nidray begins.

32. Before Passover, collect the Chametz you are removing from your house, and , using the synagogue as a drop-off point, distribute it to a local food pantry.

33. Have your synagogue and caterers adopt the MAZON project where 3% of the cost of an affair is donated to MAZON. The contributions

are used by MAZON to feed the hungry. (See #21 for MAZON address.)

34. Do your own individualized holiday food project: buy provisions for a family for Rosh HaShana, Purim, Channukah, etc. Channel the provisions through an agency who will locate a family who would need the food. (You won't need to know the recipients, and they won't know you. There's always a middle-person.)

35. Organize a "Cook for a Friend" project whereby you prepare food in your own kitchen. The agency gives you containers; you freeze the items, drop them off at the Cook for a Friend center, and they do the distributing. (Contact: Cook for a Friend, c/o Judy Schwartz, 6600 Bustleton Ave., Philadelphia, PA 19149, 215-338-9800.) Also, get involved in the local "Meals on Wheels" program.

36. Establish a food pantry in your synagogue. (Contact Congregation Tifereth Israel, 3219 Sheridan Blvd., Lincoln, NE 68502, 402-423-8569, which has one.)

37. Visit the shelters, food banks, and soup kitchens in your town and locate Jewish street people. Organize a program in the Jewish community to provide services for them. (Contact: Project Dorot, 262 W. 91st St., NY, NY 10024, 212-769-2850. They have a shelter on the Upper West Side of Manhattan.)

38. Establish a shelter for the homeless in your synagogue. (Contact: Temple Israel, 1180 University Dr., NE, Atlanta, GA 30306, 404-873-3147 or Temple Israel, 1014 Dilworth Road, Charlotte NC 28203, 704-376-2796.)

39. People involved in organizational Tzedakah work — Hadassah, ORT, Sisterhoods, Federations, synagogue, youth groups — tell your family and friends *exactly* what Mitzvah work you are doing and why you are doing it. (I am shocked by how many children of involved parents — and parents of involved children — have no idea why the parent or child is always going to meetings, making phone calls, doing mailings. The higher aspects of the Tzedakah work often get lost in the organizational shuffle.)

40. Parents — inform your driving-age children that they are expected to use the car a certain percentage of the time for Mitzvah work.

41. Organize a synagogue Tzedakah committee to cover very direct Mitzvah work. (Contact: Marlboro, NJ, Jewish Center Tzedakah Committee, POB 98, School Road West, Marlboro, NJ 07746, 201-536-2300. Chairperson: Anita Bogus, home phone: 201-536-3358.)

42. Computerize your organization's mailing list to include the members' occupations and special interests. Inquire as to what limit merchants and professionals are willing to donate goods and services for specific Mitzvah projects. (Do *not* exceed their expressed limits. Respect the bounds they set.)

43. Make your synagogue and Jewish communal buildings accessible to individuals with disabilities. (See Appendix B.)

44. Purchase large print and braille editions of the prayerbook, Chumash, Machzor, Megillot.

45. Establish a large print and braille section of your synagogue and agency library. Ask visually impaired individuals which books they might want. Publicize this service in the synagogue or agency bulletin and local newspapers. (For large print and braille books of Jewish interest, contact: The Jewish Braille Institute of America, 110 E. 30th St., NY, NY 10016, 212-889-2525 and The Jewish Welfare Board Jewish Book Council, 15 E. 26th St., NY, NY 10010, 212-LE 2-4949.)

46. Print some copies of your synagogue or agency bulletin and announcements in large print.

47. Organize a Large Print Xerox Committee to: (1) inquire which books individuals with visual impairments would want to read (2) find someone with a xerox machine that enlarges, (3) write the publisher to ask for permission to reproduce the book in larger print by xeroxing it, (4) xerox the book, (5) deliver to individuals, agencies and/or libraries.

48. Encourage Jewish book publishers to publish some, more, or all of their books in large print. Specific publishers include: Jewish Publication Society, Jonathan David, United Synagogue, UAHC, and Reconstructionist Presses.

49. Have your synagogue or library subscribe to the Large Print Edition of the New York Times.

50. Install a special sound system (infrared, audio loop, etc.) in your synagogue and agency meeting rooms for people with hearing impairments.

51. Encourage synagogues and local agencies to purchase TDD's (Telecommunications Devices for the Deaf) which will allow the community's deaf members to use the phone system to allow them to be tied into communal events. Price range: $150 and up.

52. Have synagogue services and communal events signed for the hearing impaired members of the community. Inquire which members already know sign language . . . it is often a pleasant surprise to know that such resource people are often already available.

53. Set up courses to teach sign language, or sign up for an already-established course. Be sure to learn the contemporary Jewish terms in sign language. (Contact: Rabbi Dan Grossman, Temple Sinai, Dillon Rd. and Limekiln Pike, Dresher, PA 19025, 215-643-6510.)

54. Purchase prayerbooks, Chumashim, Machzorim, etc. with Russian, Spanish, Ladino, Farsi, Yiddish, or other translations for synagogue members who will appreciate services more with these translations handy.

55. Establish a group home or group homes for Jewish retarded adults in your community. (Contact: The Jewish Foundation for Group Homes, 11710 Hunters Lane, Rockville, MD 20852, 301-984-3839.)

56. If there are already group homes in the community, make certain the residents are part of synagogue, JCC, and community programs. Help facilitate the transportation.

57. When you hear of protests against group homes in a neighborhood, organize committees of people to show your support. Particularly encourage the religious school students to take part in the process.

58. Contact local general group homes and institutions to locate Jewish residents. Provide services for them (holiday celebrations, get-togethers, visits), and extend invitations to communal events. (Contact: Rabbi Leib Heber, c/o Western Pennsylvania Auxiliary for Exceptional People, 281 Sharon Dr., Pittsburgh, PA 15221, 412-421-1757. He is a giant in this area of Mitzvah work.)

59. Have the local special needs individuals participate in Super Sunday, the UJA-Federation's annual major phonathon. Two or three of my friends from different cities indicate that this has been extraordinarily successful in their communities. Similarly, they should be invited to other fund-raiding events where their people-power may be needed.

60. Encourage synagogues and agencies to mention on stationery, bulletins, newsletters, and publicity what accessibility there is for their buildings and programs. (Holiday Inns and churches do it.)

61. Insure that as many parts of the Jewish communal building are wheelchair accessible. For synagogues, this should include the Bima, or, if that is architecturally impossible, then parts of the service should be conducted from ground level if possible.

62. Encourage all national synagogue organizations, National UJA, Council of Jewish Federations, Jewish Welfare Board, and other national organizations to publish their directories with notations indicating which buildings have what kind of access for people with disabilities.

63. Purchase for yourselves, your children, grandchildren, synagogue and/or communal agencies the special dolls that represent children with disabilities. Started as a small project out West under the "Hal's Pals" label, they are now being manufactured and marketed by Mattel, with all profits going to Tzedakah projects benefitting children with disabilities. (Contact Mattel: 800-421-2887.)

64. Downgrade a testimonial dinner to a dessert reception. Contribute the difference in cost to Tzedakah.

65. Establish a Tzedakah-Newspaper-and-Magazine-Clipping Committee to scan the papers and magazines for Tzedakah articles to be shared with your group. Review at least one article before each meeting or event. Compile a scrapbook and share it with religious school children and members of the youth group.

66. Encourage your local newspaper, or synagogue or agency bulletin to publish a regular "Be An Angel" column. Specific projects in need of specific goods and services and contributions are described, . . . encouraging the readers to take part. (Contact: Denver's *Rocky Mountain News,* 303-892-5381.)

67. Conduct a clothing drive for local individuals in need.

68. When cleaning out the closet and selecting clothes to give away, recite some formula such as, "I am now about to perform the Mitzvah of Halbashat Arumim — providing clothes for those in need of them." If you have children, make sure they are aware that this is a specific and important Mitzvah stretching back many centuries in Jewish tradition and not just a "something or other" we do now and again. Also, it is important, on occasion, to give away clothes that we would still use.

69. Organize drivers to insure that non-drivers, elderly, infirm, partially-able, or all-alone members of the community can take part in community events.

70. Seek out your local Jewish interest-free loan society. If there is one, find ways to make their work better known in the community. If there isn't, set one up. (Contact: Julius Blackman, President, Association of Hebrew Free Loan Societies, 703 Market St., #445, San Francisco, CA 94103, 415-982-3177.)

71. Get a computer whiz kid to computerize a series of projects — volunteers, times, places, and other details . . . . a good way to integrate the youth into Mitzvah work, and a fine way to use a computer.

72. Set up a local Jewish Big Brother and/or Big Sister Program for the benefit of latchkey children or any other children who might need such a program.

73. Adopt a recently-arrived immigrant family. This was a major project in many cities when the Boat People arrived from Southeast Asia. There is still a need.

74. Encourage your Jewish Community Center to make all facilities of the building — gym, pool, day care, message service — available to individuals presently seeking jobs through Jewish Vocational Service, Jewish Family Service, or other agencies. During the tense, often-depressing interim period between jobs, this can be a most welcome contribution to the well-being of the unemployed person. (Contact: Jewish Community Center, 6701 Hoover Rd., Indianapolis, IN 46260, 317-251-9467.)

75. Start a Jewish hospice program in your community. (National Institute for Jewish Hospice, 6363 Wilshire Blvd., #126, Los Angeles, CA 90048, 213-653-0795.)

76. Start a program for Jewish alcoholics, chemically dependent individuals, and gamblers in your community. (Contact JACS — Jewish

Alcoholics, Chemically Dependent Persons and Significant Others Foundation, Inc., 10 E. 73rd St., NY, NY 10021, 212-879-8415.)

77. Help revive or stabilize a synagogue whose membership has moved away. (e.g., The Stanton St. Synagogue on the Lower East Side of New York, through the efforts of Project Ezra; The Tremont Street Synagogue, Cambridge, MA, through the efforts of college and graduate students and leftover '60's people in Boston.)

78. Ask the principal of the religious school if you could come in and talk to the pre-bar/bat mitzvah groups about giving some of their money away to Tzedakah and or other Mitzvah projects they might tie in with the celebration.

79. Encourage your synagogue to establish "twinning" with Soviet Jews for the bar/bat mitzvah students. When the bar/bar mitzvah kid is assigned a specific twin, double-check with the Soviet Jewry agency to make certain the family in the Soviet Union wants to receive letters. (There have been some glitches.)

80. Encourage the bar/bat mitzvah kid to go to a jewelry store to get a special bracelet made with his or her twin's name on it.

81. Encourage bar/bat mitzvah families to invite members of the elderly community to the event, from the old age residence or independent housing.

82. Establish a special "twinning" program with Jewish special education children and adults for the bar and bat mitzvah program. Match up a bar or bat mitzvah kid with one of the special people to share the day.

83. Encourage bar and bat mitzvah celebrations for individuals in Jewish special education programs in the community.

84. Ask if your local Jewish old age residence allows pets (either visiting pets or permanent pets). If they do not, start a pet therapy program, consulting your veterinarian for details. Take your own pet for visits (except if your dog is call "Fang", or your boa constrictor, "Coil".)

85. Ask if your local zoo will bring pets to old age residences for programs. Set up an intergenerational program with the religious school, always an enjoyable and entertaining event. (The Utica Zoo, for example, has such programs.)

86. Start an intergenerational choir, choral group, or band.

87. Locate the Jewish elderly in non-Jewish old age residences and provide for them. (Contact: Jewish Chaplain, UJA-Federation, 7900 Wisconsin Ave., Bethesda, MD 20814, 301-652-6480.)

88. Approach the mayor of your community and ask to set up a bookbindery. The books would be bound by the elderly, the books themselves — the schoolbooks of the local schoolchildren. (This is how

Life Line for the Old got started in Jerusalem.)

89. Have your synagogue giftshop market the products of Life Line for the Old. (Contact: Linda Kantor, President, American Friends of Life Line for the Old, 52 Wellington Dr., Orange, CT 06477, 203-795-4580.)

90. Start your own mini-Life Line for the Old — independent workshops where the elderly make products for sale. Through the synagogue, JCC, home for the aged, or independent housing — start with one workshop, a few elderly people and a few teen-agers, making things together: challah covers, matza covers, yarmulkas, Tzedakah boxes, sweaters, . . . anything. Begin, perhaps, with products that can be used by various agencies (such as yarmulkas), to gain high visibility. (At the Jewish Welfare Board Biennial Convention in Boston, 1984, there were 500 yarmulkas, and challah covers for each Shabbat table, made by the Boston Jewish elderly.)

91. Encourage your cantor, choir, singers, or just plain people with good voices to sing at hospitals, institutions, and other places where this will be appreciated. (Contact, Cantorial School, Jewish Theological Seminary, 3080 Broadway, NY, NY 10017, 212-678-8000.)

92. Encourage your barber or hairdresser to cut and style the hair of individuals in local old age residences and institutions free of charge. Also a good project in local shelters. (If you cut hair yourself, volunteer to do it.)

93. If you are a merchant or a professional, sell some of your merchandise or give some of your services at a discount, asking the ''discountee'' to give the difference to Tzedakah. Set reasonable limits on how much you can handle, pick which friends you think will respond, and encourage them to support your favorite projects.

94. Canvass audiologists, hospital hearing centers, old age residences, and other likely sources, and collect hearing aids that are no longer being used. Have a Tzedakah Messenger deliver them to Yad Sara in Israel — they will repair them and lend them for free to people who need them. The same for eyeglass frames. Other supplies (glucometers, crutches, etc.) are very much needed. (Contact: Yad Sara, ATTN: Uri Lupoliansky, 43 HaNevi'im St., Jerusalem, 02-244-047.)

95. Encourage local physicians, nurses, and other healthcare professionals to re-cycle equipment they no longer use, or to purchase new items at discount at cost, and have them taken to Yad Sara.

96. Encourage your dentist and dental technicians to do the same with dental equipment for the dental clinics at Life Line for the Old or Yad Ezra. (Life Line for the Old, 14 Shivtei Yisrael St., Jerusalem, 02-287-829; Yad Ezra, 15 HaRav Sorotzkin St., Jerusalem, 02-526-133.)

97. Encourage your plumber, electrician, carpenter, handy-people to offer their services for free to agencies that will link them up with individuals

who need the repairs done, but cannot afford to pay. If you, yourself, are such a handy-person, volunteer your own services.

98. Encourage attorneys, accountants, and investment counselors to do *pro bono* work for (a) Jewish communal agencies, and (b) individuals these agencies might want to refer to them.

99. Conduct seminars for attorneys, accountants, and investment counselors to study the ins and outs of encouraging people to give more. (How far may one go when suggesting contributions — arm-twisting, mild suggesting, strong urging, etc.?)

100. Using your local computer whiz, establish a Furniture-Utensil-Vehicle Committee which will keep track of people who no longer need certain items, and who, on the other end, might need them. The committee can serve as the intermediary for the transfer at no cost, cost, minimal cost, or symbolic cost.

101. Hold a Marathon Tzedakah Day, combining study about the Mitzvah and specific Mitzvahs that can be done within the time frame. Eight hours is a good start.

102. Gather friends for an evening of Tzedakah storytelling. Share the stories and review together the insights gained from them. They should be stories from your own life, or from what you have heard or read.

103. Build up a private Tzedakah library: books, videos, slide shows, tape-interviews with Mitzvah heroes, and newsletters from various Tzedakah groups.

104. Work through an existing fund, or set up a special fund, to purchase Encyclopaedia Judaicas for individuals, which they will pay for in easy monthly payments, interest free (of course). Cost: $498.00; $536.36 in New York. (Contact: EJ Project, c/o Shaare Zedek Hospital, 49 W. 45th St., NY, NY 10036, 212-354-8801.)

105. Set up a seminar for highschool seniors, informing them of what kinds of Tzedakah projects are available on college campuses. (Contact: National Hillel, 1640 Rhode Island Ave., NW, Washington, DC 20036, 202-857-6560, and Los Angeles Hillel Council Mitzvah Project, 900 Hilgard Ave., Los Angeles, CA 90024, 213-208-6639.)

106. If you are a grandparent, invite your grandchildren out for an afternoon when you can tell them Tzedakah stories from your own life, and that of your parents and grandparents, to give them a good sense of the continuity of this Mitzvah through the generations.

107. Give blood.

108. With your Rabbi, research the issue of donating corneas and/or other body organs.

109. Write an Ethical Will and put it in your safe deposit box. The

document should contain your feelings about what values you consider important as a Jew: caring, Tzedakah, kindness, decency, etc. (Consult: *Ethical Wills,* Riemer and Stampfer, Schocken Books, 1983.)

110. Consult your Rabbi during the week, asking who is in the hospital, and offer to make rounds. Establish a Bikkur Cholim-Visiting the Sick Committee. Similarly, consult the Rabbi concerning making a Minyan for people sitting Shiva.

111. Establish a synagogue or community Hachnassat Orchim-Welcoming Committee, where committee members visit people new to the community, welcome them, and introduce them to the nature and structure of the community. Congregation Beth Sholom of San Francisco, at the end of services, asks new people in the congregation to stand up and introduce themselves so that members can more easily welcome them.

112. Inquire about getting involved in your local Chevra Kaddisha-Burial Society. Many cities need people to sit by the bodies during the night before the funeral (Shemirat HaMet). The movie, "A Plain Pine Box" is an excellent introduction to this area of Mitzvah work. (Movie — Adath Jeshurun Congregation, 3400 Dupont Ave. S., Minneapolis, MN 55408, 612-824-2685.)

113. Organize a synagogue or community Mitzvah Trip to Israel, doing part-time "regular" touring, and Mitzvah work the rest of the time. (Consult: Rabbi Ron Hoffberg, c/o Temple Beth El, 338 Walnut Ave., Cranford, NJ 07016, 201-276-9231.)

114. On any trip to Israel, always take a larger suitcase than you originally planned to take—fill the extra space with Mitzvah items, e.g., medical supplies for Yad Sara, clothes, etc. Bring back items from Life Line for the Old.

115. Using the computer and computer whiz kid, keep track of which groups and individuals are going to Israel and ask them to deliver some of the Mitzvah items that have been collected. Ask them to bring back items from Life Line for the Old to be sold in the synagogue gift shop.

116. Collect wedding dresses and have them delivered by Mitzvah-Messenger to people in Jerusalem who will put them at the disposal of brides who otherwise could not afford to purchase one. One of the great, unique Mitzvahs. (In Jerusalem, The Rabbanit Bracha Kapach, 12 Lod St., 249-296, or Daniel and Charlotte Kutler, 7 Keren HaYesod St., 233-991.)

Yasher Koach — strength to all who would take part in the Mitzvahs!

INTRODUCTION TO TZEDAKAH

There are no real secrets to good Tzedakah work, no magic formulas, no exotic twists of mental agility. The good will of good people -- and people who want to be good people -- can bring about grand and glorious changes in the world, and these changes can be far more dazzling and extensive than we would normally think possible. In that sense — the extent of what Tzedakah can achieve — there is something mysterious and magical, but the actual doing of the Mitzvah is the simplest-of-simple things: we just do it, and marvellous things happen.

This book is offered as a guide and aid of sorts for those who would wish to pursue the meaning and reality of this Mitzvah. It may be read by itself, before, after, or along with the first volume of *Gym Shoes and Irises*. The covers of the books show a child sharing one act of Tzedakah with her mother, putting money in a Tzedakah box. The bills appear to be torn, and the coins apparently broken, symbolically indicating that each person should give a portion of his or her money to Tzedakah, and the rest of the money is for them to keep and to use as they wish. The sum total of the bills lying on the table is $18 — Chai = Life, because Tzedakah is a Life-force, yielding vigor and insight, strength and stamina to both the recipient and the giver. The child's look is sometimes described by my readers and audiences as a look of awe or amazement, a certain joyous surprise, and, most certainly, admiration. She sees in her mother a role model for a certain pattern of living. This is as it should be: children admiring parents for substantive values, people admiring people for their openheartedness and generosity. In addition, there is a $50 bill in the Tzedakah box. When my photographer, Jay Wolke, was preparing the cover, this was the only element I insisted on, for two reasons: (1) placing it at the bottom is a way of setting the standard, that others should know that, at times, $50 is a recommended contribution, and (2) sometimes we must go beyond nickels, dimes, and dollar bills, and extend ourselves beyond what we are used to because of the great needs that exist in the world. The cover very much expresses much of what these books are all about.

I want people to have non-delusions of grandeur, to be power-hungry, but for Tzedakah power, to want to do bigger, even awe-inspiring things, in this realm, and not to settle for just a minimum of interplay in the lives of others through this Mitzvah. I would hope, in addition, that this Tzedakah work would change us all, in some ways large and small, allowing us to believe that — at least for certain moments in our lives — we are capable of experiencing sublimity, the connectedness of human beings, and the unique grandeur of the human soul.

That is all very high-sounding. But I do not want this book to be "A Philosophy of Tzedakah", nor only "A Teacher's Guide to Tzedakah". Rather, I would want the many ideas to be channeled into the practical suggestions scattered throughout the book. I want the ideas and suggestions to be taken as challenges. I want people to say, "Oh, yes, I could do that in my community." And I want them to read some of the stories and letters, and say, "I, too, could do that." I admit that the book is somewhat fragmented or haphazard. I am more a poet than a dissertation-length book writer, and it was difficult for me to organize so much raw material. And yet, I would think that people can find ideas and practical suggestions throughout the book, with a little untwisting and unbending, ideas and suggestions which are immediately applicable to everyday Mitzvah work. If more and more Tzedakah acts result from the publication of this book, then I will have considered my purpose fulfilled.

I am fully aware that Tzedakah touches on many frustrating and confusing issues, but I have attempted to stress that — despite the massiveness of so much need and the incredible complexities of human inter-relationships — that still, there are places and times where and when anyone can accomplish nearly anything. We are inundated with requests to contribute our time and money to the release of Soviet and Ethiopian Jews and Jews in Arab lands, the needs of Israel, food for the hungry, AIDS victims, homelessness, synagogue demands, scholarships, disaster relief....The list goes on and on, and yet, there is still room to do something, and, not only that, but the simplest of deeds most certainly makes a difference. And the multiplication of these simplest of deeds makes a substantial difference.

And I believe that — contrary to what some educators and many lay-people have told me — I believe that Tzedakah and Menschlichkeit *can* be taught in the classroom, and that as a result, people *can* change — adults and children alike.

I would suppose that there are really two reasons why I am motivated to keep myself involved in Tzedakah, and to attempt to get others involved to a greater extent: One, as mentioned before, is that such simple human activity can really have such an awesome effect on others, and, second, more grizzly, is that all around us we see life treated much too cheaply. We see people treated as meat (instead of flesh and blood), both when they are alive, and even after they have died. Abuses abound, and Tzedakah is meant as one way to counteract this degrading, sometimes lethal, flow of things. If we can relieve some of that indignity and suffering, then we will have done no small thing.

I would now clarify a few issues:

1. In no way do I wish to imply that people should go into Tzedakah work solely as a "feel-good" form of therapy. While it is true that doing the Mitzvah often produces feelings of wellbeing for many people, this book is not a psychology text. Tzedakah should be done because that is what human beings ought to do for others. Or, from a theological standpoint, because it is Mitzvah, literally, a Command, a form of instruction from the divine realm about the nature of people. If, as a a result of performing the act of Tzedakah, people feel good, then that is fine, too. The Talmud would state it this way, *"Sheluchay Mitzvah* - People on Mitzvah Missions will come to no harm." (Pesachim 8b) If we see Life-as-a-Jew as a total Mitzvah Mission, we are assured of protection from the dangers of loss of self-respect, loneliness, and a sense of alienation from life.

2. I have intended to stress that it is important for people to strive to achieve a degree of Menschlichkeit, and that this goal is far more impor-

tant than success in other realms of life. I am not holding myself up as a Mensch. Rather, I see myself as one who looks towards that goal and attempts, in whatever ways my own personal make-up allows, to move closer towards it. That is why I consider it so critical to seek out that quality in others, to associate with the ones who embody this quality, because these serve as guideposts in my own personal search. If, in some places in the book, I seem to brag about the Tzedakah work I have done, or sound self-righteous, this was not my intention. Not by any means. What is meant is that the *striving-towards-Menschlichkeit* is the critical issue. If anything, one of the purposes of this book is to demonstrate that, if I can do it, then *anyone* can.

Indeed, there are times when I say to myself I would have preferred not writing either Tzedakah book at all because it seems that, in places, I am flaunting the goodness of some people, and Mitzavhs really ought to be done quietly. Nevertheless, in our self-centered times, the rules of secrecy and anonymity must be carefully bent and broken. For the sake of Tzedakah education and involvement in Mitzvah work, we are forced to speak of the deeds of others, so that we may all learn from them.

3. I am a bit of a fanatic about Tzedakah. Fanatics get carried away, and, in their enthusiasm, often strew hellfire and brimstone wherever they turn. If, in my hyper-energized state I wrote harshly, I regret having given offense. For my lectures, I always carry note cards that say, "Be Nice", "Be Pleasant", "Be Up", and "Be Positive", because Tzedakah teaching should work from those emotions, and lambasting, if needed at all, should be done with great care. I have met so many people, been in so many places, I see that there are exceptions to nearly all my flaming criticisms. And yet, I had to include these negatives — cheapness, greed, egocentricity — because the negatives also instruct us. So, as a warning to the reader, I would say that what often comes across as an Absolute should be tempered with subsequent phrases (in most cases) or (often) or (sometimes). It is what I call the "Maybe-Not-Completely-So" element of Absolute Rules. There are almost always exceptions.

4. Ultimately, Tzedakah is not enough in the grand scheme of being Jewish and in the continuity of Jewish history. It is but one part — a most critical part — of being Jewish, as are Shabbat and holidays, lifecycle events, our sense of memory, Kashrut, synagogue life, commitment to Israel, the passionate study of Torah, etc. While I have concentrated my writing on this specific Mitzvah, I would not want my readers to think I believe this is all there is to Judaism and being Jewish.

5. Finally, a word about Ziv Tzedakah Fund, my personal Tzedakah project. As the story is told in the first volume of *Gym Shoes,* I fell into this work quite by accident. In a dozen years, the extent of the work has grown and grown (as has the multitude of materials to read), and there have been times that the sheer excess load of work almost caused me to close down the Fund. Ziv has been wonderful work for me, rarely arduous. But

it has sometimes been just too much to do. Since it is only one part of what I do — much of my time being spent in "normal living" — and since I do not wish to expand Ziv so much as to make it a multi-million dollar project (if it entails re-structuring and over-expansion), then I would recommend the following: (1) We always welcome contributions, however (2) I would not want people to read this and conclude, "Aha! Let's call Siegel and get some funding for our project." The projects are often most worthy, but Ziv's Board of Directors has stated, and the policy remains in force, that we are not seeking new projects to fund. Any new places that appear on our reports are found at our own initiative. I beg the indulgence of those who would want to try. We just can't do it; we are at our limit. (I am sure I have said this two or three times in the body of this book.)

What has been most pleasurable about writing this book was the constant need to call friends everywhere, to consult, gather information and materials, photographs, stories, and insights. I was in touch with so many people who helped make this happen, and they are mentioned in the acknowledgements. But the phenomenon itself — this having to be in touch, this being touched by their sensitive conversation, by their giving of themselves — this proves the point of the book: Tzedakah work ties us ever-so-closely to others, with a warm, incredibly gentle touch. I am grateful, and deeply moved.

THINGS I HAVE LEARNED
AFTER A DOZEN YEARS
OF TZEDAKAH WORK

1. There *are* simple solutions to many Tzedakah situations, some of them almost magically easy. I believe there are more simple solutions than we allow for.

The truly complicated and absolutely complex Tzedakah problems are just that: incredibly difficult, some with no solution at all, perhaps never. But those that are simply-solvable should be approached as such, and solved right away.

For example, My Friend the Ophthalmologist, Mark Mannis, linked up with Air Life Line, an association of Mitzvah-minded pilots whose members fly donated organs and doctors to places where they are needed, free of charge or at cost. Twice he has been taken to the Mexican hinterlands where he gave some peasants back their eyesight through corneal transplants, and trained local physicians in techniques that would assure safe follow-up. His services were donated, of course. Simple enough — some who could not see, and who would otherwise have no avenue for a cure for their blindness, now see.

2. There are still many openings left in this world for idealists.

Every Mitzvah has *not* been covered. Idealists, starry-eyed or otherwise, may either link up with existing Tzedakah program or individual Good Folks (Righteous Ones, Tzaddikim), or strike out on their own into the smooth, clear waters of touching people and being touched, in turn, by them. Many projects are waiting to be founded.

Were I to draw on my highschool academic triumphs in mathematics, my A's and A+'s, I would venture the following rule: there are at least as many, if not more, opportunities to soar in the realm of Mitzvahs as there are in the world of business and finance.

3. Individuals *can* make a difference.
Individuals *do* make a difference.

If anything, Tzedakah demonstrates that individuals have immense power, Mitzvah-power. Tzedakah could be considered an antidote to a sense of helplessness in the face of (a) massive numbers of people in need, (b) incredibly complex human entanglements, and (c) the secular society's obsession with power in its non-Mitzvah sense.

That people *can* make a difference is not dependent on numbers of people the individual effects: the one-on-one visits to the sick, the appropriately placed $57 interest-free loan to pay off a hard-pressed person's phone bill, the single pair of shoes, the hat, the dress given to one other person, can ease much pain, much discomfort, untold quantities of worry and suffering.

That individuals *do* make a difference is evidenced practically everywhere you turn in the Tzedakah world: for my generation and before, Schweitzer's move to Africa changed the course of so many lives, as do,

today, the people changed and moved by the many Righteous Ones, the
Saints, the Good Folks, the Mitzvah Heroes.

An example: one of my father's childhood medical stories to me —
not exactly childhood, but in my youth — was the story of Ignaz Semmelweis who, in 19th century Vienna, struggled to teach doctors to wash
their hands between doing autopsies and delivering babies. Such a simple
thing! Laughed at, reviled, he died in a mental institution, though some
had listened to him. Who would dare to calculate how many women since
then are alive today because of this Semmelweis?

And therein lies the trap: the individual should not only set his or her
sights on the Semmelweis's and Salk's and Sabin's. In quieter, less dramatic
ways, Tzedakah can change things, and allow the Tzedakah doer to live
more at peace with the world, with other people, and with himself or
herself.

On a most nitty-gritty level: in our schools, in our teachings, I believe
it is incumbent to drive out, exorcise like a demon, this Demon of
Helplessness. If we could only raise a generation of Jews who, from earliest
days are convinced that All the Power in the World is in their hands —
through Tzedakah — then surely the people they touch, and they
themselves, will know the world to be more Menschlich than we have
known it to be.

4. Though there is too much Tzedakah to be done, and though no
one person can do it all, this does not mean we should not jump in with
vigor and take on the work at hand.

Jewish law recognized the staggering quantity of Tzedakah work that
needs to be accomplished:

> The amount to be given —
> If the person can afford it, sufficient to cover all the needs of the poor.
> If the person cannot afford to cover all those needs, then
> > up to 20% is considered doing the Mitzvah to an
> > exquisite degree,
> > 10% is considered average,
> > and less is considered weak eyesight.
> > > *(Shulchan Aruch, Yoreh De'ah 249:1)*

No single individual can satisfy all the needs, so the law sets limits (with
some specific exceptions at the higher and lower ranges). Jewish tradition
rejects the cynical view that, since it can't *all* be done, then nothing should
be done. Nor does it assume that people are not by nature generous. Rather,
the Shulchan Aruch clearly says, ''Take part to what extent is traditionally
reasonable, and you will see just how much really can be accomplished.

Our tradition empowers us with so much potential and warns us not
to armchair ourselves into watching things fall apart. We are — within limits
— enjoined to repair and fix, renew and bind up.

An example: if each teen-ager took 10-20% of his or her income from
baby-sitting, jobs, allowance, and gift money, I would imagine that there

would be quite a few more million dollars in the world-wide Tzedakah box.

Another example: if as high percentages of Jews gave 10% or more of their incomes to Tzedakah as Mormons do, I would imagine there would be quite a few more million dollars in the world-wide Tzedakah box.

It would take little time to conjure up more and more examples, and more and more Tzedakah situations alleviated with the new inpouring of funds. Not all situations would be solved, but many, many more problems would disappear.

5. People who are involved in Tzedakah do not die of loneliness.

By it's very nature, Tzedakah work must be done with other people. One selection from Rabbinic literature, quoted elsewhere in this article, appears in slightly different form in some texts. Reading into the text for our purposes, the translation would then be:

> Rav said:
> The Mitzvot were given in order to tie God's creatures together.
> *(Yalkut Shimoni, Shemini 535)*

I would invite researchers to conduct an appropriate study to confirm the following assumption: the more that people are involved in Mitzvah work, the less depression, despair, sense of defeat and failure, alcoholism, drug abuse, anorexia, bulimia, and suicide. It would be important to ascertain just how much less, and to develop suggestions for integrating Mitzvah work into therapy programs of all kinds. Psychologists, social workers, teachers, psychiatrists, therapists of many schools, and other specialists could broaden the scope of their work as a result of the findings.

For example: in Israel, Yad Ezra, an array of Mitzvah projects, has a number of programs designed specifically for individuals with mental and emotional difficulties, including a printing shop, sewing and embroidery workshop, and a Yeshiva. One of the Yeshiva's particular programs is packaging and delivering Shabbat and holiday food supplies for individuals in need of them. Their success rate, judging by how many re-integrate fully back into society, is striking.

Another example: Yad LaKashish, Life Line for the Old, in Jerusalem, workshops for the elderly, has begun accepting workers from the city's mental institutions, people who now work side-by-side with the Elders of Jerusalem. Their success rate is also very impressive.

A final, personal example: in over 70% of the telephone area code regions in North America, I have at least one individual who is tied into some of the Mitzvah work I have been involved in. Practically any time day or night, by phone, by mail, or in person, any threatening loneliness can disappear through this medium of Tzedakah, through the communality and human contact of Mitzvah work.

6. The Tzedakah act itself is *sui generis,* unique, sometimes ineffably wondrous, sometimes routine, but always containing within itself a certain sublimity. That sublimity may be recalled later with warmth, insight, and amazement at how awesome life is and how awesome human beings are.

I would clarify one point: while it is true that people should not necessarily do Tzedakah work in order to reap massive personal benefits, nevertheless, Mitzvah-oriented people almost universally report that they "have gained far more than they have given". There is this human magic in the act, in the connection with others, in the rising to our Greater Selves. And there is a purity, even an innocence, and a welcome relief for many who may have felt a loss of innocence in the natural process of growing up to adulthood.

In Passover terminology, the act of Tzedakah can provide a kind of redemption, a daily Exodus from the Slavery of the Normal and Routine, the day-to-dayness of life, leading to a freedom, a bursting forth into well-being in its highest sense.

Extending this principle: no matter how brief the sense of innocence, purity, and uplift from a Tzedakah act may be, each Mitzvah always serves as a reminder that this *can be* the natural condition of being human. Conversely: boredom, senselessness and uprootedness, anxiety and melancholy need not be considered the natural human condition.

These things just happen, or can happen, as a result of Tzedakah work.

7. Tzedakah ought to be able to change certain negative personality traits (with a qualified "sometimes" added), though it does not *necessarily* change people's personalities.

One would hope — and there is some substantiating empirical evidence — that the arrogant would become more humble through Tzedakah work, the irascible more gentle, the obnoxious more pleasant, the cruel and insensitive more compassionate. People involving themselves with Mitzvahs may become more decent, nicer, and more at home with themselves through this involvement. ("Nice" and "decent" are not pejorative terms.)

That Jewish tradition advocates these personality traits is obvious from a number of sources:

1. Ravina said:
   One should train oneself to be a gentle person. *(Ta'anit 4a)*
2. The Sages have said:
   One should always be pleasant when dealing with
   God's creatures. *(Ketubot 17a)*
3. At least three medieval Jewish Bible commentators
   consider the laws of keeping Kosher a regimen to
   remove cruelty from the human personality.
   *(Ramban, Deuteronomy 14:21; Ibn Ezra, Exodus 23:19,
   Abarbanel, Exodus 23:19).*

Humility may certainly become one of the benefits of Tzedakah work, as working with other people in the fields and orchards of Tzedakah brings people into contact with remarkably sensitive people, individuals who personify, to the highest degree, devotion, caring, and gentleness, a very humbling experience.

This obsession with positive personality traits is reflected in an interesting document concerning physicians, a list of 77 characteristics of a good doctor drawn up by Abraham Zacuto Lusitano (1576-1642), a famous medieval Jewish doctor. These are the opening few items in the list:

1. A physician shall be God-fearing.
2. He shall be well dressed.
3. He shall not indulge in unprofitable chatter.
4. A physician shall not be miserly and stingy.
5. He shall not be primarily interested in fees.
6. He shall not be envious.
7. He shall not be haughty and snobbish.

Only further down the list does Dr. Zacuto Lusitano indicate the specifics of the medical skills needed for curing the sick. Indeed, had we not known the list was for physicians, a casual reader might think from the first seven items that these prerequisites could apply to a wide range of occupations. The message is clear, though: the *person* is primary, then comes technique.

I would think — though this has not yet been proven — that the success rate of personality change increases with the desire of the Mitzvah-doer to have it change. The Midrash states it nicely:

> Rav said:
> The Mitzvot were given in order to refine human beings. *(Leviticus Rabba 13:3, Margoliot 2:277)*

Tzedakah can trigger a cleansing process, a firing, a smelting, the end result being that some or all of the impurities, the dregs and dross, will have been removed and the purer, refined elements will remain.

8. Tzedakah is really another form of Teshuvah — changing, turning, repentance. At any time of day or week or season, no matter how we may judge ourselves as unkind, unworthy, criminal, wasting our lives, or worthless, the next moment — if filled with a Tzedakah act — serves as a reminder of who we are in essence, human beings with awesome power to act, move, make changes in the world. Tzedakah allows us to re-establish our balance and sense of meaning and value.

We are Someone because we are capable of doing these Mitzvah acts. We would cease considering ourselves beasts, even for a moment, as long as the humanity of our actions contradicts that self-perception so clearly. Any of the Tzedakah acts, great or small, carries with it an immense on-rush of power to change a person's self-image and life-direction, perhaps parallel in the physical world to Einstein's equation of the tremendous amount of energy contained in even the most minute masses.

9. Tzedakah work revolves around a central point — *Kavod* (dignity, respect) and *Bushah* (embarrassment, humiliation). This *Kavod-Bushah* matrix defines and explains the quality, extent, and nature of the Mitzvah act.

For the beneficiary of the Tzedakah actions, a critical criterion is: Does this act contribute to the Kavod, the self-esteem and dignity, of the recipient? Has this act been done in a fashion that prevents Bushah, any sense of humiliation or loss of self-worth?

For the person performing the act of Tzedakah, the benefits are the same: an increase in Kavod, self-esteem. A teen-ager once taught me why, according to Jewish law, a poor person must also do Tzedakah *(Shulchan Aruch, Yoreh De'ah 248:1),* explaining, "As long as you give, you know you have something to give."

If people could feel that they are of use to someone else, acting on and nurturing that feeling, if they would take upon themselves to save people's lives and dignity in big or small ways, then their sense of peace with themselves, self-dignity, and well-being would most likely rise and soar.

Two examples of this latter point, one from the old, one from the young:

Daddy Bruce, an 86-year-old barbecue man in Denver, who feeds thousands of people every year for Thanksgiving, Christmas, Easter and his birthday, does it because he loves people. Someone once sent me a tape of a radio interview with Daddy Bruce. Some things stood out in my mind: he began to weep when he recalled that as a child Santa Claus had not come to his house, though he had visited the neighbors' houses. Now he wants to be a Santa Claus to others. And, overall, you sense he is one of the most solid and stable and untroubled 86-year-olds you might ever meet, at peace with himself and the world.

Trevor Ferrell, the kid in Philadelphia who feeds and shelters Philadelphia's hungry and homeless, began when he was 11 years old. (Now he is the ripe age of 14.) Shy, quiet, and unassuming, he is one of the most solid and stable and untroubled 14-year-olds you might ever meet. When asked why he does this work, he answers, "I just wanted to help someone."

Rabbinic literature highlights this issue of self-dignity:

One who curses oneself . . . transgresses a negative commandment.
(Shevu'ot 35a)

Rabbi Yehosua ben Levi said:
An entourage of angels always walks in front of people,
with messengers calling out.
And what do they say?
"Make way for the image of the Holy One!"
(Deuteronomy Rabba, Re'eh 4)

The first text reminds us that, as there are negatives in Jewish tradition which we are instructed to avoid (stealing, giving false testimony, murder, and the like), so, too, the list includes not treating oneself with less dignity than one is entitled to "by definition". The definition: by being created in God's image, one's Self Image is the Image of God and to be treated accordingly. Considering and treating oneself as a worthless entity or as a tradeable commodity would not be particularly consistent with Jewish values. This is one text which, I believe, ought to be taught more frequently in our religious schools.

The second text, also not taught sufficiently in the schools, reminds us to look upon every other person we encounter in this light of the Divine Image. By extension, we ought to listen to the angels walking in front of *ourselves,* as a constant reminder to ourselves that we, too, are made in the Image. Not wishing to sound like the Wise Old Sage, I would still mention a most practical situation where this applies: when teachers and professors degrade or embarrass students, the student should never fall prey to doubts thinking that he or she is worthless. This applies to the workplace also. These, and other texts, teach us that we are never worthless, nor unworthy of anything less than playing a vital role in the Grand Scheme of Things. Torah and Tzedakah work teach us just how vital we all are.

10. Once again it is time to teach Tzedakah beginning with the subject of poor people. For a few years, before poverty, bread lines, soup kitchens, and shelters became so ingrained in American life, it was important to teach extended meanings of Tzedakah: Jewish educational needs, synagogue life, special needs, Israel's security, etc. Now we cannot ignore the old-time Tzedakah teaching of feeding the hungry here in North America, many of those hungry at or below the poverty line being Jewish people.

Fact: practically everywhere I go, in conversations with Jewish educators, Family Service workers, Federation people, I hear disturbing estimates of the numbers of Jewish poor.

Another fact: some communities still wish to deny that there are Jewish homeless in any significant numbers within their boundaries.

However: just as Jews came to accept the need for four shelters for battered Jewish women in Israel, there is reason to hope they will also come to grips more realistically with the needs of the Jewish poor and homeless. (And with the Jewish alcoholics and chemically dependent, and gamblers. Some significant community work has been done, of course, but not nearly enough.)

Mention "the Jewish poor" a few years ago and the community pictured elderly Jews on fixed incomes. Now there is the "new Jewish poor" — single parent families, people who have lost their jobs, individuals with mental and emotional problems, people who just can't adjust, people beaten down and trampled by circumstance — all ages.

I remember a few years back a Jewish worker intimately involved with the Jewish poor and homeless of Chicago expressing her astonishment and dismay at how many young Jews were just wandering the streets, lost souls.

Facing up to the realities of poverty is a fair beginning. The mechanisms and funding should follow accordingly, tailor-made to specific communities.

One such mechanism is MAZON: by donating 3% of the cost of a catered affair to MAZON, the donor channels funds which will be used to alleviate hunger in various communities. New, simple, and effective.

11. There is no real "them" and "us".

Years back I remember witnessing the bar mitzvah of a young Russian Jewish immigrant. He was standing in front of this huge open ark somewhere in Arizona giving a moving talk about being free, and I kept thinking, "That could have been me. Had my ancestors not left Europe 80-100 years ago, I could have been waiting for someone to try to get *me* out." Later on I would meet someone who had come to this country on the St. Louis, the same boat that — on a later trip — was sent back to Europe with its cargo of Jews who had been trying to escape Hitler. The same feeling: it could have been my family. The same when the Ethiopian Jews left the refugee camps in the Sudan for Israel - them, us . . . . we're the same people. And finally, the spooky sense that Raoul Wallenberg arrived in Budapest just two days before I was born. I, born in Washington. Them-us.

A similar emotion strikes me when I take teen-agers to Life Line for the Old's workshops in Jerusalem. We're the same people, except for a few decades of aging between us. *We* work. *They* work. *We-they* work. (Someone has offered the term "chronologically advantaged" as a substitute for "senior citizens".)

The same when relating to individuals with disabilities — we all have some limitations, and theirs might be just more pronounced than ours — but they're not "them" and we "us". (In a book about disabilities, *Tips for Tabs,* George Alderson speaks of these "Tabs" — "Temporarily able bodied", a nice linguistic connection between the so-called different groups, disabled and not disabled.) ("Partially able" is another term sometimes used for "disabled".)

And when buying food for the hungry, the rule is: we ought not to buy for "them", what we wouldn't eat ourselves, because they're not "them" and we "us".

And when giving away clothes, we also ought to consider giving clothes that we could still wear. What's good enough for us, is good enough for them, because it is us-them as a single unit.

I believe this we-they unit all stems from the sense that, as we have been recipients of the beneficence and goodwill and kindnesses and fair gestures of others, when we were sick, or mourning, or lonely, or weary, then we should be able to identify easily with all those who, for now, find themselves in difficult or delicate circumstances. But it's just not "them" and "us", but rather a Klal, a totality.

In sum, high-sounding as it may have seemed, this we-they is a basic axiom of Tzedakah work. We are not really the "helper" and they the "helpees", which brings us back to the root-meaning of Tzedakah: the right thing, the just thing to do, the Menschlich thing.

12. Nothing beats having a circle of friends who share your interest in Tzedakah.

The idea of Chevra — your associates, your friends, your close friends — is paramount to intensified Tzedakah work. When discouraged, there are people to turn to; when exhilirated, there are people to share the joys with; when tired, there are others who will jump at the opportunity to join you in some Mitzvah work, energizing you, and when you are confused at the immediate and ultimate meanings of these acts, they are there to talk with you, listen to you, listen patiently and sympathetically.

One good test of this kind of Chevra is to ask yourself, "what Tzedakah could I get done from making just two phone calls?" If it is money, consider whether or not two calls would find $18 or $100 or $5000; and if it is bodies and minds to help you start a Meals on Wheels program, what two calls would get you the best connection?

The Rabbis praise again and again the idea of Chevra-for-the-sake-of-

Tzedakah . . . . Rabbi Akiva says, "Whoever attaches himself to Mitzvah-doers — even though he did not do as much as they did — even so, he still receives a similar reward." (Avot deRabbi Natan A:30) And, "if you see a group of righteous people, stand up and hug them and kiss them and hug them again." (Ecclesiastes Rabba 3:5,1) And, Abbaye said, "All kinds of good things for the righteous, and all kinds of good things, too, for the neighbor!" (Sukkah 56b)

Perhaps it was said best more than 18 centuries ago by Rabbi Tarfon, speaking of his friend, Rabbi Akiva. His words have been transmitted to us in two versions, varying only slightly . . (1) "Akiva, whoever separates himself from you — it is as though he disconnects himself from his own life" (Zevachim 13a), and (2) "Akiva, whoever separates himself from you — it is as though he disconnects himself from Life Itself." (Kiddushin 66b) This intimacy that people build through the vehicle of Tzedakah gives meaning to one's own life and to Life Itself. Tzedakah acts gain more significance when performed in intimate contact with friends, and the richness of the friendship grows through the Mitzvah acts done together.

13. Real-live Tzedakah is best understood when viewed in action, while watching a Mitzvah hero ("One of the Good Folks", "Tzaddik", "Righteous One") at work. A Mitzvah hero is not to be followed blindly; rather, he or she is a teacher-by-deed.

Linking up with Mitzvah heroes eliminates too much stultifying over-analysis and abstract philosophizing and brings home the immediacy and flesh-and-blood reality of Tzedakah work. Tzedakah is people, very human people, doing supremely human acts. Jewish texts give us perspective and sharpen our sense of the boundaries and unbounded infinites of Tzedakah, but seeing it happen, and taking part in the action under the aegis of a Righteous One, brilliantly clarifies the essences of the Mitzvah, and the Jewish texts come to life through the deeds.

Tzedakah, because of its very nature, and because of an individual's increased contact with these Inspired Ones, then lets us set our own personal goals much higher than we ever considered possible. It also changes some of our goals and helps us re-define what is meant by "personal fulfillment".

Just as neuro-physiologists tell us we use only a small portion of our brains, so, too, the Mitzvah Maestros and Maestras show us how our human capabilities can lead us to greater, more personally inspired and inspiring possibilities.

I would add: sometimes a Mitzvah project becomes calcified or ossified because of a loss of intimate contact with an Inspired Mitzvah Personality. The project workers then assume that whatever they are doing is whatever can be done. Whether it be work with the elderly, the partially-able, the poor, the hungry, or homeless — until they refresh their insight by watching the Good Ones at work, they will keep within those well-defined expectations . . . in good faith, and justifiably so, because the commonly-accepted definitions of human excellence are different than those of the Mitzvah hero.

One positive example: Project Dorot, a Jewish project for elderly Jews living on the Upper West Side of Manhattan, established a shelter for homeless Jews. In the first two years they successfully re-located into permanent housing a full 65% of the people who came to the shelter. Whenever I ask audiences what they would estimate a fair re-location rate to be, they usually guess 10% or 5%. They find it hard to believe that 65% now no longer live on the streets of New York.

Those are the facts.

There are many other examples readily available.

14. The quality and extent of the Tzedakah accomplishments is not a factor of the income, college degrees, IQ, sex, or age of the Mitzvah doer.

My negative grumbling: society holds up too many status criteria which are not in consonance with the realities of Tzedakah. From all my readings and conversations with people, it is incontrovertibly evident that great, masterful strokes of Tzedakah work have been carried out by young and old, wealthy and dirt-poor, male, female, PhD laureate or highschool dropout, and people with average or below-average (whatever the scales are) IQ's. Tzedakah crosses all lines — social standing, academic standing, wealth, whatever — The Great Equalizer. Indeed, I would advocate that individuals desirous of freeing himself or herself from artificial societal categorizations would do well to get deeply involved in the world of Tzedakah.

One more grumbling: if we do not break down these artificial categories and re-establish our value system on the basis of Mitzvah accomplishment, we are cheating ourselves in the long run. We will be left, I believe, with a plethora of talented, intellectually bright, well to do, rich people, self-absorbed and uncaring. It is a bitter and angry statement, but it is at the crux of the full meaning of Tzedakah for society's welfare.

A revealing, warming example: Janet Marchese of White Plains, NY, with her husband, adopted a child with Down's Syndrome. Subsequently she helped place more than 300 other babies with Down's Syndrome in adoptive homes. The article I read said that she is a part-time waitress, he, a New York City policeman. To me — holder of three college degrees and other symbols of achievement — this is very humbling, enlightening, and uplifting.

What human beings need, people in their loneliness, despair, dismay with life's eventualities — what they need is more Janet Marchese's. The rest is secondary.

15. Seeking out unforgettable experiences is one of the most effective ways to gain a full sense of the meaning and reality of Tzedakah.

Frequently, I ask my audiences to name an unforgettable positive experience from their formal Jewish education. I am often met with silences and blank stares. I expand the question to unforgettable experiences in general, sometimes leading them with questions like, "Where were you when President Kennedy was shot?" "When Roosevelt died?" "When Shcharansky was released?" "When the Challenger exploded?"

Discussions often open up readily from there. People begin to recite:

• I was at a bat mitzvah for a learning-disabled child . . . (I, myself, was once in a synagogue when a young retarded woman read from the Torah.)
• I received a Safe Pass from Wallenberg.
• I was raised as a Catholic . . . (The woman proceeded to the story — the first time she had ever spoken of it — of how her parents, about to be shipped to the Camps, left her in the care of the non-Jewish neighbors.)

More and more stories pour out. By no means is The Unforgettable Experience the only way to move into greater insight and Tzedakah involvement, but, if:

• We placed ourselves into situations where we would encounter these experiences more often,
• Our educators would program more of these into the curriculum,

the positive, sweeping effects, if properly directed into patterns of Tzedakah, can leave incredible impressions. Ask the people who have visited the newly-arrived Ethiopian Jews in Israel, the ones who have visited Ma'on Latinok or Life Line for the Old, the ones at Jewish Vocational Service who have seen shattered, unemployed people rebuild their lives in their new jobs.

A useful exercise would be to take a group of friends and to ask how many of them are in their present occupations by accident or because of an encounter with some unusually influential person in their lives. Many people have said, "Yes, now that I think of it . . ." and then they explain how they came to be professors, or social workers, teachers, physicians. One friend switched from Rabbinical school to medical school because years back, when he was being treated for cancer, the doctors showed such compassion for him, he knew that he wanted to become a doctor.

Again, this is not a rush for "highs", and Unforgettable Experiences don't stand on their own. But they can serve as turning points (regardless of our age) upon which to build later courses of action.

The best examples for little children I can think of include:

• Every Friday night, before candle lighting — having everyone put some money in the Tzedakah box.
• Adopting The Tzedakah Habit — having the children pick out one extra item for Tzedakah everytime the child grocery shops with the parents.

It might be wise for Tzedakah professionals and volunteers, educators and teachers, to begin compiling a list of potentially unforgettable experiences and how they can be programmed into the lives of the members of the community. Everyone will benefit.

16. You can't do $1,000,000 worth of Tzedakah work with only $500,000 (large scale).

You can't do $5,000 worth of Passover food packages (250 x $20/package) if there is only $3,500 in the fund (medium scale).

You can't buy a decent pair of shoes for someone for $48 if there is only $27 in the Tzedakah box (modest scale).

Numbers, numbers — many organizations are (justifiably) criticized for being concerned for the figures of donations rolling in, and leaving other elements of the Mitzvah of Tzedakah in the dust. It is irrelevant whether or not we are speaking of $100 or $100,000,000 — the principle is the same — an obsession with Tzedakah cash. I agree with the critics, if money is the *only* concern.

HOWEVER, I stand with those who bolster their work with hard-research figures, and the wild dreamers, who both need certain amounts to do their work: there is no denying that the amount they need is, indeed, what they need, and the work will suffer without it.

Personally, I enjoy giving a "pitch" to the hilt, speaking to the point, urging, twisting an arm here or there with an audience, encouraging this way and that, wheedling, so that the money figures go up.

Here are a few numbers from my personal scorecard — about which I openly brag as I begin to hit my stride:

Documented: personally helped channel over $700,000 to Tzedakah to people and places I am personally involved with. In addition to these statistics:

Federation Women's Division, Bridgeport, CT — pledges up 22%
Federation Women's Division Board, Baltimore, MD — up 22.89%
Federation Women's Division, Omaha, NB (lunch event) — up 18%
Federation Business and Professional Women's Division, Omaha, NB
    (dinner) — up 40%
Federation Young Women's Division, Metrowest, NJ — up 50%
    (though this group was different than the others; thus the higher
    figures).

Two more personal examples:

I had lunch with an individual in New York, arranged by a friend. After explaining my interests, I left the table feeling he had not responded particularly well. We both were interested in Tzedakah, but it seemed to me his particular interests lay elsewhere. Later on I found he had contributed $30,000 to a place I had been involved in, though I had not suspected he was so wealthy, so generous, so interested in that particular project.

And, the synagogue where I have worked for the High Holidays: Marlboro, NJ, the Marlboro Jewish Center. In 1985 I appealed, low-key, for money for respiration monitors for Yad Sara, to prevent crib death. These machines are lent out for free. We got four of them, at $540 each. Two people bought a whole one, twenty bought 1/10 each. In 1986 I dropped the low-key approach because I had committed myself to getting 60 more monitors (at a slightly-higher price [$560/monitor]). They came up with 25-30 monitors.

It is a unique feeling being a part of that process, turning money into Mitzvahs and watching others share that exhilaration. I remember, as a teenager, being asked to speak about Israel in synagogue on Yom Kippur. It was part of a Bonds Appeal. I suppose those good feelings lay latent for years, and they are now beginning to go into full swing.

But the fact remains, perhaps a little hard and cold: you can't do $1,000,000 worth of Tzedakah work with only $500,000.

17. Tzedakah can serve as a neutral ground for individuals and groups at odds with each other.

An example: the old adage used to go that the only thing that could pull all Jews together was a war in Israel. In recent years we have seen a unification, uplift, and jointly-shared enthusiasm concerning other events when (a) Natan (Anatoly) Shcharansky was released and arrived in Israel, and (b) when the Ethiopians first came to the land, their safe haven.

Another example: Yad Sara, the organization in Israel that lends medical supplies free of charge to people who need them, was honored with the government's first award for *Achdut Am Yisrael* — "Unifying the People of Israel". And this after only ten years of Mitzvah work.

Something there is about Tzedakah that allows for differences to fade into insignificance, sometimes temporarily, often permanently. When there is a grand, noble task to be accomplished, some Mitzvah act large or small, all gaps and abysses can be bridged.

18. Tzedakah keeps people attentive to the issues of Tzedek — Justice.

By being in constant contact with Mitzvah heroes and Tzedakah work, a person focuses more sharply on the many injustices and wrongdoings whirling around in the media, the streets, the air. Frequently, it is white-collar crime that rubs with such irritation. For example, R. Foster Winans, the Wall Street Journal reporter convicted for insider stock trading was quoted as saying, "It had occurred to me that a whole lot of people were making a whole lot of money on Wall Street and that I wasn't one of them." Outrageous.

Extortion and bribery in the Chicago court system and the New York City government, savings and loan scandals that have kept thousands of people from their deposits, causing irreparable losses and damage to people's lives that cannot be quantified . . . . People corrupting a system so much that it leads the "person on the street" to the ultimate enemy — cynicism, an acceptance that people are bastards, that crookedness is an acceptable definition of people as people. The Prophets, though, did not become cynics. They screamed in sympathetic pain for the sufferers, and with high shrieks set out to set things straight. (The Hebrew word "Tzedek" also means "straight".) Ralph Nader, unfortunately unknown to younger people today, followed in their footsteps. So many of the protective laws and regulations we have today, we owe to him, the Man of Justice.

One more example: computer piracy. Some would say, "Well, that's the way people are. As long as there are ways to beat the system, people will try to beat the system." Rather than succumb to that pessimistic, cynical approach, a young friend of mine, Reuven Lerner, sent me a three-page document, a print-out of a reasonable proposal concerning this issue which he posted on a computer bulletin board. He makes it abundantly clear that he considers this piracy wrong (he wrote the piece at age 16), and then offers a well-reasoned, lucid alternative.

The cynic might call a Mitzvah-oriented person naïve, but the Mitzvah people continue to move on, at greater or slower speed, naïve or not.

This juxtaposition of Tzedakah work and injustices regularly brings into incredibly strong relief the sadness and pain engendered by the cheaters and cheating, the stealers and stealing, the debasers and debasing. Tzedakah is not the only cure to this malaise, but it *is* one of the courses of therapy.

19. It is only of secondary importance to examine people's reasons for doing Tzedakah work. There are lengthy controversies in the Talmud as to whether or not Mitzvot have to have a certain intent attached to them. Tzedakah is a definite exception, where the motive is secondary to the act. Tzedakah is defined as taking of your resources and transferring it to another's possessions for that other person's benefit. Maimonides includes in his 8th Level of Tzedakah "giving grudgingly" (resentfully, grumpily) (Hilchot Matnot Ani'im 10:7-14). Grudgingly, yes, but still Tzedakah. And giving from a sense of guilt is still Tzedakah.

It would be fine if everyone gave for the highest idealistic reasons, but Jewish tradition is very realistic, allowing for all kinds of motives for giving. One text reads:

> Rabbi Elazar said:
> The full impact and richness of the Tzedakah act depends
> on the amount of lovingkindness put into the act.
> *(Sukkah 49b)*

That is on the highest level. Nevertheless, even if a person does his or her Mitzvah work largely for ego-gratification, still, the beneficiaries benefit, and there is always hope that the motivation will change with the passage of time and repetition of the Tzedakah acts.

One proviso: it would seem that the Jewish community sometimes overplays it testimonials, offering many rewards of being honored and honored again in the presence of one's peers. Most will agree — even those in the honoring organizations — that a note of moderation might be appropriate at this juncture.

And as for the often-heard line, "He/she is doing it only for a tax deduction," two answers fit well within this context we have discussed: (1) We should be grateful American tax laws make it easier for people to give, and (2) It still costs people to give their money away. Even in the old-time 50% bracket, it still costs $500 to give away $1000. The donor could have still kept it, paid tax, and still had $500 to buy toys with. Perhaps I am naïve, but someone who gives away $1000-which-costs-$500 must have *some* sense of Tzedakah.

20. For contributors to include Jewish Tzedakah projects, the same rules apply for large or small organizations and for large or small contributions:

1. Are they honest?
2. Do they use the funds wisely?
3. Is their overhead reasonably low?
4. Are they *ultimately* (the word occurs again and again in Tzedakah writing) concerned for the human issues of Tzedakah — dignity, sensitive care, compassion, or are they so

bureaucratized that it prevents the humanity from coming through?

5. Is their Jewishness a significant part of their work?

I can recall receiving letters from religious-school children asking about my fund's overhead, and whether or not I got a salary from the work (which I don't). I am delighted that they are aware enough of the real issues to ask.

21. Yuppies have not done well with Tzedakah.

A recent study for the Rockefeller Brothers Fund by Yankelovich, Skelly & White Inc., substantiates what has been suspected all along by fundraisers: Yuppies are indeed very self-centered and give well below their potential. The survey actually studied a group of Baby Boomers (born between 1946 and 1964), not all of whom have become well-to-do rising stars in their fields. Still, the study indicates that the sub-group of Yuppies gives disappointingly low percentages of their incomes to Tzedakah. Yes, of course, indeed, no question — there are exceptions, but "Yuppie" remains essentially a negative term in the Tzedakah world. And I don't believe fundraisers begrudge the successful ones their name-brand clothes, their pools and fine houses. They just want the benefits shared more extensively.

The special sub-group — those who rallied and protested against the Vietnam War and advocated love and peace: they are the most difficult mystery to crack. Why, with all the sensitivity they demonstrated not so long ago, why have they turned so self-consumptive?

No answer.

22. Many people resent being told to give. This, despite Jewish tradition's teaching that Tzedakah is a kind of Mitzvah-tax rather than a voluntary "give from the heart" idea. I assume this resentment has been true since the earliest days when the concept of Tzedakah was introduced into Jewish life in ancient times.

It is not so hard to understand. Yet, at the same time, it is hard to understand. The not-too-hard-to-understand part is that people work hard for their money, or that their time is precious, and their money and time are theirs to do with as they wish. The hard-to-understand part is that, according to Jewish tradition, our talents, our abilities to earn money, life itself, *ultimately* go back to a Divine Source that only asks in return 10-20% of our incomes and some of our time and effort to pass around to others in less advantaged situations.

I know the argument-from-appreciation is weak, religious as it is in tone in the secular-based environment we live in. Nevertheless, a quote from the poet, Edwin Markham, might be appropriate:

"Giving is living," the angel said.
"But must I keep giving again and again?"
My selfish and querulous answer ran.
"Ah, no," said the angel, her eye pierced me through,
"Just give till the Lord stops giving to you."

I have no further particular insights into this matter, other than to say that the battle to raise consciousness and to sensitize is, in my opinion, not being won in any particularly impressive fashion.

23. When it comes to Tzedakah money, there are always going to be some incorrigible non-givers.

Originally, I was not ready to accept this assumption, but after hundreds of conversations with people "in the field", it has become apparent to me that there are some people — more in some places, less in others — who do not give of their money (nor of themselves) to anything, for anything...either because of greed or self-consumption (a fine descriptive term) or cheapness — whatever. (Greedy and cheap are not the same.)

A corollary to this principle is that there would be more people willing to give than we would normally expect, if they would only be brought into contact with the right Mitzvah person or Tzedakah encounter. These might open them up to the glories of Tzedakah work.

Another corollary: perhaps the Great Righteous Ones *(Tzaddikim Gemurim),* those select few Righteous-of-the-Righteous who tower above all Mitzvah people, could reach everyone. Perhaps. There have been no recent test cases that I know of, though.

In the non-Jewish world a generation or two ago, Father Flanagan of Boys Town believed "there's no such thing as a bad kid". I have heard of a few others in our own day, Jewish and non-Jewish, who believe there are no such people who are totally deaf and blind to Tzedakah work. The late Rabbi Aryeh Levine of Jerusalem believed it; perhaps Rabbi Leib Heber of Pittsburgh believes it, and others I have not been privileged to meet. But they are the rare ones. The everyday reality, too widespread for so few to cover, leaves the facts as facts: some people are unreachable.

24. One I cannot make any sense of at all:

If people hate being treated lousy, why would they want to treat others lousy?

Conversely: if they love being treated well, with respect, care, and caring, why would they not throw themselves more extensively into doing the same for others?

No answer.

25. One more I cannot make any sense of at all: Why is most of this material on Tzedakah not obvious?

This is not meant — not by any means — in a self-righteous tone. (I always invite my audiences to call my mother or my good friends to hear why there should be no suspicion of self-righteousness. They'll provide the long list of shortcomings.)

In all-serious voice, though, it appears that making life more livable through Tzedakah would seem to be a better option than perpetuating cruelties, indecencies, and human-wrought disasters. Use any fancy words that come to mind: existentially, ontologically, phenomenologically speaking . . . the idea remains the same.

I do recall one specific speaking engagement where the obviousness of the ideas came through clearly. I was teaching at a retreat for participants in the Los Angeles Hillel Council's Mitzvah Project, about 20-25 students. Some had been visiting regularly at old-age residences or hospitals or hospices, some had worked at Sova, the Los Angeles Kosher food bank, some did other Mitzvah work. Listening to the students tell their stories and pour out their feelings, their sense of uplift and perspective, their mature grasp of many shades of reality, I knew that a significant amount of the material I had prepared was superfluous. They already knew, and felt in their gut, most of the insights I had wanted to share with them. What remained for me to do was text study about Tzedakah, to refine and sharpen the direction of their efforts. It was a wonderful pleasure for me, to be slightly outmoded. (I can brag, though, that the director of the program is Marci Fox, a former Tzedakah apprentice of mine.)

In most settings where I speak, though, there is generally only a small percentage of the people who find little surprizing material in my talks. For most of them, sadly, it is all or mostly new to them.

ADDRESSES OF PLACES AND PROJECTS MENTIONED IN THIS ARTICLE

1. Air Life Line Assn., 1722 "J" St., #14, Sacramento, CA 95814, 916-442-5165.
2. The Ark, 2341 W. Devon St., Chicago, IL 60659, 312-973-1000.
3. Daddy Bruce's Barbecue, 1629 E. Bruce Randolph Ave., Denver, CO, 80205, 303-295-9115.
4. Dorot, 262 W. 91st St., NY, NY 10024, 212-769-2850.
5. Trevor Ferrell, c/o Trevor's Campaign for the Homeless, 120 W. Lancaster Ave., Ardmore, PA 19003, 215-649-6400.
6. Rabbi Leib Heber, c/o Western Pennsylvania Auxiliary for Exceptional People, 281 Sharon Dr., Pittsburgh, PA 15221, 412-421-1757.
7. Life Line for the Old, 14 Shivtei Yisrael St., Jerusalem, Israel, 287-829.
8. Los Angeles Hillel Council Mitzvah Project, 900 Hilgard Ave., Los Angeles, CA 90024, 213-208-6639.
9. MAZON, 2288 Westwood Blvd., #200, Los Angeles, CA 90064, 213-470-7769.
10. Sova, 3007 Santa Monica Blvd., Santa Monica, CA 90404, 213-453-4606.
11. Yad Ezra, 15 HaRav Sorotzkin St., Jerusalem, Israel, 926-133.
12. Yad Sara, 43 HaNevi'im St., Jerusalem, Israel, 244-047.

MITZVAH HEROES

At my lectures on Tzedakah, I usually ask the audience who their heroes are, who the heroes of their childhood might have been, who their children's and grandchildren's heroes are. Often there is a general silence. Once things get rolling with older crowds, some of the more common names include Eleanor Roosevelt, Henrietta Szold, Helen Keller, Golda, John F. Kennedy, if we are doing well, and, if we go the popular route, talking of the kids' heroes, the list includes sports figures, movie heroes, and some media personalities. I like to break the tension by using Allan Gould's and my humor book, *The Unorthodox Book of Jewish Records and Lists* to read about the mythical Danny Rose. He became the hero of many kids because he supposedly came to Hebrew school with chicken pox, infected everyone, and forced the school to close down for three weeks. That eases the tension.

I, myself, enjoy occasionally reading popular biographies, having covered, at least, Elvis Presley, Lenny Bruce, Hemingway, Loretta Lynn, Hank Williams, Johnny Cash, poets Dylan Thomas, Delmore Schwartz, and John Berryman, Henry Ford, Charlie Chaplin, Phil Ochs, Woody Guthrie, Bob Dylan. I suppose I am looking to see what people do or did with their lives.

In the past five years or so, though, I have switched my interest to looking for individuals who are involved some way in Tzedakah work, big time, small time, quiet or well-publicized. The variety is staggering. My first list, actually, was printed in the dedication to the first volume of *Gym Shoes and Irises:*

1. Myriam Mendilow
2. Hadassah Levi
3. Reb Osher Freund
4. Uri Lupoliansky
5. The Rabbanit Bracha Kapach
6. Si Levine
7. Dr. David Weiss (the Jerusalem Dr. Weiss)
8. Eva Michaelis
9. Curt Arnson
10. Meyer and Hannah Bargteil
11. Daniel and Charlotte Kuttler
12. Uri Cohen
13. Miriam Itzkovitch
14. Avital Shcharansky
15. Rachel Guron
16. Dr. Kurt Meyerowitz
17. The late Irene Gaster
18. The late Ya'akov Maimon

It is a very personal list, people I have met through my Tzedakah work over the last dozen years. Some of my friends and readers have gotten to meet some of them through my writings or through visits to their projects or through just meeting them, some place, some time. I would like to present some other lists of people and projects, hoping that it will be an influence on others to delve more deeply into Tzedakah work.

or through just meeting them, some place, some time. I would like to present some other lists of people and projects, hoping that it will be an influence on others to delve more deeply into Tzedakah work.

THE CAJE TZEDAKAH PROGRAM LIST:

CAJE — the Conference for Alternatives in Jewish Education — is the largest gathering of Jewish educators anywhere, anytime, and probably the most important Jewish convention of the year anywhere, anytime. At their 11th Conference in 1986 at the University of Maryland, the participants had the opportunity to meet the founders, directors, or workers of Tzedakah projects that dazzle the imagination in large and small ways. By all accounts, the encounters with these people was enriching, enlightening, and moving. The Mitzvah people included individuals from my *Gym Shoes* dedication list: Mendilow, Hadassah Levi, Lupoliansky, and others familiar to some from my annual Tzedakah reports. CAJE seemed to be a most appropriate forum for this event, a ready atmosphere of people hungry for learning and Jewish values, an enthusiasm to explore a program so new, so radical, so — in the final analysis — obvious. Here are some of the other people and projects from The Night at CAJE, though the descriptions are too brief:*

1. Rabbi Aaron Weitz of ECHO (Ezrat Cholim Organization — The National Jewish Institute for Health): a vast network for medical referrals throughout the country, finding the best physicians and locale for the best treatments.

2. Joan Hooper of the Beit Tzipporah Battered Women's Shelter (Isha L'Isha) in Jerusalem.

3. Aaron Lansky, founder of the National Yiddish Book Center, Amherst, MA, which has gathered over 600,000 Yiddish books, saving them from oblivion.

4. Rabbi Leib Heber, who has worked for years providing visits and Jewish needs to Jews in mental institutions and other places throughout Western Pennsylvania.

5. Terry Friedman of Bet Tzedakah: The House of Justice, a group of lawyers in Los Angeles providing free legal services to individuals with low incomes.

6. Rabbi Aharon Fried, founder of CHUSH, The Jewish Center for Special Education in Brooklyn, a Jewish day school with extensive auxiliary services for students with learning disabilities.

7. Trevor Ferrell, the "kid" in Philadelphia who feeds and shelters the homeless, along with his father, Frank.

8. Larry Phillips, President of Phillips-Van Heusen, one of the founders of the American Jewish World Service, a Jewish humanitarian

---

*Since many of these projects are discussed in other parts of this book, I will limit descriptions of the work. The master listing of addresses in Appendix A will allow people who are interested to obtain information directly, if they wish to write or call.

group funding small-scale agricultural and primary healthcare projects in Africa, Asia, and Latin America.

9. Allen Ray, President of the Board of The Ark, the super front-line Mitzvah project for poor and homeless Jews in Chicago.

10. Marci Fox, Director of the Los Angeles Hillel Council Mitzvah Project, involving college students from many campuses in Tzedakah work.

11. Reverend John Steinbruck, director and mainstay of the N Street Village of Luther Place Memorial Church, Washington, DC, providing a full range of services to poor individuals: food, shelter, clothing, medical care.

12. Gary Moskowitz, founder of the National Association for the Jewish Poor, New York, involving over 450 students in providing services, immediate and long term, for the Jewish poor, social services, educational, and recreational programs.

And representatives and activists representing Tzedakah work on behalf of Soviet Jews and Ethiopian Jews.

MY FIRST PRELIMINARY LIST GATHERED FROM NEWSPAPERS AND MAGAZINES:

Taking my own advice from a previous article, I began gathering articles about people, big-time, some doing long-term work, some now and again, some young, some old, some strange and others so-called "normal", some very, very famous, some hardly known outside of the small circle of people they work with. They come from all walks of life and do all kinds of things for a living. I usually xerox this list for my audiences, and this was my first occasion for using the term, "Some of the Good Folks":

WHAT DO PAUL NEWMAN AND BRUCE SPRINGSTEEN KNOW ABOUT TZEDAKAH THAT WE DON'T KNOW: ORDINARY PEOPLE CAN BE MITZVAH HEROES, TOO —

SOME OF THE GOOD FOLKS

1. *Bruce Springsteen,* "The Boss", gives away $10,000, sometimes $25,000 at concerts to local foodbanks and worker relief funds.*

2. *Elizabeth Yanish,* Denver sculptress: collected 10,000 overcoats for the needy.

3. *Daddy Bruce,* barbecue man: free dinners, Denver.

4. *Paul Newman,* Movie Star: Proceeds from Spaghetti sauce, popcorn, and salad dressing to Tzedakah.**

5. *Kenny Rogers,* Country Singer: cans of food from each fan at concerts. (2,000,000 + pounds)

6. *Celeste McKinley,* Las Vegas singer-comedian (retired): free supermarket for the poor.

---

*Nearly $500,000 on his last concert tour.

**$9,000,000, including establishing a camp for children with leukemia and similar diseases.

7. *Veronica Maz,* sociologist for the hungryWashington, DC: Martha's Table — food and rehabilitation for the hungry — sociologist.

8. *Sister Margaret McCaffrey,* Shreveport, LA: food, jobs, clothing.

9. *Trevor Ferrell* (age 14), student (with reading disability): works with Philadelphia homeless.

10. *Rabbi Dov Levy,* Jerusalem: special education for ultra-Orthodox children.

11. *John Fling,* Columbia, S.C.: "The Everyday Santa" — general Mitzvah man, delivers auto parts for a Chevrolet dealership for a living.

12. *Yitzchak the Gingi,* restaurateur, 48 Montefiore St., Tel Aviv: food for anyone at any price, free whenever necessary.

13. *Patrick T. Murphy,* Public Guardian, Cook County, IL: gained release for an Oriental man wrongfully institutionalized for 31 years; brought injunctive action against Nobel prize winner, University of Chicago Medical School, and drug companies for abuse of mentally ill.

14. *Rabbi Leib Heber,* Pittsburgh, PA: personal and religious services to mentally ill and retarded individuals in group homes and institutions.

15. *Sam Sutker,* Asheville, NC (occupation unknown): gleans food from farmers' markets for the poor.

16. *George Halzel,* Randolph, MA, retiree: hand-makes toys for children in institutions.

17. *Dr. Joe Kramer,* physician: front-line medicine on Lower East Side.

18. *Ron Schultz,* maker of Christmas Spice Tea, California: All profits to Tzedakah.

19. *Jerzy Kosinski,* author, winner of National Book Award: visits sick in hospitals, reads and tells them stories.

20. *Betty Feldman,* 75, Baltimore: clown.

21. *Mani Roy,* restaurateur (Indian cuisine, Atlanta): 200 meals to Atlanta Union Mission for Thanksgiving.

22. *Joseph Kennedy II,* founder of Citizens Energy Corp.: sells home heating oil in Massachusetts 30-40% below market price to the poor, over 30,000,000 gallons to 300,000 households.

23. *Bill Sample,* security guard, Philadelphia: president of the Sunshine Foundation, providing trips and gifts to dying and chronically ill children.

24. *Terry Runyon,* Buffalo, nuclear service engineer: magician at hospitals.

25. *Dr. Sherman Woldman,* pediatrician, Cheektowaga, NY: has lending- library of infant's and children's seats for those unable to purchase their own, free of charge.

26. *Jerry Starr,* high school teacher, Buffalo: fills in jobs on Christmas day so people can be home with their families; free of charge.

27. *Tom Carney,* truck driver (known as "Blue Max" on the road): on the long hauls has saved more than a dozen lives in car accidents and similar situations; spent thousands of dollars assisting stranded motorists. According to Carney, "Anybody would have done the same."

28. *Louis* (New York City patrolman) and *Janet* (part-time waitress) *Marchese,* White Plains, NY: A few years ago they adopted a child with Down's syndrome. Since then, Janet has helped find adoptive homes for nearly 300 babies with Down's syndrome.

29. *Bob Geldof,* rock singer of the Boomtown Rats — Live Aid, Band Aid. Recently knighted by the Queen of England.

Yitzchak's Kitchen, 48 Montefiore Street, Tel Aviv.

THE LIST OF THE PRESIDENT OF ISRAEL'S VOLUNTEER AWARDS, 1986:

Each year the President of Israel presents awards to individuals who have accomplished great things in the area of volunteering. Most, if not all, of the recipients express hesitation about receiving honors and plaques, though some make peace with it because it gives their work added publicity and encourages others to involve themselves in their particular work, or other Mitzvah work, as the spirit moves them or as their own personalities dictate. In another list I will present later, a name is omitted: the woman received the award on the condition that there would be no pictures of her nor publicity about her achievements (her picture does not appear in the pamphlet issued for the ceremony.) She did not want the publicity to interfere in any way with the purity of her work.

Here is a partial list — Jews and non-Jews — of the 14 recipients for 1986:

1. Myriam Mendilow, founder and director of Life Line for the Old.

2. Shalom Azulai, Haifa, owner of a fruit and vegetable stand, has delivered fresh produce anonymously to needy people for 10 years.

3. Golan Musai, Kfar Saba (age 14), a person with disabilities himself, works with other severely disabled individuals who use their disabilities as an excuse, helping them re-orient their thinking and actions.

4. Shimon and Ronen Sharvit, of Holon. Two days a week they close their barbershop and go to various institutions to give haircuts to the elderly and to children with disabilities, free of charge.

5. Dr. Zvi Rothenberg (one of the founders of the Rubin Academy of Music), Jerusalem, teaches violin to children with learning difficulties and motor problems. His method has gained wide recognition among others in the same field of interest.

6. Lea Mardor, Tel Aviv, pioneer giving support to women who have had mastectomies. Her influence is felt in all the hospitals in Israel where such surgery is done.

7. Neli Wertman, Haifa, has recruited and trained innumerable volunteers to serve as hospitality-welcoming committees for new immigrants. She is known as "Mother of the Olim." (Many such individuals earn nicknames.)

THE OCTOBER 13, 1986, *NEW YORK MAGAZINE* LIST:

New York Magazine devoted the feature part of it's October 13, 1986, edition to people and projects and analyses of Mitzvahs. They listed opportunities for people to get involved, wrote most thoughtfully about the Society People who conduct the large fund-raising balls for various institutions such as the Metropolitan Museum of Art, spoke of the realities of poverty in the Big Apple, and covered a number of other insightful topics. One of the projects mentioned is Dorot, working with elderly Jews on the Upper West Side of New York, and with homeless Jews. On the down side, the one piece called "Doing Good" (which is also the title for the whole issue), speaks of generosity and benevolence and care for the weak and disadvantaged as being "built into all religions". Pete Hamill, the author, then proceeds to quote from the New Testament and the Koran, unfortunately omitting the much earlier, basic sources in the Jewish Biblical texts. An unintentional oversight, for sure.

The following is a partial list of some of the individuals featured in brief sketches in tht issue of the magazine:

1. Judith Peabody, former Park Avenue debutante, is doing extensive inspired and inspiring work with people with AIDS.

2. Sukey Rosenbaum, brings food packages, sandwiches and fruit, and other items, to the homeless living in Grand Central Station. The Coalition for the Homeless is the sponspring agency. (One individual refers to her as "Our Lady of Grand Central".)

3. Mark Chinitz, an attorney for Weil, Gotshal, volunteers at Covenant House, the center for lost and wandering and floundering kids under the age of 21. Chinitz's firm gave him time to do *pro bono* work for Covenant House, and he organized a pool of lawyers to do additional work for the place free of charge.

4. George Martin, defensive linebacker for the New York Giants, specializes in visits to children at hospitals. He has also put together a program to help his teammates work on their college degrees.

5. Bette-Ann Gwaithmey, whose teen-age son died of a form of childhood cancer, has already raised over $2,000,000 to establish a pediatric cancer research laboratory at Sloan-Kettering.

6. Joe Gilmore, minister of South Church in Dobbs Ferry (a well-to-do suburb of New York), does "midnight runs" with food and blankets to Manhattan's homeless. He concentrates on those outside the system of shelters in the city.

7. Judy Wyman, who works for an accounting firm, goes once a week to Joselow House, run by the Jewish Guild for the Blind. There she meets up with Jimmy, a blind and mentally retarded adult, for outings around the city. (Judy, herself, had a vision loss for a number of months, so this particular Mitzvah struck home with her.)

8. Ed Gallowitz, an executive for Van Heusen, visits elderly individuals who live alone as part of one of a local church's Visiting Neighbor programs.

THE LIST OF RECIPIENTS OF THE ISRAELI MINISTER OF LABOR AND WELFARE'S ANNUAL AWARD FOR OUTSTANDING VOLUNTEER WORK, 1986:

I was fortunate enough to be in Jerusalem for these very moving ceremonies. I note that in previous years, two people with whom I have had a great deal of contact, have been recipients of the award: Myriam Mendilow and The Rabbanit Bracha Kapach.

These are some of the people who were honored. (Because the program is printed in unvocalized Hebrew, I hope I will be forgiven for any mistakes in transliterating the names.) —

1. Esther Obermann, Kibbutz Lavi, does outstanding work with prisoners and families of prisoners in Tiberias.

2. Rivka Saraf (age 85) and Miriam Zubrov (72), Migdal HaEmek, devote themselves to the well-being of the lonely and homebound elderly in their town.

3. Eliezer Beetchkov, age 18, Hod HaSharon, for two and a half years has been intimately linked with an Israeli soldier, who because of a head wound, has become disabled. Eliezer originally began his work through a highschool volunteer program, now far exceeding the program's expectations.

4. Chana Goldberg, listed as a "chronic volunteer" from Hod HaSharon, covers so many areas, the pamphlet lists only a few: working with children in need, new immigrants, the elderly, individuals with mental disabilities, Magen David Adom. (The Hebrew says, Ve'od — "And more".)

5. Yitzchak Suleiman, 32, hairdresser from Rishon LeTzion, for five years, once a week, has done the hair styling for elderly women free of charge at various centers for the elderly, and gives talks on personal appearance for this specific age group. Other people who work in his salon who join in his work still receive their salaries for their time away from the salon — he does not want to interfere with their making a living.

6. Students at the Miftan School in Nahariya were cited for a number of projects:

    a. adopting a kindergarten
    b. getting involved in Magen David Adom work
    c. providing a mobile repair service for elderly homeowners
    d. actively working in a project providing security for elderly people in the community and other projects.

7. Nechama Pikrash, foster mother (grandmother? great- grandmother?) *par excellence* (her age is listed only as "advanced in years"), has extended herself to many, many children who need her unique touch. Her house is open not only to them, but also to young people about to enter the army, and, I would imagine, just about anyone else. (The Hebrew text indicates the openness of the house is "unbounded".) (Visit Tiberias and see.)

8. An organization of widows called *Irgun Almanot She'ayrim,* reaching 11,000 families, 35,000, individuals, for:

    lobbying for changes in laws relating to widows
    setting up frameworks to overcome the sense of loneliness among widows
    mutual assistance between long-time widows and those recently widowed to ease the adjustment and help restore the recently-widowed to a more normal life

9. Rafi Ginat, producer of Israel's most widely-watched television show, Kolbotek (estimates are that 95% of the viewers watch the show), is best known for bringing issues of consumer justice (Tzedek) to the attention of the Israeli public. In the last three years, he has integrated into the show a program called *Pinat HaTzalash* — "Commendation Corner", through which he publicizes and draws attention to people-in-the-street types of volunteers who are working wonders within Israeli society. (During the ceremonies, he was the first to receive the award because he had to return to the studio to prepare the program. The applause was thunderous — a real-live Israeli national hero.)

It was an astounding, inspirational afternoon at the Jerusalem Theater. The place was packed; many of the people who had come were people whose lives had been touched by the honorees. You walk away from events like these thinking things like, "It works. Life works. Society works. People care and put out for others. Tzedakah is alive and well." Incredible uplift, sublimity — all the good words Tzedakah can call to mind — came to mind that afternoon.

AN ADDITIONAL, RECENTLY-BEGUN LIST OF MORE PEOPLE, COLLECTED FROM THE NEWSPAPERS, MAGAZINES, TV, AND CONVERSATIONS WITH FRIENDS — NOT NEARLY COMPLETED:

"Gloves" Greenberg, the man who gathers gloves all year in New York and distributes them to the homeless and poor of the city as the weather begins to turn cold.

Dr. Robert Peter Gale, Los Angeles, chairman of the International Bone Marrow Transplant Registry — the physician who flew to the Soviet Union to care for victims of the Chernobyl nuclear reactor accident.

Dr. Gerald Friedland, leader of the AIDS treatment team at Montefiore Medical Center, New York. Newsweek, July 21, 1986, wrote pages and pages about his insight, courage, stamina, and gentle human touch.

Eugene Lang, addressing the graduating sixth grade students of Harlem's P.S. 121, a school from which he himself had graduated 50 years previously, made the following proposal: any child who continues on through high school — he would assure payment of their college tuition. One subsequent article indicted that as a result, very few dropped out, that he had built up a personal relationship with many of the students, and that powerful people in other cities were following his lead and establishing similar programs.

Two friends in California with calligraphic skills, who offer, within their time limits, to do work for others — the check for the fee goes to Tzedakah.

Two photographer friends of mine who give me photographs to sell when I am on the road, the sales money going to Tzedakah.

Another photographer friend who carries a camera attached to a long pole, which he holds, photographs himself with another person, and then gives them the picture — a self-devised project which has been particularly well received in old age residences.

Matthew Starr, Baltimore, a young man with Down's Syndrome, featured subject on the poster for the National Organization on Disability, addresses the freshman class of the University of Maryland Medical School, speaking of himself, of Down's Syndrome, sensitizing them at the earliest stages of their medical careers about this specific issue, and, more important, the human beings who live fully, actively, despite the limitations.

The members of the Alpha Omega International Dental Fraternity, more than 10,000 Jewish dentists around the world. Alpha Omega is specifically oriented to Tzedakah, having founded the Hadassah-Hebrew University Dental School, funded the re-building of the Tel Aviv University Dental School, and many other projects. (I am delighted that an old friend of mine, Dr. J. Steven Kahan, was the chairman of the 1986 international convention in Washington, DC.) And to members of other professional fraternities who share their skills, time, and money in such fashion.

The members of Beged Kefet, a Jewish music group that gives all its fees to Life Line for the Old in Jerusalem. Based in New York, the group began performing in Jerusalem, for Life Line, and for other audiences. Unique in style and harmonies, the seven singers and musicians (four from the original group), contribute $6-7,000 a year to Life Line, not counting additional funds that come in from the literature they distribute about the super Mitzvah project for the elderly in Jerusalem.

And to all members of similar musical groups that may do the same kind of Mitzvah work, I would accord the status of Mitzvah hero.

STRAY CONCLUDING COMMENTS:

1. I do not mean to imply that other kinds of heroes are not heroes, too. It is just this: missing out on this kind of hero, the Mitzvah hero, means we might miss out on some unique, glorious aspects of being alive.

2. One need not admire everything about these heroes. Some of them are incredibly difficult to work with; the fanaticism of others may make them momentarily abrasive in the heat of the Mitzvah moment; still others are so strange it is difficult to spend leisure time with them outside of the Mitzvah realm, and others still may be quirky, inconsistent, unreliable, making it difficult to sustain a long-standing relationship with them. Some of them have off-balance personalities or weak dispositions, failings of other kinds, but they all have two things in common: in their Mitzvah work they personify the best that human beings have to offer, and their dedication to their Mitzvah work is worthy of admiration and imitation. Human, flawed, and wondrous.

3. Not infrequently, after a talk on heroes, someone will come up afterwards and say, "My mother is/was my hero in Mitzvahs", "My grandfather", and most strikingly, "My husband", "My wife", "My child".

4. Some people are suspicious (though not necessarily maliciously so) of the Mitzvah heroes. I would only say that, after meeting so many of them, the best thing to do is to link up with some of them, watch them at work, and the skepticism will quiet down. I, too, was skeptical of Trevor Ferrell, the 14-year-old in Philadelphia who feeds and shelters the homeless. Meeting him drove out all doubts: normal, nice, pleasant, quiet, just doing naturally what he thinks is right — that's how I would describe him. I have a picture of him with Mother Teresa. He has been to Calcutta, cared for the sick and dying, shared Mother Teresa's work. I see nothing warped in that for a 14-year-old, nothing morbid, or too-heavy-for-his-own-good. Rather, there is this pleasant aura around him, a warmth that touches everyone who comes near him.

5. Labels and nomenclature are still a problem. Some of the people on the lists are true Tzaddikim — Righteous Ones. Others are Good Folks, Mitzvah people, Inspired Ones. As you meet them more and more, you learn to affix whichever seems most comfortable.

If I were a Rabbi, and a student came to me and said, "Bless me, Rabbi," I would say, "May the Almighty grant you as many glorious moments in the presence of these people as I have been fortunate to have spent with them. They are the greatest of blessings."

LETTERS, STORIES

We can learn from stories. The Bible, Talmud, Chassidic teachers, Elie Wiesel — they all teach us with their tales. And yet, it is the *form* of the instruction that is so important. The stories are *stories,* and reducing them to "the message" adulterates their power.

I have included stories and letters — barely a small part of what has accumulated in my files and in my mind over a dozen years of Tzedakah work — to be thought-provoking to the reader. Even more than that, they are meant to give us a chance to pause, to be inspired and moved, to flash on new insights or to recall old ones that lie neglected in our sub-conscious, to give us perspectives. In transcribing these passages, and even in the proof-reading for typographical errors and punctuation, I found that I was mov-ed again and again. As a poet, I thought that many of them should have been re-told in poetry or song, but, as a compromise, I would suggest that many of them are best appreciated if read out loud, slowly, capturing the rhythms by voice what no printed words can accomplish, i.e., bringing the stories closer to a re-lived moment, re-creating the reality behind the words.

I have come to think that everyone should pick the half-dozen or dozen stories that are their favorites, the tales that have changed them, made them more what they are as human beings than anything else in life. They should choose them, tell and re-tell them to themselves and their most intimate friends, record them on tape, record them in the form of written words, act them out, perhaps. They are signposts and milestones for us, and torches that light pathways leading to great distances, warm, comforting, as gracious a gift as the Creator of human beings to his creations as I can imagine — the telling of stories, the sharing of words that tie one person to another.

Each of us has his or her own tales. It is my hope that some of these letters will encourage others to record their own, engendering many, many more enriching, enlightening, and life-touching documents, oral and writ-ten, supremely human testimonies to the sublimity of being alive.

Some of the letters and stories may even be the genesis of new Tzedakah projects. So much the better: more Mitzvah work, more tales to tell; the cycle continues.

Jerusalem, an Outdoor café on Ben Yehuda Street:

Just a leisurely afternoon, towards the end of my summer trip. I am sitting with good friends: Rabbi Ron Hoffberg, Arnie Draiman, a couple of others we have picked up along the way over or invited to our table as they walked by.

Since they turned Ben Yehuda Street into a *Midrechon,* a promenade, dotted with nosh places and coffee shops, we've developed this theory that, if you sit there long enough, everybody in the Jewish world you ever wanted to see would walk by. It always works — one day, someone from Tucson you haven't seen in years; a kid you taught in Chicago who now lives in Jerusalem with his wife and six or seven children, an educator you know from Washington, whom you never see at home. Only in Jerusalem.

So Hoffberg, Draiman, the others, and I are just sitting there, having our seltzer, our juice, our coffee, our ice cream sundaes, and Hoffberg looks up and says (a little casually), "Oh, there's Shcharansky."

There's a group intake of breath, a disbelieving silence, a glance. Indeed, there's Shcharansky and his pregnant wife, Avital, just strolling up the side of Ben Yehuda Street, windowshopping, like any other free Jew would do in Jerusalem.

Shcharansky, arrested March 15, 1977, freed in the year 1986, casually strolling up the promenade, glancing at the window displays of the stores, chatting with his wife who was thrown out of the Soviet Union the day after their wedding, who fought, and screamed, and organized, and travelled everywhere to free him.

Just strolling up the street, minding their own business, out for a walk in the late afternoon sun.

From my friend, Louise Cohen, who spent a summer in Netanya learning Hebrew at Ulpan Akiva. Some of her classmates were newly arrived Ethiopians. After the summer, she sent me letters and pictures:

The pictures are of kids you may have met when you visited the Ethiopians in Netanya. One of the American kids on the Ulpan bought bubbles for everyone on the last day of class, and these guys just went wild. I explained to the little girl (Gila) how to make more solution form shampoo or soap, and she immediately taught the younger kids. They were probably still blowing bubbles when you got there.

The boy in the pink shirt made me swear to send him pictures, and as usual, I was blown away by the thought that a year before he probably could have posed for one of those swollen-belly, flies-in-the-face, starving-child-in-Ethiopia shots, and now, for a little while anyway, he can be a little kid with nothing more important to do than watch bubbles float in the sunlight.

The rescue not only gave him life and a home, it gave him back his childhood. His name, incidentally, is Matan - "gift". I'm not sure who chose it or what specifically they had in mind, but spending time with him and the others was certainly a gift for everyone who had the chance.

(I think every major mission to Israel should take time off from high level briefings and spend an afternoon blowing bubbles with Ethiopian kids.)

And from another of Louise's letters:

Welcome back to the USA. Here's a present: pictures of the Ulpan Akiva trip to the North.

About the pictures - I had hopes of taking dramatic shots of the Ethiopians gazing proudly at their new flag with panoramic views of Israel in the background. They were going to bring a lump to every Jewish throat, and turn Osnat into the Operation Moses poster girl. I did sneak in one like that of Gila in Haifa, but the Ethies kept faking me out by jumping

Ethiopian Jewish kids blowing bubbles. Netanya, Israel.

in front of the camera and smiling "just like any other tourist". At first I was very frustrated, but after I got past my need to win a Pulitzer Prize with an Instamatic camera, it began to get to me that the real miracle is that just six months after escaping from horrors we can only imagine, they are so darn normal. That may be just what Israel should be, a place where Jews can finally relax and be just as normal as everyone else, which wouldn't be so terrible if we could simultaneously hang on to some of the good stuff about being the Chosen People.

To flesh out the pictures for you — the couple giggling on the cable car are Osnat and Erez. They are 18 years old and have been married 4 years. (They think it is a quaint funny custom that Americans stay single so long.) Erez was in my class and looks like a little kid, but he has an intelligence and *ziesskeit* that came through even in simple, Alef-plus Hebrew.

Osnat and I talked one day on the trip for over an hour (half-Hebrew, half-pantomime), and she told me that when they were in the refugee camp in the Sudan, all of her friends died, and she simply did not want to live any more, but Erez forced her to eat every day and literally saved her life.

I was curious to know how the whole rescue was orchestrated, and she told me that one day someone said, "Tonight's the night," and a bus showed up and took them to an airstrip just as a plane was landing. They were whisked on to the plane and took off in minutes. Osnat said she was too sick and unhappy to be afraid, but she was really shocked when they

landed and she saw all these white people jumping up and down and crying and kissing them, and saying "Yehudim, Yehudim!" (Jews, Jews!) That
was one Hebrew word she knew from before, but it took her a while to
understand that they were saying, "We are *all* Jews," because she hadn't
realized that there were white Jews!

Her next big shock came when they were taken to the hospital. She
said that in Ethiopia the doctors were all non-Jews, and if they treated a
Jew, the Jew inevitably died. (This may be because the conditions were
so bad, and medical care so scarce, that by the time anyone saw a doctor,
he was already on the way out, but she was sure it was murder.)

Osnat said that when the first Israeli doctor gave her a shot, she was
convinced that the whole trip was just a weird hoax, and that she was going to die. It wasn't until after a lot more shots and medicine that if finally
became real to her that she was in a place where, not only were there white-
skinned Jews, but Jewish doctors! She couldn't imagine such a thing in
Ethiopia. I told her that in America it was practically a requirement that
Jews be doctors (or vice versa). She understood that was a joke (in spite
of everything, she and Erez have a sense of humor).

Erez also appears in pictures I took of the Museum of Clandestine Immigration. Our teacher was afraid that the Ethiopians were not understanding what they were seeing, but Erez let her know that he did, by pointing
to the pictures on the wall and saying, "These people came on this boat,

Erez and Osnat.

we came on a plane.'' The absorption centers have been trying to catch the Ethiopians up on 2000 years of history, and they seem to identify strongly with Holocaust pictures, which probably remind them of their own lives last year. We probably have yet to hear all the gory details of what life was like in Ethiopia, but once, when someone asked Osnat what made her leave, she did *not* say, ''Ayn ochel'' (No food) — but, rather, ''HaGoyim'' (the non-Jews).

Finally, the girl with the incredible smile is Gila, whose big problem now is that she has no idea how her parents are, or if they are alive, and whether or not she'll ever see them again. She is about 14 years old, and came to Israel completely alone. Just think of the difference between her life and the USY kids you work with. She told me she'll be going through a day studying, learning about buses, etc., and suddenly she'll think about them and fall apart crying. She has yet to get a full night's sleep, because she generally dreams of her parents and wakes up crying. Anyone who thinks the Ethiopian absorption is going slowly should have a chat with Gila, and think for a while about the emotional baggage that she carries along with the results of years of famine (she has some bone problems), her first attempt at literacy, Hebrew, plumbing, etc., etc.

In spite of all that, Gila had fun on the trip, and wanted her picture taken every five minutes. (I almost fell off a cliff at Rosh NaNikra in the classic one-more-step-backwards routine.) She was absolutely thrilled when I gave her the copies of the pictures of herself, the scenery, etc. She told me that she used to have a lot of pictures (I'm not real clear about exactly what they did or didn't have in Ethiopia). . .but they were lost or stolen in the Sudan.

It seems like such a simple thing, but when you think about it, it's just like the question you pose, when you are teaching about Tzedakah, ''Why irises?'' It's vital to make sure that people have food, clothes, medicine, but there are also little extras in life that make a person feel more like a Mensch. I had been shy and cautious about taking pictures because I didn't want anyone to feel that she was on display or an object of tourist-curiosity, but for Gila and the others, it meant a lot to have something as non-basic as ''pictures of my trip''. That marks a step up from survival towards real living, and boring, blessed, wonderful *normalcy*.

I could go on and on, but you've got the idea.

A medical story that, because of its intricacies, will be be written up in the journal ''Obstetrics and Gynecology'':

Jay Masserman is an obstetrician-gynecologist in Orange County, CA, in practice with his cousin, Louis Weckstein. Jay and I go back many years, since he was a medical student in Ann Arbor. No, even before that. For a decade and more now, we have had an agreement: I teach him some of my latest discoveries in Talmud, and he returns the favor with great medical stories. I am convinced — I, son of a physician, — that my father's medical tales are among the most powerful memories I have of my childhood, and Jay is just picking up on this critical aspect of my Education in Life.

One of Jay's stories was so powerful, I re-told it in a poem in one of my early books: his sitting through the long, long last hours with a young woman dying of leukemia, her anger, her sadness, his humanity. Other tales of his I bring to mind for myself and my audiences whenever I or they need to be reminded of the intensity of life and the exhilaration of being human.

In the Spring of 1986, I was out on the West Coast for some speaking engagements, and Jay and I had our now-annual reunion. I couldn't possibly describe all the surgical details and complications of his latest story, but these are the things I remember:

He began his story by saying, "I have never seen so much blood." That is the phrase that I hear over and over again from him. At 1:30 or 2:00 a.m., Jay is awakened by Lou who is seeing a patient in the emergency room. When Jay arrives, and this pregnant woman is moved to an operating room, she begins to hemorrhage horribly. Lou and Jay work to stabilize the situation. The baby is delivered and is safe, but they can't see what to do next because there is so much blood. At one point the anesthesiologist tells them there is no blood pressure or pulse, but they continue to work away at it. Jay tells me that somewhere along the line Lou had ten seconds to decide just what to do. Ten seconds.

They have no clear view of the damage that has been done. Fortunately, another physician sticks his head into the operating room (fortunately — it was late, late at night, a fluke) and asks if they need any help. Now I couldn't say if Lou or Jay told him to put his hands on the aorta like you might see on some M.A.S.H. re-run, but this extra set of hands held the bleeding back sufficiently for Lou and Jay to see the burst bladder and other complications. They sewed up the bladder and did whatever else was necessary, closed her up, and waited those excruciating many hours to see if this diminutive, slight mother was strong enough to live.

She lived (though the stories don't always end this way; there's the young woman with leukemia, others).

Later, the nitty-gritty of fees came into the picture: the mother's medical insurance would barely pay for the hospital costs, if that. Lou and Jay could live with that. All they wanted was for the parents to bring the child in every year on the child's birthday.

It's a long Tzedakah story. Chassidic stories usually last only about thirty seconds or a minute. Jay's latest tale is longer, and six months in my mind, and I go over it again and again, picturing myself standing there at a slight distance from the operating table, watching the two of them at their awesome work, picturing the clicks and switches moving and shifting in Lou's and Jay's minds as they labored to save this baby and this mother, seeing angels.

From a college student:

Dear Danny,

I was one of the participants in the Mitzvah Project retreat week-end which you helped to lead last January. This past year has been amazing!

For me to attempt to explain how this project has touched me and affected my life is impossible. I only hope that my carefully chosen words and experiences will exude my enthusiasm and love for the many people and activities involved in the project. Looking back, I almost feel guilty that I have reaped more from the Mitzvot I have performed than those who received them.

This is really evident in my volunteer work at Cedars Sinai Hospital in Los Angeles. This past year I was able to compile a sixty-five page paper on the art of visitation in a hospital. I wanted to produce a work that would explain what I had learned about the experience of being a visitor and being a patient. I had hoped that it would make visiting a less frightening, more empathetic experience.

I had no idea how much of an impact I was making until the death of a cancer patient I had been visiting. Being an inhabitant of the hospice, there was little that I could do for him except to sit with him, possibly hold his hand, and give him the respect that he deserved. As he grew more ill, I was only able to leave him notes stating that I had come, as he would not permit visitors. The week before his death, his brother phoned me to let me know that he had taken a turn for the worse and wanted to thank me for making his last few months pleasant. At his funeral, his brother mentioned me in the eulogy, stating that I had given his brother the strength to live longer.

Other, less dramatic experiences than this one have happened to me since I have begun to visit patients. Patients have physically sat up and opened their eyes by the time I leave their rooms; others directly tell me that they thank G-d that I had come. Some merely squeeze my hand or smile just to let me know. One man, on a respirator and very ill, simply lifted his fingers off the bed as I left. For him, this took much co-ordination and much strength. I cannot tell you how elated I feel that I have touched even one person with whom I have come in contact. If I have just brightened the day of one person, then I feel accomplished.

I have also spent the year volunteering at Sova — a Kosher food pantry in Santa Monica. For me this experience has been as eye-opening as it has been fulfilling. I have been sensitized to the needs of the hungry as well as the Jewish values of taking care of one's kinsmen. This summer, while working at a Jewish day camp, I realized how ignorant my local Jewish community was to the problem of the hungry. I felt that I could make a difference by holding discussions with the children, stressing the concepts of Mitzvot and Tzedaka. I was met with criticism from my co-workers who felt that young children could not comprehend Mitzvot nor the concept of pain and suffering. Not only did I receive a terrific, positive reaction from the children and their parents, but I became constantly bombarded with stories from the children on how they had "made a difference" the day before. In seven days following my talk, my campers had brought in two carloads full of bags of food to Sova that they had collected. Further-more, they *personally* unpacked their bags which filled the previously emp-ty shelves at the pantry. The highs that I got from this experience and the feelings running through me about Pesach when I helped to pack bags for hundreds of families cannot be bought or achieved through any drug.

Overall, the Mitzvah Project has not only sensitized me and involved me in the human experience, it has also given me a blueprint for a way to conduct my life and to touch others. My time spent doing Mitzvah pro-jects has served to make me complete as a person.

Fondly,
Stacy Bunnage

A letter from some teen-agers in New Jersey to Hadassah Levi, founder and director of Ma'om LaTinok, a home for infants and children with Down's Syndrome in Israel:

Dear Mrs. Levi:

We are a group of high school students from Essex County, New Jersey, who were chosen as Teen Leaders from the Jewish community. Through the YM-YWHA of Metropolitan New Jersey we organized a fund raising event to raise money for *Ma'on Latinok.*

Several of us had visited Israel and were able to spend time in your home. We were deeply touched by the children and found it difficult to leave them. As a way of sending a part of us to the children we decided to raise money to be used in any way to make their lives better.

Our fund raiser was a 'Battle of the Bands' where four local high school bands performed and competed for a prize. The event was very successful and we were happy to be able to teach others about the work that you do.

We send this contribution of $600.00 with love and hope that it will in some way make a difference in improving the lives of the children.

Sincerely,
The Teen Leadership Group, Lori Weiner, Advisor

. . . Steven Birnbaum, Neil Zirkes, Robert Klein, Jill Perlstein, Andrea Rose, Sara Bucholtz, Nicole Collins, Ilene Schlanger, Scott Bolton, Robert Shapiro, Andrea Cytron, Amie Cohen, Scott Miller, Melissa Selke, Ian Scheinman

Another letter to Hadassah Levi:

I am enclosing a contribution which was given by a young man who chooses not to be named. Although he is young, he will probably not live many more years. He is blind and diabetic. He is also on a limited Social Security income and has many medical bills himself. This small contribu-tion represents a large amount of money for him to send.

However, when I told him about what you are doing, he insisted that I send this money for him . . . .

We wish you well in the very important work which you are doing.

Some notes written by participants in the United Synagogue Youth Israel Pilgrimage to Hadassah Levi, after visiting Ma'on LaTinok, her home for children with Down's Syndrome. (I have two albums full of these letters):

To see this tiny world, the world of the children, special children in many ways, shows how love, devotion, and a true sense of caring can change their lives from what would be despair to joy. These children immediately erased our fears and reservations and replaced them with warmth, affection, and, most of all, an understanding of the importance of the work done at Ma'on LaTinok. It is a struggle, against small funds and closed minds, but a struggle well worth the fight. Thank you for opening our minds, and our hearts.

USY Group 2, 1982

I love what you are doing more than you can possibly imagine. I wish that I were older, so that I could also do the same (now I have other obligations such as school). When I come here to live — in 4 or 5 years — I would like to help out on your ḳibbutz, and if possible, adopt a child. I really love children. Thank you for giving them a place to live. . . .

Rachel Brown, Group 4, 1982

It is the few with a firm purpose in mind, Mrs. Levi, who give faith to the rest of us. Your mission is one of compassion and love and you set an example for the rest of us.

Strength, Success, Health, and *Love,*

Adam Weiss, Group 4

I wish everyone could share the incredible amount of love that these kids shared with us. Thanks for the beautiful experience.

Laura Denenberg, Group 7, 1984

If anything is worthwhile, this place is. The kids are beautiful and so are you who started it. It's full of love.

. . . . (no name)

We are forced to face reality, in the fantasy world of a small child.

Jocelyn Seitzman

I held a little girl and she kissed me. I can't tell you of the feeling that went through me. I didn't want to put her down.

Neil Cantor, Group 5, 1984

I think Ma'on LaTinok is a beautiful place for young people to appreciate how lucky they are.

Faith Fishler, Group 5, 1984

And one from a Member of Rabbi Ron Hoffberg's synagogue group from Cranford, NJ:

Being here makes one think many things — many of them personally painful, others full of hope. . . . It fills me with hope and joy to see that people — my people — have individuals who are capable of this special kind of love. The process of thinking about these problems — our problems, and the introspection it causes, strengthens us all. . . . We count our blessings for healthy children, and count you as a blessing for helping us take care of the children — our children — who are born with Down's Syndrome. . . . God bless you.

A sadly-noted postscript from the Detroit Free Press and The Jewish News of Detroit . . . . In the Spring of 1982, a soon-to-be-occupied group home was gutted by arsonists. It was the second arson fire in two months in different homes in the Detroit suburbs. In the second case, the Jewish Association for Retarded Citizens was not intimidated and promised to continue to open such homes in the future.

An excerpt from an article in the CAJE Newsletter, written by Hanan Alexander, a member of the faculty of the University of Judaism, Los Angeles. The article is entitled "On Special Education: A Dog's Life and Priorities." (Originally printed in The Jewish Newspaper, I:2, 3/14/85.):

I recently heard a radio commentator who claimed that most people would save the life of a beloved dog before that of a stranger. I was skeptical until I had occasion to visit two day school classes in which this very question was asked. That the third graders voted overwhelmingly in favor of saving the dog did not surprise me. Many of them have dogs. They are still young and have yet to learn the true value of a human life.

When the overwhelming majority of an eighth grade class responded in the same way, I began to get very nervous.

When I look at a school with accelerated academics whose students would save a dog's life before a human life, I begin to wonder what we are teaching our children both at home and at school. And, when I consider the stresses this orientation creates and the children it leaves out, I begin to have some serious doubts about our educational priorities.

From Louise Cohen, my friend in Boston:

Just in case you forgot, or didn't jot it down, here's my contribution to the list of 100 (actually 116) Mitzvahs. . . .

#87 or whatever (actually #59) — make sure that JCC special needs clubs come out and work at Super Sunday, the Federation Phonathon. We started this about four years ago with the Tikvah Club, learning-disabled and mildly to moderately retarded late teens and early twenties. At first there was some resistance. The staff person at CJP was unsure of what kind of assignment they could handle, but finally came up with snapping apart the pledge cards and putting them into the envelopes to mail out. They worked so well that they kept getting ahead of the people making the phone calls, who couldn't keep up with them. The first year there were some unpleasant looks and remarks from at least one kvetchy lady who was concerned that they would make too much noise and distract her and her friends from whatever assignment they had. Since that whole section of the hotel ballroom had always been known as 'the boiler room' anyway, noise was clearly not the issue. As time passed, everybody got so involved in their tasks that even the lady who was so nasty forgot whatever had offended her (probably insufficient cuteness), and now it is a given that Tikvah people work at Super Sunday.

At the end of that first year when the members evaluated the year's programs, Super Sunday was the one thing they unanimously agreed they would repeat again. They loved the excitement, and food (super sundaes), and the visiting celebrities. Most important, they loved being part of the community and being able to do something that would help other people. Their leader had explained what fundraising was all about and how the community is organized including where their group fit into the JCC picture, and most of them grasped the implications of what they were doing at least as much as anyone else there. A few members wanted to try getting on the phones, and some of the more verbal people have, in fact, called their own families and friends. (Incidentally, many of them are from families that are active in the community, but they just never thought that the retarded kid might also some day want to do some fundraising.)

I like to think we go one step higher on the Tzedakah ladder than even teaching people to support themselves — when we put them in a position that they can also start helping other people.

From Barbara Bermack of the Pomona Jewish Center, Pomona, NY, recounting her experiences learning Hebrew. The first of two letters:

I'm writing today to fulfill your request as to my reasons for wanting to learn Hebrew and become a Bar Mitzvah a "few" years after my 13th birthday.

In 1983, with our son Steven's Bar Mitzvah a year away, I started to attend Shabbat services with him as is required by our Temple. Not knowing any Hebrew, I followed the service in English as best I could, but I wanted to chant with my fellow congregants and found myself picking up words and phrases due to constant repetition. It was at best frustrating for me, but Steven tried to help me along. A few weeks into our routine, Steven tried to teach me the Bracha for the Torah so that I could have an Aliyah on the day of his Bar Mitzvah. It was extremely important to him that I stand alongside my husband and pronounce all the words correctly.

He wrote the words out phonetically and tried to teach them to me. I think that's when I realized that not only was my learning this important to him, but it was equally important to me. I knew then that the best gift I could give my son on his Bar Mitzvah was to understand the service and be able to read along as he chanted the Haftorah.

Rabbi Kieffer had an adult study class that had been meeting for two years, and I needed outside tutoring to catch up to them. I hired Steven's Hebrew teacher to give me private lessons once a week. Rabbi Kieffer recorded the Shabbat services for me so that I could reinforce my learning each time I attended services. The only family member who knew what

I was doing was my husband. I wanted this to be a surprise for Steven.

I progressed rapidly and in six months, I joined the other women in Rabbi's class. Meanwhile, I started to read along each Shabbat morning as the Haftorah was read. I lent my voice in song, and Steven thought that I had picked up a great deal by just sitting in on the service. A few months before his Bar Mitzvah, I found Steven looking at my eyes as I scanned the prayer book, and I knew that I could not sit next to him and still keep my secret. So my husband started attending services with us and putting himself in between Steven and me so that I could use my fingers in following the words of the books.

One Shabbat morning, about 2 months before Steven's Bar Mitzvah, my husband could not attend services, and I had to sit next to Steve. As I was following the Haftorah, Steven lost his place and absent-mindedly asked where we were up to. I, just as absent-mindedly, pointed to the word. I waited for some reaction from him, but there was none. That night at dinner, he suddenly put his fork down, looked at me, and exclaimed, "You knew where we were this morning. You can read Hebrew!" I had no choice but to tell him what I had been doing. An onrush of tears and hugs and kisses from my eldest child made every hour of study worth it. He beamed all evening and bragged all day to his friends and urged me to keep going.

After Steve's Bar Mitzvah, I continued in Rabbi's class for my own sake. A little knowledge led to a desire for more, and it was my suggestion that the five women in the class share a B'not Mitzvah ceremony.

After a date was selected and we started studying together, we alternated between moments of elation and days of despair. One of our compatriots dropped out, and the remaining four of us plodded on, each bolstering the other, each bringing to bear her own inner sources of courage. Rabbi Kieffer exuded such confidence in us that we finally started to believe that we could indeed get through our Haftorah as well as the service for taking the Torah from the Ark and returning it, and the Musaf service.

My family was so encouraging and so proud that I knew I could not drop the idea no matter how terrified I became. My husband called friends and relatives to share the day with us.

The four B'not Mitzvah became very close. We had been acquaintances before, but now we were friends.

We divided the service so that each of us felt secure in her own part, and we planned rehearsal times together as well as numerous lunches. We organized a luncheon at the Temple for all who could attend the service and we doled out pieces of the service to our families and very close friends. A total of 24 people (not counting ourselves) had something to do or say that day.

We hit a number of small snags along the way, but with four of us to share the problems, the solutions were quick to fall into place. Rabbi had us do the service for taking the Torah out and replacing it and the Musaf service on the Shabbat preceding our B'not Mitzvah so that we developed some confidence in facing the congregation.

Three days beforehand, we were to meet with Rabbi one last time to go over everything. We arrived at the Temple at 7:30 p.m., but Rabbi wasn't there. We called Barbara, and she said he went to the library with their son, Efraim. He had forgotten about us. Panic set in, but we realized this was "bascherrt," destined for us to make it alone. We opened the Ark and did the entire service, on our own, for the first time. Rabbi walked in on the tail end, and he was beaming. We all had tears as well. We had finally made it through. Shabbat day was icing on the cake.

The actual service is but a blur to me. I remember that Rabbi stopped us in the middle of our Haftorah because someone was chanting with us. It was a terrifying moment, but it passed quickly. I tried not to look at my family or friends because I would have started to cry. I fought back the tears often that morning, but my eyes were glazed over most of the time.

The four of us shared a wonderful day together, each having her own reasons for being there. I can tell you that my family and I still attend services regularly. My enthusiasm is infectious. Steven now goes to Hebrew High School and will be attending Camp Ramah this summer. My husband and I, along with our daughter and son Steven, make no social plans on Friday evenings anymore.

One of the most rewarding results of that Oct. 13th date was the outpouring of love from our congregation. Ten families purchased a leaf on the Tree of Life in our honor. My dearest friends had a tallis woven for me, and each had a hand in the weaving. Prayerbooks were bought to commemorate the event, and a new Hebrew class has started with 9 new students learning the Aleph-Bet. I am one of their most ardent supporters.

My goodness, Danny. I just re-read my letter, and I think you may have gotten more than you bargained for. I hope this helps you in some way.

Barbara Bermack's Second Letter — The Tzedakah Story:

Dear Danny,

Hearing from you yesterday was a pleasant surprise. I am flattered that you wish to use my letter in your next publication and you most certainly have my permission to use it as you see fit along with my name and any contents of this letter as well.

This gives me the opportunity to bring you up to date on events since our B'not Mitzvah which will interest you. The four of us presented the Temple with the promise of a permanent Tzedakah Box as our gift to the Congregation. We commissioned an artist in Monticello, New York, to design and build one out of brass and wood. The finished product was quite beautiful and we were very pleased with the result.

However, we realized that a lockable clear case would have to be built to protect the Box along with its contents. That proved to be more difficult than getting through Hebrew school. The cost was so prohibitive that we almost despaired of ever seeing this well-intentioned gift hanging in our building. It also had been a year and a half since our B'not Mitzvah and our spirits were dampened by our dilemma.

Then a thought occurred to me. My parents live in Florida and my dad had lately been making some beautiful mirrors and lamps out of cut

Pomona Jewish Center, New York. Tzedakah box and Joe Zuckerman's case.

glass and lucite. His neighbor, Joe Zuckerman, eighty years of age, had been his instructor. Joe has golden hands but has had very little mazel in his life. His only joy is in his creations of wood, glass and shells. He was a master carpenter by trade and the love that he puts into his work is all that seems to keep him going.

I brought the Box to Florida and showed it to Joe and my dad. Joe's eyes lit up and he immediately set to work putting his ideas on paper for the case design. The following morning he had detailed drawings worked out and he begged me to leave the Tzedakah Box with him so he could build its case.

Three weeks later the Box and Case were shipped to me. The handiwork is magnificent and the love that built that case cannot be purchased at any price. My dad called to tell me that we added five more years to Joe's life by allowing him to feel useful and needed. The first recipient of the Tzedakah Box was the builder of its case!

It hangs proudly now at the entrance to our Sanctuary at Pomona Jewish Center and it has taken on an even greater meaning for the four of us. The Congregation has heard the story of the Box and Case and rejoiced in its happy ending.

I thought that the continuation of our story would interest you and I'm grateful for the opportunity to share it. You have my permission to tell it again and again.

Be well and happy.

One of many letters from someone I have not yet met; a Passover story:

At one of my Sedarim this year, we ransomed the Afikomen for Tzedakah. The person who found the Afikomen named the Tzedakah collective of her choice to whom we would donate. Here is my contribution! Please send me an updated report. Thanks!

A Federation event:

Thought I would pass on one item for future workshops. We returned to our big fundraising event, black tie and the whole works for the Jewish Welfare Federation. The centerpieces did not consist of the usual flowers, etc., but rather all the money that would have been spent was spent to buy toys (to be sent to Beit Shemesh), bingo sets for our apartment complex for the elderly, books given to the BJE library, etc. Can you picture black ties, long gowns, and basketballs on the tables or blocks of Legos or Tinker Toys?

Don't you love it?

From David Milkes, Long Beach, CA. Attached to the letter was an article from a local newspaper reporting on college scholarships awarded by the Bar Association. Also attached, a check for $50.00:

Dear Mr. Siegel:

The last time I contributed to your fund was after my Bar Mitzvah. I was very glad to share my good fortune with others who were less fortunate.

Now that I am graduating from high school, I would once again like to share my good fortune with others. I am honored to be able to donate some of the money I have won from recent scholarships. Having read your latest newsletter, I am confident that you will find a worthy cause for this donation. I hope you can bring as much happiness to others as has been brought to me.

From one of my friends in the Rabbinate:

One day I was speaking to our maintenance man — an all-around-good-guy. He is a church-going active Catholic. I believe that all of his children are adopted. His adopted son has very great emotional problems. That child has to be under constant supervision. Our man has given so much love and caring to this child under the hardest of circumstances that this story alone would be inspirational.

But that's not why I am writing about him. One day, I was talking to him about Tzedakah, and he told me about his Kaffeeklatsch. Every Saturday, he and his buddies go over to somebody's house (on a rotating basis). The host provides the coffee and donuts. The men just sit around and talk. At the end of the session, each man donates $1.00 to a special bank account. When the account reaches a tidy sum of money (I forget how much), the men sit down and decide to which local charity they will give the money. The Shriner Hospital, Open Pantry, and soup kitchens have been the recipients. All in all, this group of men has given away over $5,000 above and beyond their normal commitments.

From a 9-1/2 year-old girl, on a piece of paper decorated with a teddy bear:

Dear Sirs:

Our Chavurah has collected some Tzedakah and would like to give it to you. $12.40 worth of it. (check enclosed) We hope it helps.

Sincerely,
Leah Horowitz (9½) & The Newport Chavurah

From Louise Cohen, my friend from Boston, after a conference in Los Angeles:

Remember the yarmulkas you gave out with the stipulation that anyone who took one had to give $10 towards food for someone? After the conference, I went to see a play at the Huntington Hartford Theatre, and there was a neatly, but shabbily dressed, gentleman out front with a sign asking if anyone had any yard work, maintenance, etc. that he could do. He seemed more or less for real (although to tell the truth I'm not sure how much he really wanted work), and I was so impressed by his dignity in asking for jobs and not money, that I couldn't resist. I explained that I was leaving L.A. the next day and didn't have any work to offer him and slipped him the ten, which he didn't refuse. If you happen to know anyone in Los Angeles who needs a gardener, he may still be there . . . .

From Rabbi Marc Wilson, Temple Israel, Charlotte, NC:

Did I ever mention our "Parent's Hostel" Program to you? We have a list of congregation members who, on a moment's notice, will provide lodging for needy people whose children are brought to Charlotte for hospital care. There isn't much of a demand for it, but the hospitals are grateful to know that we are there, and it's gratifying to know we can accommodate. This might be an interesting project to encourage in communities where there are children's hospitals that serve a large regional area (like Eggleston in Atlanta and Children's Memorial in Chicago).

(Rabbi Wilson's suggestion is similar to the Bostoner Rebbi's project called ROFEH = *R*eaching *O*ut *F*urnishing *E*mergency *H*ealthcare, 1710 Beacon St., Brookline, MA 02146, 617-728- 0521.)

From my own family:

Hachnassat Orchim — hospitality, one of the major Acts of Lovingkindness outlined in the Talmud, along with visiting the sick, comforting mourners, burying the dead, providing clothes for those in need of them, and assuring young brides and grooms in need of a decent beginning to their marriage.

I've been travelling well over 20 years and have been the recipient of the kindnesses of hundreds of hosts and hostesses everywhere, but my upbringing has given me the craving to become the host.

I remember — and college friends keep reminding me — that my father has a lovely custom when people come to our home for Passover or some other holiday. When the guests would arrive — my college friends, for example, he would have them call home. California, New York, Chicago, Toronto . . . . it made no difference. He encouraged them to talk as long as they wanted to, knowing that they missed being home with their families for the holidays.

For years he has done this, a small gesture, to be sure. I think he sensed then that I would remember this household custom, and that my friends would remember it, and we would all recall it and record it somewhere down the years. Just recently someone reminded me again how much this meant to him.

Now, typing this story, I can see Steve Vinocor, sitting in my parents' bedroom, dialing "O", saying, "I'd like to place a long distnace call to. . ."

Such a little thing.

A story I learned from two sources: Trevor Ferrell, and from some literature on Sanctuary:

A Rabbi once asked his students how they could tell when the night had ended and the new day was beginning.

"Could it be," one student asked, "when you can see an animal in the distance and can tell whether it is a sheep or a dog?"

"No," answered the Rabbi.

Another asked, "Is it when you can look at a tree in the distance and can tell whether it is a fig tree or an orange tree?"

Again, the Rabbi answered, "No."

"Well, then, when is it?" the students asked.

"It is when you look on the face of any man or woman and see that he or she is your brother or sister. If you cannot do this, then no matter what time it is, it will always be night for you."

An old Arab woman performs a great act of Tzedakah:

Life Line for the Old, my favorite hang-out in Jerusalem. So many workshops for so many old people to come to, to make their gorgeous products. I know that in thirty years or so I'll retire and come here myself, to be at ease in old age, learning new skills, sharing my time with my friends, inspiring children, as this generation has inspired me and so many thousands of others.

This morning I am in one of my favorite workshops, down below the big room for people who have some kind of disability. It's a small workshop, maybe five or six people, but some of my favorite Elders are here, and particularly Chemda, the Favorite among Favorites, working at her sewing machine.

Chemda, well into her seventies, came from Aleppo, Syria, more than a half century ago. Every time I am in her workshop we schmooze a little. This morning she decides to tell me her sister Yaffa's story. I already knew that Yaffa somehow managed to get out of Syria just four or five years before. For almost forty-five years the two sisters hadn't seen each other — I knew that already. I often talked to Yaffa, through Chemda's translation into Arabic, because I admired her delicate crochet work so much, and because the two of them were such a pleasure to be with, Chemda at her sewing machine, Yaffa with her needle.

I knew that somehow Yaffa managed to get to Turkey from Syria, and from there to Israel.

Chemda filled in the rest:

My sister, Yaffa, lived in the same building as Assad's mother. Assad, grand dictator of Syria, no friend of the Jews . . . .But Yaffa and his mother were friends. She'd make things for his mother, have tea with her. Yes, they were friends.

Yaffa asked her to speak to her son — she told her she wanted to visit some relatives in Istanbul. Would she please speak to her son and see if he could arrange it?

Assad's mother, Yaffa's friend, knew Yaffa wasn't going to stop in Turkey, knew that she would go on to Israel, but she arranged it anyway, and Yaffa was free, re-united with Chemda, her sister.

I like to think that this is The Story of Israel, right in one room, but that is too abstract. This story is too human — two sisters sharing their later years together through the Mitzvah-intervention of a Jew-hater's mother.

And there is a postscript, 1986:

One of my mornings there, I am talking to Chemda, as usual. She tells me her brother, Yosef, is getting out soon.

How, when exactly, through what connections — I don't ask.

By the time I left Israel that summer, Yosef had left Syria and arrived in Israel, though I didn't get to meet him, because he was in Tel Aviv visiting other relatives. But I'll meet him next year.

Yaffa said, "He looks so old, so tired."

She last saw him as a teen-ager. Now he is in his sixties.

Arnie Draiman, a recent Oleh to Jerusalem, used to work for Congregation Ahavath Achim, Atlanta, GA. This is a column he once wrote for the synagogue bulletin:

THE TZEDAKAH HABIT . . .

"Rabbi Tanhum, though he needed only one portion of meat for himself, would buy two; though he needed only one bunch of vegetables, he would buy two . . . one for the poor and one for himself."

(Midrash Kohelet Rabbah 7:30)

In response to Danny Siegel's Scholar-in-Residence presentations, we would like to urge members of our congregation to get into the Tzedakah habit. Although financial contributions to worthy organizations are always important, so too, are other types of Tzedakah work. The projects listed here can involve the entire family on a very regular basis. In cooperation with the Jewish Family Services (formerly Jewish Family and Children's Bureau) Ahavath Achim members can help with the needy of our Atlanta community. Our "Adopt-A-Family" program will enable you to share resources with those in need.

Get into the Tzedakah habit by adopting one of the families/persons listed below with their needs:

(1) A young man under care for schizophrenia, who is currently gainfully employed and adjusting to a 'normal' lifestyle, needs tubes of oil paint, wood-framed canvasses, turpentine, and other miscellaneous items, for a meaningful and therepeutic hobby: painting.

(2) A woman needs supplies necessary to complete cross-stitching of pillowcases, which is her craft.

(3) A woman needs food items (staples, canned goods, beverages, etc.) paper goods, books, (novels, stories of Jewish interest), and dog food for her only companion. These are needed about every two weeks.

(4) An older woman is in need of food items on a bi-weekly basis.

(5) New Russian immigrants are in need of food items and certain sewing supplies on a monthly basis.

(6) A Non-Jewish Ethiopian Family needs food items especially for their two year old — on a monthly basis.

(7) Donations of food items for emergency kits for people with needs on a limited basis. For example, individuals, during inclement weather who

can't get out to get food, or individuals who become infirm at home for a few days, etc.

For information on how to help the above, plus others, please contact me.

From The Voice, *November, 1984, the bulletin of Congregation Kol Emeth, Palo Alto, CA, where my good friend, Sheldon Lewis, is the rabbi. This is an excellent example of how to install a special sound system in the synagogue for individuals with hearing difficulties, and how to provide receivers for members and guests. Every effort is made to avoid embarrassment concerning the cost of individual receivers:*

INFRA-RED SYSTEM APPROVED: The infra-red hearing enhancement system that we tried on Rosh Hashanah was approved by the Board of Directors at the October 25th meeting. The response to the trial on the holidays was overwhelmingly positive. Questionnaires were sent out to those who tried the system; 82% of the questionnaires were returned! Comments from the others were obtained by phone. Many users reported that until they used the system, they had never enjoyed a service so much. Others commented that they did not realize how much they had been missing.

Half of the respondents said that they would like to own their own receiver. One person offered to buy four receivers, one for personal use, and three that would belong to Kol Emeth for long-term loan use by people who could not afford their own. The Board decided that the distribution of these receivers would be handled confidentially by the same three-person Financial Panel that makes dues adjustments. This panel consists of the treasurer, financial secretary, and membership officer. The congregation will have two receivers on hand for guests and newcomers to try. The Religious Practices committee will make these available at services.

Owning a receiver provides several advantages:

a. the individual will always have a receiver in working order

b. the ear pads need not be changed or washed after each use

c. the owner will be sure to turn the unit off after each use to preserve the batteries

d. the owner can use the receiver at the Geary and Curran theatres in San Francisco, which are equipped with infra-red systems.

The infra-red system will operate automatically whenever the public address system is on; at services, Sisterhood functions, lectures, school assemblies, etc. We plan to install the system so that it can be moved to Gunn High School auditorium for the High Holidays.

The Board has established a special fund for the purchase of receivers for those who could not afford their own. Contributions can be sent to the synagogue office marked for the Hearing Enhancement Receivers. The gift will be acknowledged in the VOICE, and if it is in honor of someone, the honoree will be notified of the donation.

Once the system has been installed, we plan to have Pro Media come to Kol Emeth with samples of all the receivers that will work with this infra-red system. Those who participated in evaluating the system will be invited to come to choose the style of receiver they like best. The synagogue will then buy all the receivers as a group, to take advantage of quantity purchasing. The members will then pay only our cost for a receiver. Even those who will be obtaining receivers on a long-term loan basis can choose their receivers at this time. If you did not participate in trying out the system but would like to try or buy your own receiver, please call the synagogue office at (415) 948-7498 and leave your name and phone number so we can contact you when the receivers are available.

From Mark Picus of Houston:

I enjoyed hearing you last August at the CAJE Conference in San Antonio. I have also enjoyed reading your books *(Angels & Gym Shoes)* and am adapting much of the material for use in my religious school class (5th grade in a very reform synagogue)....

Your ideas have given me an idea. I'm getting married in December. Both my and my fiancée's family are large, we have many wonderful friends, and our wedding is going to be large by necessity (about 400 people). We are keeping it modest, as befits our style, but nevertheless, a tremendous amount of money will be expended on our simcha. I am hoping to make arrangements so that on the day after the wedding, the centerpieces (all 40 or so of them) will be brought to the Jewish Home for the Aged. I am frequently torn when I think about the huge sums of money being spent so that 400 upper middle class people can enjoy themselves for a few hours, even though sharing a wedding with well-wishers can hardly be considered wasteful of anything. I hope I'll be able to share my happiness with some who can't attend.

From the Nemers, friends from Minneapolis; a note accompanying a check:

By the Grace of G-d we have had a good year. In the name of G-d, we would like to share with others.

BeAhava-Love,
The Nemers

From Addie Levy of Arlington, mother of Howard Levy ז״ל. Howard was a friend of the founders of Ziv, a Hebrew school and USY contemporary for many years. A few years ago he passed away, and left some money for the Ziv Tzedakah Fund:

Enclosed is a check for $2,040.88 from Howard.

I am sure that he would have wished it to be spent in Israel to help Jewish people.

Thank you for your help.

From Dr. Abraham J. Gittelson, my mentor in Jewish education, from Miami:

I want to tell you about a project I just heard about in my neck of the woods, or palm trees, at least. A long time friend, Adophe Greenbaum, told me the other day that he gathers the flowers that adorn the bimah of the reform congregation he attends, and takes them after Shabbat and holidays, usually on the Monday following Shabbat, to what is called "The Gathering Place". It is a JCC program for frail elderly Jews, who are brought to the JCC every day during the week for an all-day program of study, crafts, lunch, and entertainment. He puts the flowers on the tables where they meet each Monday, and thus enlivens the physical, and psychological setting.

I would imagine that many synagogues put flowers on the bimah each week, and probably throw them out the next day. Here is a wonderful Mitzvah that might be publicized for the use of these flowers in all sorts of settings — senior citizen centers, old age homes, nursing homes, etc.

From Joe Williams, a friend I first met at a Federation Young Leadership retreat in Houston. I noticed that he wore a hearing aid, and we talked about getting some for Yad Sara in Jerusalem, which would lend them to people for free. Letter dated May 24, 1982:

Enclosed are two hearing aids which I'm glad you will be able to put to good use. As I recall, one of them works O.K., but I believe one needs some repair work.

Joe's second letter, September 15, 1986, after I made additional inquiries, asking him to find further supplies:

I have discussed the issue of old hearing aids with our Jewish Home for the Aged and they will start sending us whatever used aids they have. They indicate there aren't very many because they are able to recycle them from one patient to the other. In the past, when they occasionally had an old aid available, they donated it to an organization in Houston which does the same thing in our community that Yad Sara does in Israel. They would rather make those donations to Yad Sara and will do so in the future, although they indicate there aren't that many that become available.

I also talked to the Commercial Hearing Aid Company I use and hopefully they might send us some in the future, although they have also been using the local agency for that same purpose. They indicated most of their used aids are returned to the factory and that they also don't have a large volume available.

From Robert Fishman, Director of the West Hartford Community Relations Committee:

I think about you often and hope you are doing well.

I heard about a terrific Tzedakah story recently and thought you may want to use it or better yet - get it straight from the source. My friend, Miriam Hochman, the wife of an Orthodox Rabbi and mother of 4 proudly told me about one of her daughters who spent a year in Israel and decided upon her return to help clothe the needy young girls' in Israel. This daughter is Bat Mitzvah in age.

She discovered a New York garment outfit was going out of business and she got friends and family to buy up all remaining skirts for a huge discount. Then she arranged to send them to a girls' school in Israel where they outfitted all those who were needy.

You can write or call Miriam Hochman directly because I do not know which New York Yeshiva her 13-year-old daughter is attending.

CAJE, the GA, My New Suit, My New Contact Lenses:

CAJE — The Conference for Alternatives in Jewish Education, largest gathering of Jewish educators in the world.

Attendees from Lincoln, Nebraska, decided to invite me out. I know the rabbi and his wife from before; the laypeople are young, enthused — an optometrist and his wife.

A few months later I am in Lincoln, and a while later, we arrange to have new gas-permeable hard contact lenses made for me. At cost. The difference between cost and retail goes to Tzedakah.

The GA — The General Assembly of the Federations. Hundreds and hundreds of laypeople and professionals, obsessed with Tzedakah.

I am doing a Lunch and Learn — over box lunches, about 100 people study Tzedakah texts with me. We are on a roll, swept up by the rush of texts. In preparation for one piece of Midrash, I ask the students what some of them do for a living. One says, "I have a men's clothing store in Sioux City, and you'll be coming out there soon."

I reply, "Good! You'll sell me a suit at discount, the difference going to Tzedakah."

A few months later, I am in Sioux City. Straight from the airport the rabbi takes me to the store. One suit, two shirts, two ties, substantial discount, good money to Tzedakah.

Alterations are quick. Friday night, already the suit is ready, which I model to honor The Sabbath Queen. My Tzedakah suit.

The GA, A 5-Second Pep-Talk From One of the Honchos:

Before my talk on Tzedakah to about 150 Federation Young Leadership people, I consult with a good friend, one of the Leaders of the Leaders. He is ten years my junior, a very successful businessman, well-respected, and well-liked. We have become good friends; he is *Ziess* and *Edel* — a very sweet and gentle person. I ask him what message he would like me to get across to the group.

He says, "Tell them that the greatest thrill of closing a big deal is all that extra Tzedakah money you have to give away."

From the Regional NCSY Youth Director, Baltimore-Washington area. Long beard, broad heart:

I have just finished a seminar with his teen-agers. They were tired from being up late the night before, so the program goes unevenly. Some perk up on some of the Mitzvah projects; some fade in and out. The staff and I don't feel wonderful about the program, but it wasn't so bad. I keep forgetting what it was like to be a teen-ager talking late into the night with friends.

The director, Reb Itchie, talks to me as I sit in my car ready to go back home. He has a story to tell me.

"My father was a baker. He died when I was about 10, but here's a story for your talks.

"There was a man from our community who had been sent to jail. Everyone shunned him when he got out, dissociating themselves because of the embarrassment of it all.

"My father, the baker, went over with a big cake he had baked, welcoming him back to freedom."

End of story.

I like stories when they end like that. The silence afterwards just hangs there, and the listener has to deal with it. No Big Boom ending, no clever turn of phrase, no punch line. Nothing....Just a story for me to remember, to carry with me, re-tell, as I am doing now for my readers.

The following is an obituary for Frances French Harris, known as "Auntie", who was an unassuming, generous woman who personified the highest human values. Auntie, granddaughter of Frederick French, a slave freed by Abraham Lincoln, died in her nineties in April, 1985. She raised many children besides her own — members of the extended family — including Ethel French, a woman who has worked for my family since before I was born. Ethel, one of those raised by Auntie, has passed on many of those values to me. The obituary was written by her great-nephew. Ethel's son, Paul Jones, Jr., another one of those fortunate ones to have been raised by Auntie. It is a grand and most appropriate tribute to this quiet giant:

Frances French Harris was born in Fairfax County, Virginia, on October 13, 1890. She was the oldest daughter of seven children born to the late Edmund French and Elmira Washington French. Frances received her public education in the Fairfax County "Colored" school system. She attended a one-room school house in West Falls Church, Virginia, and she finished her education at a one-room school house in Merrifield, Virginia. During her school years and a short time after then she would do day domestic work; however, most of her time was spent doing the chores which would help the family structure — washing, ironing, gathering wood for fuel, and caring for the family in general. The position of the oldest child during this time, at the beginning of the new century, was a position of great responsibility.

Beyond this position in the family structure, Frances did find a life of her own. She was married by Rev. Walter S. Jackson at the Simpson Memorial M. E. Church to Edward Harris on October 27, 1909. They remained married until his death in 1962. She joined the Galloway Methodist Church in 1918, which at that time was under the leadership of Rev. T.

P. Thomas. She was a member of the Providence Club for the Church and the Household of Ruth. Frances attended this church until her health would not allow her to do so. However, she continued to support it in her own way.

Although she had no children of her own, she can be given credit for helping her niece Ethel raise, guide, and care for her three sons: John Emory, William Edward, and Paul Lawrence Jones.

Frances remained at home and in Fairfax County all of her life. She did not venture to many other places except with trips sponsored by the church. But what she did do was to establish herself as the strength or backbone of a multilevel family. She remained in this position until the day she died, Saturday, April 20, 1985. Frances was in her 95th year. Her two nieces, Ethel and Arlie, supported her during her time of need, and most fittingly she died at home in her family's care where she devoted her total life. She leaves to mourn her nieces Mary W. Alexander, Ophelia F. Crowner, Ethel French, Arlie L. Hart, Vergie F. Jackson, Eleanor Washington and nephews Paul French and Daniel Washington, other relatives and many friends.

The Family

From Elyse Winnick, a former student at the State University of New York at Albany. This note is from her days there as a student:

. . . . I met you when you spoke at SUNY Albany . . . . I've been talking with my friends about Tzedakah a lot, and I think we're all beginning to share an inner excitement, a burning desire to give and share. We've done some work in the past, when we were all together in Young Judaea (Project Dorot, singing at nursing homes), but it was just a little and just when the movement provided opportunities. I think we're starting to get our acts together now. We'll be searching out things to do over intercession and try to implement them when we return to our respective schools in February. I've already started my plans. For one, I'll be doing community service through the university at one of the conservative synagogues here. I don't know yet what my specific responsibility will be, but my inclination is to have them place me wherever I'm needed most.

I've also made a bigger (and what is for me more involved) decision. My long distance telephone bills tend to be rather high (none of my friends from home is in the area). I plan to give up the phone for the ever useful 20¢ stamp and give at least $5 a week (depending on the week's expenses) for Tzedakah. It's not tremendous, but it's better than being idle. I usually prefer hands-on helping, but I've realized that the best help is whatever help you can give.

Changing Times:

When I was in USY, the United Synagogue Youth group, going away to the week-long encampment at the end of August was one of the highlights of the year. It was fun, educational, filled with Yiddishkeit. Now times have changed. Camp is still fun, educational, and filled with Yiddishkeit, but there is an extra element in some regions, Metropolitan New York and Seaboard (and perhaps others) in particular: one day is devoted to bringing in residents of nearby institutions for people with mental and physical limitations to share in a carnival and other activities. I am jealous. By all reports from the staff and the teen-agers, the day is a powerful experience that will be remembered long into the future. A little scary to many at first (I would be scared, too). But previous attendees ease the newcomers into the day, and drained and thrilled at once, by late evening, everyone knows something remarkable has happened, a new connection, an inner change, a maturing and joy. Yes, I am jealous that we didn't think of that back in the late '50's and early '60's.

The Book, The People:

From the earliest stages of our Jewish education, most of us knew that if we dropped a prayerbook or some similar holy volume, we should pick it up and kiss it. I would suppose that the message from Project Dorot's shelter for Jewish homeless in New York and Trevor Ferrell's work with the homeless in Philadelphia — the message from them would be, "Yes, continue to pick up the books and kiss them. But do the same for fallen human beings." The Dorot people have never told me that, nor has Trevor, but that is what they are saying.

After a Teacher's Seminar on Tzedakah:

A woman speaks to me about her course preparing her to become a Jew by choice. She recalls how charity was such an important part of her Christian upbringing, and that, unfortunately, nothing about Tzedakah was covered in her studies in preparation for becoming Jewish.

End of story.

After a talk I gave in Maryland, one of the rabbis sent out the following letter to parents of the congregation's children. A most gratifying follow-up to one of my talks.

Dear Parent,

Several weeks ago the Jewish Council of Howard County sponsored a stimulating talk by Danny Siegel. Danny's talk on tzedakah challenged our community, and particularly our young people to be "mitzvah heroes" — to do good deeds on behalf of Jews less fortunate than ourselves.

A group of youngsters in our community, members of the Patuxent chapter of AZA and B'nai B'rith Girls has accepted that challenge and wants to call on other young teens to do the same. Their project is to help raise money for tzedakah through the ongoing United Jewish Appeal campaign being conducted by the Jewish Council of Howard County.

In addition to contributing money themselves, these youngsters will be soliciting contributions from their peers. I heartily endorse this worthwhile initiative and ask that you discuss tzedakah with your children.

Please encourage them to give a gift of their own when called by a teen volunteer. Setting aside for tzedakah a portion of their spending money or bar/bat mitzvah money can give a youngster an important sense of participation in our community and instill fundamental values so important to Judaism.

If for personal reasons you are uncomfortable with your children being called on this basis, please write or call the congregation office. Should your child wish to make a gift directly, please send a check made out to

_____

Please give this important effort your support and encourage your children to be "mitzvah heroes!"

Thank you in advance for your support.

A question of Jewish Law I addressed to my Rebbi, Rabbi David Weiss-HaLivni. The question is posed in the form of a She'aylah, a formal question on matters of Jewish Law:

To My Teacher, Rabbi David HaLivni,

A She'aylah:

While lecturing recently at a synagogue on Long Island, the conversation turned to the needs of individuals with disabilities.

The questions arose: is one permitted to lower the Mezuzot on one's doors for them to be accessible to individuals in wheelchairs?

Would it be preferable to have two Mezuzot on the doors, one higher up, and one lower down?

Bechavod — With Great Respect, Your Student,

Danny Siegel

Rabbi HaLivni's reply:

My dear student!

It would be preferable to lower the Mezuzot — if *it is obvious* that. it was done for the sake of the disabled.

Bi'didut — In Friendship,

David HaLivni

From the Chicago Tribune Magazine Section, June 11, 1986, an interview with dubutante Cornelia Guest, god-daughter of the late Duke and Duchess of Windsor. She published a book that same month, The Debutante's Guide to Life, *Two pre-publication quotes:*

"Scratch a debutante's finely groomed surface and you will not find Mother Teresa of Calcutta underneath. Debs do charity work because their friends do. Anything can be fun if you get to gossip at the same time."

And —

"Respect for education is a characteristic of immigrants."

From the Chicago Tribune, November 15, 1986, about Ivan Boesky, King of the Arbitragers, shortly after he was ordered to pay a $50,000,000 fine

and to give up another $50,000,000 in illegal profits from insider trading. A quote from a column by Herb Greenberg:

A few years ago arbitrager Ivan F. Boesky stood before a standing-room-only group of University of Chicago business students and said, ''It's okay to make money. It's a good thing. You go to heaven if you do it.''

A LITTLE CASE IN KINGSTON, ONTARIO

*Allan M. Gould**

This is a story about medical ethics. But unlike most stories of this kind, there are no deaths, no embryos thawed out or thrown away, no life support systems switched off. In fact, there was no one actually harmed, at least to the best of our knowledge, except perhaps a doctor who was put through a long and distressing trial. The so-called "victims" in the case have not complained about any pain from their unnecessary treatment, perhaps because they are mentally disabled.

There are no heroes or villains in this story, either, as there often are in similar cases. The doctor who was on trial is by all accounts a superb physician; the medical student who blew the whistle on what she considered unethical conduct would just as soon forget the whole thing; nearly everyone involved feels apologetic about the incident and has taken steps that it will not occur again.

But there is a victor, a winner in the case of Her Majesty The Queen vs. Doctor Ruth Wiens, which concluded before His Honour R.B. Batten at the Provincial Court House, City of Kingston, Province of Ontario, on the 22nd day of June 1984, in the forenoon — quite a few winners, in fact. This is a victory for all the mentally and physically disabled of Canada, for everyone who ever steps foot into a hospital, for everyone who lives in Canada, even doctors.

The cast of characters is simple; the case is not like one of those windy Russian novels of the last century where you need a list of *dramatis personae*. There is the doctor in the dock, Ruth Wiens; her lawyer, D.K. Laidlaw, Q.C.; the prosecuting lawyer, David Newman; the medical student, Laura Muldoon, who'd prefer not to be mentioned, since this has all been dreadful PR for Queen's University Medical School.

There are lesser characters, of course: Robert Seaby, the Executive Director of Ongwanada Hospital, where the assaults took place; Dr. Boston, the Chief of Pediatrics at Queen's; Elaine Newman, a lawyer with The Advocacy Resource Centre for the Handicapped in Toronto (ARCH);a few others. We can't list the names of the teenaged boys on whom the examinations/assaults were done/committed, however, since no one ever managed to find out what they are and that is one of the points of this law case.

The chronology of events and the events themselves are also straightforward, even if the questions which have arisen from them are not. For we are discussing here nothing less than the education of medical students and their need to be taught. These are the future doctors who will ease your

---

*So much of Tzedakah is tied up with the issue of human dignity, I decided to include my good friend Allan Gould's article about the abuse of retarded people in this volume. It is a devastating piece and stands in the stongest contrast to the items about Hadassah Levi's work with infants and children with Down's Syndrome in Israel. The article originally appeared in Canadian Forum, August/September 1985.

pain, operate on your spouse, cure your child. Call it a case of ends and means with a necessary trade-off somewhere in between the doctor's need to know and the patient's right to say "no."

Here is what happened before the case came to trial:

On November 4, 1982, Dr. Ruth Wiens, a lecturer in the pediatrics department at Queen's University since the late '70s and a member of the Medical Advisory Committee of Ongwanada Hospital since 1979, toured the facility with 10 students from the second-year class of Queen's University Medical School.

Ongwanada is a temporary building from the Second World War, built as the barracks for Alcan female munitions workers. After the war, it became the Kingston home for the Department of Veteran's Affairs; then it became a TB sanitarium. By the late '60s TB had been mostly eradicated: in 1967 the Ontario Ministry of Health decided to move disabled children into Ongwanada. By 1970, there were 100 mentally and physically disabled youths in the building; today, there are around 85, since some have recently moved to group homes. In 1977, Ongwanada merged with the Penrose Centre, "a 19th century monstrosity," to quote the parent of a mentally disabled child, making the place the home for over three dozen chronically ill adults, as well.

November of 1982 marked the third consecutive year that Dr. Wiens had taken her students — there are about 75 in the second year — to visit the disabled children and youths, to sensitize them to the physical and mental problems of the disabled, and to study their conditions. "It's hard to be depressed when you're in Ongwanada with Ruth Wiens," says one medical student who, like nearly all, wishes to remain anonymous. "Dr. Wiens is a wonderful person! She'd pick up kids who are drooling, and kiss them all the while she'd talk to us. She is truly warm."

Wiens would show the students how this child had Tay-Sachs, this one was hydrocephalic — noting the head and how it was filled with water. "We did knee reflexes," recalls the student; "we lookied into the eyes of many, which is a reasonable thing to do, if a kid is blind. A lot of kids there are blind. But at not time was there ever a hint of any rectal exams."

But there was in Laura Muldoon's group, in November, 1982, as there had been in groups of two previous years. All second-year students at Queen's Medical School practise what are called "clinical skills," in which a different part of the body is studied each week; one week it will be the ear/nose/throat area, the next week the cardiovascular system, and so on. Patients at Kingston hospital are asked if they mind if a medical student taps their chest or looks down their throat; most say yes.

Muldoon and two other students were troubled that their trip to Ongwanada coincided with the week they were to do their examination of the abdomen and a rectal. They spoke with their teacher about their concern, and Dr. Wiens apparently assumed they were being squeamish about handling genitalia.

On the day Muldoon and nine fellow medical students visited Ongwanada, "Dr. Wiens handled the children there with care, love, compassion and concern. She was a good doctor," says Muldoon, now 24. But after watching her teacher perform the first rectal, the three students left the room, refusing to participate and Dr. Wiens accepted their decision.

Few medical schools in Canada have compulsory courses in ethics, but a growing number, like Queen's, let students run their own. By coincidence, Laura Muldoon had been placed in charge of a symposium on "The Voiceless Patient" — patients such as children and the mentally disabled — and a panel discussion was held on March 10, 1983. The fifth case was the Ongwanada incident.

Dr. Georgina Harris of London, Ontario, was at the discussion as a clinical psychologist who works at University Hospital at the University of Western Ontario and as the mother of a mentally disabled child. "I didn't know what Ongwanada was," she recalls. Dr. Wiens was invited to describe what she had done, and those on the panel thought it was all right to use mentally disabled children in teaching medical students. All the others thought it was wrong.

Nick Bala, an associate professor on the faculty of law at Queen's, declared it was "assault," and said that Dr. Weins and the students could be tried in a court of law. (A group of medical students approached Bala after the symposium and were overheard asking him, "Can we say that we were just following the orders of our teacher?" The law professor reminded them of the Nuremberg trials.)

"Dr. Wiens never once said, "Oh my God!" or "I never thought of that!" recalls Dr. Harris about the symposium. "She seemed to wonder what all the fuss was about. But to say that a physician doesn't know that she didn't need consent is unbelievable to me! And what was so bad was that not only was there no consent to do these non-therapeutic exams but these children had no possibility of refusing!"

Harris recalls Wiens saying that parents who have children in institutions expect that they will be used in this way. At that point, Laura Muldoon asked Dr. Harris if, as a parent of a mentally disabled child, she thought that was true."I said 'certainly not!' And that as far as I was concerned, no other parent would feel that way, either!" The psychiatrist on the panel agreed that he would be astonished if parents expected non-therapeutic examinations.

Someone at the symposium stood up and said that rectals should be learned in the proper fashion, with experts, at which point another student cried out, "Come on! You know what goes on with people coming out of surgery!" Then another doctor on the panel asked, "Why don't you medical students practise on each other?"

There was a great roar of laughter.

Professor Bernard Dickens, of the University of Toronto Law School, who lectures and writes extensively on the question of consent and medical ethics, comments: "The reason why those medical students would not examine each other is precisely why they should not do it on retarded adolescents! One does not use a vulnerable population when a non-vulnerable population can be used just as well."

"The penny dropped," as Dr. Wiens would later put it in court. The word got out from the symposium and was soon in hundreds of newspapers and broadcasts: QUEEN'S UNIVERSITY STUDENTS USE RETARDED YOUTHS FOR MEDICAL EXAMINATIONS! The response, as one can well imagine, was universally negative.

"I don't think it happens every day," says Dr. Arthur Schafer, a professor in the department of philosophy at the University of Manitoba and a lecturer on bio-medical ethics in the faculty of medicine, "but it's not as infrequent as it should be." Schafer recalls being told by medical students at the University of Manitoba that they had been invited to perform rectals on unconscious patients. When the students began the examinations, patients groaned in pain, and one student refused to continue. "The teacher became belligerent and insulting and said that it showed how badly they did it, and made them feel stupid." Through discussions with his students, Dr. Schafer has gotten them to agree that "to do any sort of procedure on unconscious patients without previous consent is first of all battery, and more importantly, immoral." Students may learn medical history or technique from such procedures, but they are also learning "that it's legitimate to use patients for one's own convenience."

Echoes Nick Bala, the Kingston lawyer on that fateful symposium panel discussion, "It was not necessary to have mentally retarded children as the subjects. It was a question of convenience of it all. The fact that they didn't know who the children were!" exclaims Muriel Clarke-Beechey of Kingston, who was on the board of Ongwanada from 1972 to 1982, and whose son Rob lived there from 1968 to 1972. "That means that they walked in and said 'We'll take you, and you, and you,' like meat in a grocery store. And they chose multihandicapped children, who couldn't push them away. They maintain that it didn't hurt them, but you don't know if it hurts them or not. Some only make little sounds and faces, and only if you know them do you understand. I'm sick to my stomach when I think of this incident."

Other parents reacted with more than revulsion. Some laid charges against Dr. Weins and Ongwanada. Or at least, they tried to. A great deal happened between the symposium and the time the case came to trial in the spring of 1984, but in brief, the facts are these:

Elizabeth Hilhorst, the mother of a mentally disabled youth at Ongwanada, read of the incident in the papers and was concerned that her son Glen, now 18, had been involved. She contacted the Ontario Association for the Mentally Retarded (OAMR), the Kingston Association and eventually the Canadian Association for the Mentally Retarded (CAMR, which has recently changed its name to the Canadian Association for Community Living) and retained Elaine Newman of ARCH to defend her. "Glen is at the level of a one-year-old," she later told the court. "He doesn't cry easily for pain. He once was burned through his skin and only sniffed; you have to know him. Dr. Weins said, 'none were in any discomfort' from the rectals, but how could she know?"

Newman wrote to the attorney general of Ontario, then Roy McMurtry, to investigate the matter, on March 30, 1983. An investigation followed by Officer Pellisaro of the Ontario Provincial Police, who had difficulty discovering the names of the mentally disabled youths, and even the names of the medical students. He recommended that no charges be laid. (On the stand, during the trial, the prosecuting attorney asked the officer whether, if he had been able to find credible evidence and witnesses, he would have recommended that it go to court. ''No,'' he replied.)

The attorney general decided that ''the public interest would not be served by a criminal prosecution in this case although it is quite possible that a technical assault took place.''

On May 4, 1983, Elaine Newman wrote to the attorney general: ''We are dealing with completely helpless and totally vulnerable people — people who can neither call out for help nor complain. Does the attorney general conclude that a crime committed against a voiceless victim is no crime at all? . . . It is the helpless and the vulnerable segment of our community that most requires the protection of the criminal justice system. To deny them that protection in so clear a case as this has certainly served to bring the administration of justice in this province into ridicule and disrepute.''

On the last day of the six-month period during which charges could be laid, May 3, 1983, a private informant, John Osborne of the Kingston Association for the Mentally Retarded, swore out a complaint against Dr. Wiens before Justice of the Peace E.B. Hare of Kingston. Hare refused to pursue the criminal charges, forcing the three associations to file notice with the Ontario Supreme Court and asking them to issue a writ of mandemus requiring the justice to deal with the case. ''On every front we have been roadblocked,'' declared Jim Montgomery of the OAMR at the time. ''We are frankly appalled by the wall of inaction we have run into,'' added Dr. Hugh Lafave of the CAMR. ''An important issue is at stake here. Does the justice system of this province with all its power protect the rights of mentally handicapped people as vigilantly as those of other citizens?''

Finally, on October 6, 1983, another justice of the peace, Peter Philip, decided that there was sufficient evidence against Dr. Wiens, allowing the associations to abandon the writ action. On November 23, it was announced that Dr. Ruth Wiens would be tried in provincial court the following April 12, on five charges of assault.

The Ontario Health Insurance Program building in Kingston, Ontario is spanking new, officially opened by William G. Davis, former premier of the province, on October 24, 1983, shortly after his attorney general had told the various association for the mentally disabled of Canada to forget about pursuing that Wiens affair. Just inside the sparkling white building is an abstract mural incorporating the words:

When health is absent wisdom cannot/reveal itself art cannot become/manifest strength cannot fight/wealth becomes useless and intelligence cannot be applied/The health of the nations is more important/than the wealth of the nations/Life is an adventure in forgiveness/Any life however long is too short if the/mind is bereft of splendor/Our awareness of what goes on within/ourselves is the most illuminating/of all our experiences/The greater the ignorance the/greater the dogmatism.

On the trip from Toronto to Kingston for the opening of the trial, the two prosecuting attorneys expressed their hopes and concerns for the case. "They want to quash it because of abuse of process," said Michael Code, the young co-counsel. "But I think our case is so strong, they'll have real trouble."

"I'm not so sure," said co-counsel David Newman, the older of the two lawyers. "I've defended six doctors, and never had one convicted. They're just a touch below Jesus Christ. People talk of doctors in hushed tones, even at cocktail parties." "You know, it's unusual for someone as big as Laidlaw, a two-grand-a-day man, to get involved in a provincial court trial." "It's devastating, hurtful, what those students did!" exploded Code. "No dignity! Totally demeaning! And those institutions use consent forms to take the kids to a picnic! If they need permission for a trip, then surely they need it for anal exams!"

As the courthouse, the regular judge was away for some reason, and Provincial Judge R.B. Batten came into the courtroom, which has wood panels everywhere and a big, glassed-in area for the court artists ("Be careful: his right side is best!" the secretary kibbitzes with them). The seal of the province of Ontario hangs on the wall: *A Mari Usque Ad Mare*.

Doug Laidlaw, at the time one of Canada's most prominent lawyers — shortly after the conclusion of these proceedings he was killed in a Toronto traffic accident — rose and took control. Tall, handsome, stately, his hair thinning, his thumbs often sliding into his pants gunslinger fashion, Laidlaw moved to stay the proceedings on "abuse of process." He argued that the prosecution was using the courts wrongly, that it was attempting to punish a fine doctor when the problem had already been corrected, and was only interested in publicizing the CAMR and OAMR's attitudes toward the mentally disabled.

If Laidlaw succeeded in getting the case thrown out at this point, his client, Dr. Ruth Wiens, would never have to go through a full trial. But in order to prove his abuse of process argument, he'd have to call witnesses, including Dr. Wiens, which for all intents and purposes would make the motion a trial, in which most of the arguments and concerns would get aired.

Dr. Boston, of Queen's Medical School, argued that a new, "very careful set of guidelines between Queen's and Ongwanada would insure that any teaching henceforth at the hospital would be beneficial and at no time harmful." Under cross-examination by David Newman (the lights of the room reflected off the lawyer's balding head, making his sharply-angled face look disconcertingly like Pierre Trudeau's), the uncomfortable Dr. Boston declared: "Dr. Wiens said that the patients had no objection to the examinations." "But they couldn't give consent because they couldn't talk," shoots back Newman. "No further questions."

The problem of consent in medical care is hardly limited to the mentally disabled, of course. "I've heard far worse horror stories than the Wiens case," says one medical student at Queen's. "Tales of women under anesthetic, and five people come in and do pelvic exams." "There's a lot of anecdotal evidence of pelvic exams being done without consent," echoes Bernard Dickens of the University of Toronto law school. A Toronto nurse tells of non-therapeutic spinal taps being done on premature infants without their parents' knowledge, and the story is echoed by the mother of such a child.

Other people question just how informed consent can be when one is in a hospital and so very grateful to the doctors. "We never asked patients who were really sick." recalls Dr. Peter Rempel, a recent graduate of Queen's. "The majority of patients would say "yes." Patients are flattered if they are paid attention to by doctors!" Nick Bala agrees: "There are a large group of people who are more or less coerced, although a voluntariness is theoretically there. It's difficult for people who are less sophisticated and less educated to refuse their doctor."

Most doctors and lawyers are concerned about this, and have gone out of their way to avoid gentle persuasion. "We make sure that the family doctor is not the one who requests that the child be checked by students," says Dickens, "so there is no sense of manipulation. At the Hospital for Sick Children, we are working to make sure that the vulnerability of parents is not exploited." Dr. Heshy Sturm, a general pediatrician at that hospital, concurs: "I ask parents, 'in order to benefit other doctors it would be helpful if your child was seen. But don't hesitate to say no. If you're not comfortable with it, tell me. It will in no way affect your child's medical care.' " Sturm claims that only "one in 10 parents says no."

Robert Seaby, a pleasant-looking, bespectacled young man, was called as a witness by Laidlaw. He agreed with the defense attorney's statement that "this prosecution is harmful to Ongwanada," of which he is executive director. Newman later read a quotation of Seaby's to *The Globe and Mail* in which he said: "The doctor carried out the examinations with care and compassion. It was an error in her judgment not to have obtained consents from the parents but I don't feel there was any malicious intent on her part or the students'. At no time do we condone teaching procedures without obtaining consent. We'll take every step to ensure that it never happens again."

Dr. Ruth Wiens was then called to testify. She is an attractive woman of 50, with severe, short-cropped brown hair, and was handsome in her grey suit.

Her lawyer examined her: "At that point in time [when the question was raised at the symposium], what was your opinion as to the ethical consideration involved?"

Wiens answered, "Ethically I had no problems with it because it was in no way, as I could see it, an abuse of the children. They were not distressed or disturbed or hurt . . . Certainly the legalities of the whole thing had not intruded themselves on my mind at all until — until that ethics seminar, I guess, is when the penny dropped."

In cross-examination, Newman referred to the exams themselves and asked Wiens, "Do you know from the course of your medical practice that . . . there is a large segment of the population that finds a certain discomfort from receiving a rectal examination?"

"If there is an abnormality or if they are very tense," Wiens replied.

Dr. Harris, who lectures about pain at the University of Western

Ontario, commented later: "It was clear that the children must have had cerebral palsy, which means great tension. And the more tension in the body, the more pain you feel."

Later, Newman's voice grew harder. "Do the students ever, for instance, in clinical studies, practice on themselves, on one another? In examining each other's glands or . . ." "Yes," said Wiens.

"But you wouldn't think of having them examine each other rectally, would you?" Newman pressed.

"We encourage them to do whatever they can to improve their skills," said Wiens.

"Yes, but do you recall ever inviting the class to examine one another rectally?"

"No, I have not."

"It wouldn't be received in a — I wouldn't think — by the students in a very receptive manner?"

"I can't say."

"Come, Doctor, surely you could say. You can anticipate what it would be if you told the class, 'Well, I want half of you to lie down on the examination table and the other half of you are going to perform rectal examinations on your lab partner here.' You can well imagine what the response would be, can't you?"

"I would assume that there would be some who would object, certainly; maybe most."

"Yes. Most probably would. Thank you."

The unpleasant aspects of the case — the fact that these were rectal exams, performed on mentally disabled children who lacked the capacity to refuse the act — were certainly important to both sides. "People seem to think a rectal exam is such a terrible fucking thing!" complained Doug Laidlaw after the case was complete. "And the prosecution tried to turn it into a horror scene! Sure it's an invasion of privacy! So is an electrocardiogram!"

Laidlaw is correct, of course; any act of touching another person without his or her consent is assault, under our criminal code. And had it been only an ear examination, it may never have seen the light of day, much less the light of courtroom. But the image of the mentally disabled being used is what cuts deeper. "That people who can't fend for themselves are used as guinea pigs by the medical profession - it's diabolical!" says Nicola Schaefer of Winnipeg, the author of the best-selling biography of her severely disabled daughter, Catherine, *Does She Know She's There*. "Medical students should meet the handicapped in homes, not in institutions. I was able to say "fuck off!" to doctors in the hospital: my daughter could not."

"Technically, Ongwanada is their home," echoes Kathleen Ruff, the human rights advocate for the CAMR, and former host of CBC TV's *Ombudsman*. "It is only called Ongwanada Hospital because of the few dozen chronically ill elderly who live there." (Ironically, Ongwanada comes from an eastern Canadian Indian dialect, meaning "Our Home.") "You don't learn about the mentally handicapped in an institution; if you want to know native people, you don't go to a prison! There is a danger that in an institutional setting it is very easy for people to become dehumanized."

Two weeks later, on April 26, the two lawyers were still arguing on the abuse of process motion. In his closing argument, David Newman, for the Crown, tried to tie the numerous strings together: "Good motives do not excuse someone from criminal liability. Dr. Wiens' intentions were good intentions. She said that she didn't realize at the time that it was an offense. How many doctors are there like Dr. Wiens? The penny hasn't dropped for them. The news will travel fast, and they will not commit this offense. The victims could not speak or walk. They could not find for themselves a justice of the peace. Ongwanada is the home of these children! Into their home came a well-meaning doctor who performed rectal exams. If it were my child, and my home, I know what my reaction would be. The Bill of Rights still exists. We are here to protect the liberty and security of people, even if they cannot protect themselves."

In his conclusion, Doug Laidlaw was equally passionate: "If this were assault with a deadly weapon, or assault with attempt to cause bodily harm, then be concerned. But when we deal with a very trivial, technical offence, then you ask yourself, why move the machinery of law here? . . . Why punish a doctor? They want you to say, 'Medical profession, you will be guilty of an assault every time you touch a patient without his consent!' They want a trumpet blast from the court to frighten the medical profession. You would be saying to doctors, 'practise at your peril!' It would be destructive to the medical profession in this province . . .

"The prosecution used words like "victims" and not "patients." They never mentioned that a medical school and teaching was involved. They want to tell doctors, 'Practice at your fear!' The confidence that people have in doctors is that they do their very best to practise their profession."

At this point, Laidlaw drew an analogy which left the people in the crowded courtroom open-mouthed. "Suppose a husband and wife are alone at night and get into an argument. The husband slaps his wife. They are contrite, and make up. Outside the window, a neighbor looks in, from a private interest group for women. Without the wife's agreement, the husband is dragged before our courts. A husband and wife must be left alone to solve their problems! To insert a criminal procedure would damage that relationship. The parallel is precisely the same! It's exactly parallel! The medical profession has a very sensitive relationship with its patients."

The court was adjourned until June 22, at which time Judge Batten was to rule on the abuse of process motion.

"The elitist approach of Laidlaw was evident in the submission he made," said Elaine Newman of ARCH after the proceedings. "This is a man who does not have insight into the present and possible future abuse of the mentally handicapped. He sees the same about women: He argued that a battered wife should not have status in the courts. It's the Bay Street view of rights. It's a second-citizenship notion. And he's not the only one in the world who feels that way."

Newman's feelings towards Laidlaw were mutual. Although the Advocacy Resource Centre for the Handicapped was praised in Judge Rosalie

S. Abella's 1983 study, *Access to Legal Services by the Disabled* (''ARCH
deserves to be strengthened and encouraged in its work''), Laidlaw wrote
a withering letter on May 10, 1984, to the Legal Aid Committee of the Law
Society of Upper Canada, urging them to ''take whatever steps are necessary
to terminate the services of such organizations insofar as they go outside
the appropriate boundaries of proper legal aid.'' This was six weeks before
the case concluded.

On June 22, 1984, Judge R.B. Batten ruled on the motion to stay.
Reviewing the various argument of both lawyers, he quoted from Elaine
Newman, who was on the stand on the first day of testimonies: ''Certainly
it was hoped that the criminal process would deter this individual from
repeating the offence, [and that] it would deter this institution from repeating
the practice. But, on a more general level, [it was hoped] that a general
deterrent effect could be achieved through the criminal process . . . It makes
a statement to the community about appropriate and inappropriate
conduct.''

The judge denied Laidlaw's application to have the case thrown out.
David Newman asked Dr. Wiens to be arraigned on the first count. The
clerk of the court read the information pertaining to the charge: '' . . . that
Doctor Ruth Wiens on or about the 4th day of November, 1982, did at
Ongwanada Hospital, in the said city, commit a common assault upon a
male person, referred to as John Doe #1, whose name is presently unknown
to the informant but who, on November 4, 1982, was a patient at
Ongwanada Hospital, contrary to Section 245(1) of the Criminal Code of
Canada. Dr. Ruth Wiens, how do you plead?'' Douglas Laidlaw leapt up
and said ''Guilty.''

Laidlaw, Wiens and the medical profession seemed to have lost. Laidlaw
argued for Wiens' character and urged an unconditional discharge. Newman
agreed, but ''tempered'' Laidlaw's remarks: ''The act itself,'' Newman said,
''as opposed to the actor, is not, I would suggest to the Court, as flighty
and insignificant as my friend has characterized. The act is an evil act
although the doer is not an evil person. The act contravenes a very important
principle that has been upheld in our courts. And that is that the body of
every individual in our society is inviolate, subject, of course, to various
consents . . . The Court must be certain that the dignity of all individuals,
dignity particularly in this case of mentally retarded persons and
handicapped persons, can never be sacrificed for whatever purpose. It can't
be sacrificed at the altar of academia, no matter how noble teaching is, and
how important it is; the right of the individual and the maintenance of their
dignity supercedes all that.''

The judge agreed with both lawyers, giving Dr. Wiens an absolute
discharge while making a finding of guilty.

What of the trade-off? How will our future doctors learn their
profession? Doug Laidlaw was completely unrepentant: ''There's been no
lesson taught, except to terrify a few doctors, and steer them away from
working with the retarded. Don't you think that that sort of thing will
continue, except that now paper will be neatly stapled? It's not going to
change! Won't rounds still be continued? Won't doctors still have to

improve training? The message of the case is do your paperwork. That's all."

Maybe so, but other commentators are more circumspect. "To educate our medical students effectively will sometimes conflict with patient care," admits Dr. Schafer of Winnipeg, "but patient care is more important than promoting student education. I think that they can win patient cooperation by showing that the patient will gain. Students have the time. They can offer the patient the opportunity to ask questions. They can offer sympathetic understanding." Adds Professor Dickens of the University of Toronto law school, "We acknowledge as a community that the teaching of medical students is an important priority. But we should minimize the inconvenience. At Ongwanada, they were using and abusing the children for teaching material. But there comes a point of needing hands-on with patients."

Has any good come from the Crown vs. Wiens? "This case has done much good for the medical community," declares Dr. Margaret Somerville, a full professor in both the faculties of medicine and law at McGill who teaches compulsory classes on medical ethics to first and fourth year medical students. "Doctors will be forced to learn how to teach ethically." Somerville is the author of the study *Consent to Medical Care,* which was prepared for the Law Reform Commission of Canada. In the 186-page book, Somerville writes on "Institutionalized Children": "These children deserve special mention and special protection, which means they should never be subjected to non-therapeutic medical interventions or used in non-therapeutic medical research . . . " The chairman of the commission at the time Somerville wrote her report was Francis C. Muldoon, Q.C., the father of Laura, who made the penny drop.

"The fact that it went to court and a guilty verdict was rendered is a good thing," agrees Dr. Schafer. "I am enormously heartened that some medical students, to the threat of their careers, were willing to protest. Increasingly they do protest, and educate their teachers." "I think teaching hospitals have gained instruction from this case," adds Bernard Dickens. "It was time for it. The attitude toward doctors as holy is being eroded. It's a shame, though, that we have to learn from cases where doctors are pilloried."

True. But as Elaine Newman of ARCH comments, "This case deals head-on with our revered relationship with our doctors. And we respect the needs and aims of the medical profession. But Laidlaw tried to establish that that relationship is beyond the purview of criminal law, and somewhere along the line, someone has to say "No!""

In June, 1984, a provincial court judge looked at one of the top lawyers in Canada, and at the medical profession, and said "No."

THE VOCABULARY OF TZEDAKAH

Sublime, inspiring, exceptional, extraordinary, uplifting, wonderful, incredible, ineffable, unique, warm, great, lovely, exquisite, caring, loving, sensitive, awesome, amazing. Again and again these words and similar combinations of them appear in the telling and re-telling, the writing and re-writing of the nature and workings of Tzedakah. The inner essence of Tzedakah flows freely in a universe of human acts and encounters that do, I believe, inspire, amaze, uplift, and leave both participants in the act and observers moved, to tears, to joyous dancing, to amazed, dumbfounded whispers. An idea-made-real that summons up such lyricism points to other strings of words: hope, trust, faith, and more. In a sense, Tzedakah is Judaism's Life-force, the mode of behavior that enlivens both giver and recipient, energizing, sometimes rejuvenating, revivifying — bringing to life those who may have been downtrodden, defeated, weary to their bones and souls. So many words, so much of the human being and the raw basics of what it is to be alive are associated with Tzedakah.

On the other hand, the basic vocabulary of Tzedakah terms is relatively small, easily mastered. They are critical to a Jewish understanding of the Jewish way of giving, but once integrated into a person's essential store of words the boundaries and limits of that person's life experiences can change; different lightings color events; hands, faces, the totality of a body all move differently, and the communicability of words-as-deeds and deeds-as-words becomes an everyday astounding reality.

The following list of terms should become a starting point. Some are discussed at greater length in other pieces I have done and others have done. As time passes and the individual experiences more and more Tzedakah events, the words will take on new depth and breadth and assume new combinations of interplay. The dynamism of this vocabulary goes in two directions: the words should direct the person to seek out, identify, and take part in more and more of these experiences, and the Tzedakah experiences should cause the person to call to mind the words by immediate association, saying, "This dazzling moment is a Tzedakah connection", or "I see now that Tzedakah means people are more than people. This human, giving moment proves it."

TZEDAKAH-GEMILLUT CHASSADIM-MITZVAH:

TZEDAKAH- צדקה: the right thing to do, the just thing, what people do for each other because that's what people ought to do for each other, the Menschlich act. In the time of the Talmud, Tzedakah referred specifically to giving one's money away to those in need, 10-20% of one's income being the recommended amount. Later on it carried the connotation of any form of giving: time, money, effort, energy, talents. In my writings I use the term in both the restricted and the extended meaning of the term.

GEMILLUT CHASSADIM- גמילות חסדים: acts of caring, lovingkindness. Again, strictly Talmudically speaking, this term refers to a person's giving time, effort, talents, energy for the benefit of others, such as visiting the sick, comforting mourners, providing for poor couples who are getting married, hospitality, and the like — the complementary giving-word to Tzedakah as money. Tzedakah *money* is often used to give people the resources to do Gemillut Chassadim. Again, strictly speaking, they are two separate Mitzvot, though, and giving money would not, technically speaking, fulfill the time-energy-effort Mitzvah, and vice versa. One reason why doing Gemillut Chassadim alone is not so all-inclusive is that money gives the giver geographic range, time range, and talent range, i.e., the money can be used anywhere in the world, not just where one's local talents could be employed, it gives one the opportunity to "invest in futures", wherein the money can be established for projects to live long after one's own lifetime is over, and "talent range" meaning, for example, since I am not a surgeon, and could not perform delicate heart surgery for someone, at least I can pay to have it done by someone else. (This was, indeed, the case, once, when I and many others were called upon to finance the surgery and post-operataive care for an Israeli child brought to New York for a delicate operation. The ½ of 1% that I could help gather gave me great geographic and talent range far beyond anything I could have done personally to cure the child.)

Jewish tradition does not prescribe a specific percentage of our time, effort, energy, and talents for Gemillut Chassadim. Each person's limits are different, each human situation dif- ferent, each day different, and are to be adjusted accordingly.

MITZVAH מצוה: literally, a commandment. A Mitzvah refers specifically to any number of acts described as our obligations towards other human beings and towards God. Over the centuries — through the Bible, and more extensively, through the Talmud and Law Codes — Mitzvot have come to be the critical outline of human actions. Sometimes in the Talmud the word 'Mitzvah' is synonymous with "Tzedakah", and in later times, and in my writings, Mitzvah is sometimes used interchangeably with both Tzedakah and Gemillut Chassadim, any act of giving. Thus, "Mitzvah work" will mean "Tzedakah work" and "Mitzvah hero" will mean "Tzedakah hero".

Frequently associated with the word Mitzvah is the phrase *Simcha Shel Mitzvah-* שמחה של מצוה, the unique joy of doing a Mitzvah.

Ma'asim Tovim- מעשים טובים, good deeds, is another term often used to describe Mitzvah activity. "Tzedakah" itself is often defined as "a good deed".

MENSCHLICH-EDEL-EHRLICH-ZIESS-SHAYN-FEIN-HOMBRE FINO-HOMBRE BUENO-REGALADO:

Tzedakah is intimately bound to the finest human qualities. It can also serve as a sensitizing agent for personality development. Torah study, which can make us more aware of Mitzvah work, often serves as a foundation for Tzedakah awareness, which may lead to a refining of the soul. In graphic terms:

Torah ⟶ Tzedakah ⟶ Menschlichkeit.

Many Yiddish terms help clarify the meaning of Tzedakah:

MENSCH- מענטש (noun; adj. = *MENSCHLICH;* abstract = *MENSCH-LICHKEIT*): a fine, decent, caring, sensitive, loving, concerned, compassionate, empathetic, sympathetic, generous human being.

EDEL- איידל (adj; abstract = *EDELKEIT*): noble, gentle, genteel — referring to qualities of the human being and human soul.

EHRLICH- ערלעך (adj; abstract = *EHRLICHKEIT*): honest, upright, having integrity.

ZIESS- זיס (adj.; abstract = *ZIESSKEIT*): sweet, as in a sweet human being, having a sweet soul.

SHAYN- שיין (adj.; abstract = *SHAYNKEIT*): beautiful, as in a beautiful soul, a beautiful human being.

FEIN- פיין (adj.; abstract = *FEINKEIT*): fine, as in a fine human being.

To say in Yiddish, "Er iz a Mensch" "That person is a Mensch" is the highest compliment you can pay someone. To say "Zie iz menschlich, edel, ehrlich, ziess, shayn, fein" "She is menschlich, edel, ehrlich, ziess, shayn, fein" is of the same order. . . .a dazzling array of human qualities.

Having consulted my good friend, Rabbi Abraham Morhaim, I list three Ladino equivalents used by Sefardi Jews:

HOMBRE BUENO: just like it sounds — a good person.

HOMBRE FINO: just like it sounds — a fine person

REGALADO: somewhat more colloquial — a precious, outstanding person.

PRECIOSO may also be used in more formal situations.

(Feminine forms: *MUJER BUENA, MUJER FINA, REGALADA, PRECIOSA.*)

ENGLISH INTERLUDE:

Many words in English help us clarify the meaning of the word Tzedakah:

sympathy, empathy, pathos, and (negatively) apathy — from the Greek.

passion, passionate, impassioned, and (negatively) passive, and dispassionate — from the Latin.

Each of these words, based on original meanings of emotion, feeling, suffering, invites comparisons and contrasts with Tzedakah feelings, depending on the prefixes and suffixes English has added to the root. The ancient Jewish prophets opted for passion, pathos, sympathy, the highly charged positive, life-urging words, those words that make adrenalin flow and voices rise, over the more passive approach to life. Sometimes highstrung, often in deep trouble with the authorities because of their screaming for caring and just values, they, as it were, "Chose Life", rather than becoming passive observers within society. They spoke out and acted on their words, and urged others to do the same.

Also from the Latin, two words, and their English metamorphoses: altruism (Latin: alter - other) egotism (Latin: ego - I).

Tzedakah is altruistic, other-directed, not egocentric.

And one more from the Greek:

Cynicism — an opposite of Tzedakah. Tzedakah provides Life forces, vital energies, positive sensitivities, an embracing of the Mitzvah work to be accomplished in Life. Cynicism, in its modern sense, contrasts sharply, advocating, "Oh, hell, that's the way Life is. That's the way people are — bastards," and "Oh, well, what can I do with things such a mess?"

Finally, from the world of Big Business: ruthless, aggressive, tough, assertive, sharp, clever.

After consulting with my friend, Marc Sternfeld of Morgan Stanley & Co. Incorporated, we have clarified that only the first term, ruthless, is by definition a negative. Ruthlessness implies no value system and a willingness to trample on people to attain certain goals. The other terms are not *necessarily* negative, though, abusively personified in some people, they assume negative connotations. For example, there are many methods and means for doing a Mitzvah appropriately and fully. That is the positive sense of the words. However, when "aggressive" becomes a euphemism for "ruthless" and "clever" for "tricky, slimy", then the meanings stray far from the ideals of Menschlichkeit. Listening well to the common usage of these terms helps sharpen our sense of Tzedakah and Jewish personality and values.

And one last, sorely abused phrase: Quality of Life. The media floods us with medical stories where quality of life, by their definition, is the central issue. The specific category of events that interest me relates to retarded newborns — severely retarded, and not-so-severely retarded. Court case after court case has dealt with whether or not it is appropriate to withhold or withdraw medical attention, even feeding, from such infants, the main contention being, "What kind of quality of life does this infant have to look forward to?" It would appear to me that Jewish tradition does not evaluate quality of life on the basis of IQ. How deep and how far one would wish to delve into what Judaism calls quality of life is another matter, but it is clear, as far as I can ascertain, that mental capacity is not the essential criterion. Tzedakah moves in other realms, with the healthy and the sick, with the partially able and the totally able, the mentally capacitated and the mentally incapacitated considered — all of them — appropriate people for our attention. Enough said.

KAVOD-BUSHAH:

KAVOD- כבוד: dignity, self-dignity, honor, self-worth.

BUSHAH- בושה: humiliation, embarrassment, debasement, shame.

Tzedakah work fosters a sensitivity to human dignity, Kavod, both during the Mitzvah activity and in everyday living. Tzedakah also inculcates in the Mitzvah person an obsession with avoiding Bushah-humiliation, not only for the Tzedakah recipient, but in all possible human situations. Judaism reflects this in its many root words for humiliation, three of which are זלל, קלל, and בזה. By Talmudic times, the Rabbis wanted to be certain that Jews would be experts on dignity and humiliation.

TCHATCHKAS- AVODA ZARA -KAYLIM:

TCHATCHKAS-טשאטשקעס (Yiddish-toys): things, objects, playthings. Nothing I have gathered from my study of Tzedakah indicates that a Rolls Royce or Rolex watch is *by definition* a project of The Evil Forces. (To be continued, next two entries.)

AVODA ZARA- עבודה זרה (Hebrew-worship of other gods): When the tchatchkas are worshipped, believed in or loved in and for themselves, then the phenomenon becomes Avoda Zara — the worship of a strange god, materialism. College degrees and Nobel prizes can also be tchatchkas, if they are worshipped and sought out as *ultimates.* Worshipping good grades, achievement in business or school or professions, awards and prizes *per se* is also Avoda Zara. Our relationship to these things is what determines whether or not there is an element of Avoda Zara. Popularity and coolness can also be objects of Avoda Zara. That is why there are fame- crazed and achievement-meshuggeh people in the world, and fame-unfazed and achievement-for-the-sake-of-mitzvahs people in the same world.

KAYLIM- כלים (Hebrew-vehicles, instruments, tools, utensils, devices, sometimes - clothing): All "things" are potentially Kaylim — instruments or vehicles or tools for Mitzvahs. Fancy computers can just as easily be used to organize 100 volunteers for Passover food package deliveries as for illegally gaining access to bank records or school grades. So, too, the Rolls Royce mentioned under "Tchatchkas" — Jewish tradition does not differentiate between a Rolls and a Dodge when it comes to driving lonely people to a hot lunch program at the Jewish Community Center or taking others for chemotherapy or riding in a funeral procession to pay the last respects to a deceased friend or relative. Both cars can be used for Mitzvah work.

A blender, a telephone, microwave, scissors, a big-screen TV, a $10,000 stereo system, a backyard swimming pool — all may be subsumed under the category of Tchatchkakeit, or Avoda Zara, or Kaylim, tools-for-Mitzvahs.

That is why Jewish tradition prescribes the "Shehecheyanu" blessing when one purchases some new thing. A Jew recites, "Blessed are You, O Lord our God, Ruler of the Universe, Who has allowed us to reach this time." "This time" meaning "purchasing something new which has Mitzvah-potential."

TIKKUN OLAM-תקון עולם (Hebrew-fixing up the world): In modern Hebrew, Tikkun is used for fixing anything from a car motor to a washing machine — anything. Tikkun Olam would imply that by Mitzvah hammers, screwdrivers, ratchets, wrenches, and the like (namely: ourselves, our selves, our efforts, time, money, talents, hands, feet, faces), we can fix up the world to make it a more Menschlich place to live.

ISH KASHER - CHASSID - TZADDIK:

ISH KASHER- איש כשר (Hebrew-a fit person, an appropriate human being): On occasion, the Talmud uses this term, the most likely modern equivalent being "Mensch".

CHASSID- חסיד: Talmudically, this term is used sometimes synonymously with Tzaddik, Righteous One. A sub-category of this term is the one I wish to discuss — *CHASSIDAY UMMOT HAOLAM-* חסידי אומות העולם the Righteous Non-Jews of the World. This term specifically applies nowadays to non-Jews who saved Jews' lives during the Holocaust. King Christian of Denmark and the Danes who took their Jewish countryman by boat to safety in Sweden; Raoul Wallenberg; Oskar Schindler, who saved more than 1000 Jews in his factory; Fritz Graebe, "The Moses of Rovno", who saved many; Pastor Andre Trocmé of Le Chambon, France, who protected the Jews in his care, Father Ruffino Niccacci and the nuns and priests of Assisi, Italy, who saved 300 Jews, and all those others, known and unknown to us, who risked their lives to save and protect the Jews of Europe. A walk down The Avenue of the Righteous at Yad VaShem in Jerusalem will fill in more names for anyone strolling through, names of people who personified Tzedakah to the highest degree.

Ironically, some of these Righteous are living in poverty, and a few people and organizations, among them Rabbi Harold Schulweis's Foundation to Sustain Righteous Christians in Los Angeles, are working to alleviate this situation.

TZADDIK- צדיק (Hebrew-Righteous One): This term approximates the phrase, "Mensch First Class" — someone who goes beyond being a Mensch, who gives more of himself or herself, obsessed constantly with the well-being and welfare of others, always doing things to change the world through acts of Tzedakah and Gemillut Chassadim.

In my writings I use many translations of Tzaddik, ranging from "Righteous One", to "Mitzvah Hero", to "One of the Good Folks", to "Mitzvah-Maestro/Maestra", depending on the context.

The Talmud seems to struggle with the term "Tzaddik", adding another term, "Tzaddik Gamur-צדיק גמור"— a Total Tzaddik, to differentiate apparently between a select few in a class by themselves and other Tzaddikim. I believe they wanted to focus on two Mitzvah types: the rarest of rare, few-in-a-generation Tzaddikim, and the others, the "Regular Tzaddikim" ("Good Folks") who are everywhere, doing their Mitzvah deeds.

Graphically, the spectrum of Mitzvah people would appear as follows:

Mensch ——▶ Tzaddik ——▶ Tzaddik Gamur.

I object to the pejoratives sometimes applied to Mitzvah people: do-gooder, goody-goody, bleeding heart. One Tzedakah project might be to set the cynic who uses these terms straight by exposing him or her to the real-live Tzaddikim and Menschen.

In my writings I am usually referring to the mid-range Tzaddikim. They come in both sexes, a variety of sizes, all hair and eye colors, with and without beards, a full range of IQ's, shorts, suits, expensive and bargain-basement dresses, and an array of body shapes from ectomorphs to mesomorphs to endomorphs.

Jewish literature abounds in references to Tzaddikim. I will mention only three, to flesh out certain aspects of their nature.

1. "Though the Tzaddik may fall seven times, he will always rise again."
    (Proverbs 24:16)
    This verse succinctly expresses how the inner strength of the human
    being is reinforced through living a life of Tzedakah acts. Emotional
    resilience, tenacity, fortitude are all potential benefits of the Tzedakah
    lifestyle.

2. "May I be counted among the Tzaddikim" (From the Shabbat morn-
    ing service, taken from Zohar, VaYakhel p. 369.)
    This phrase expresses our desire to live and to have lived lives filled
    with deeds that would make us worthy of the title "Tzaddik".

3. If a person says,
    "I am giving this coin to Tzedakah
    so that my child will live"
    or "so that i will make it into the Future World" —
    that person is complete Tzaddik. (Pesachim 8a-b)

A very strange text. Nevertheless, it appears that the Talmud is saying that
it is possible that giving — even with less-than-exalted goals in mind (such
as getting into the Future World) — is enough to confer the title "Tzaddik" on the giver. Rashi, the most famous of the Talmudic commentators,
remarks, however, "Complete Tzaddik: for this act. We don't say he did
not do the Mitzvah for its own sake, since he did, indeed, perform the commandment of his Creator to do Tzedakah...even though he intends to
derive personal benefit — to merit being in the Next World or that his
children shall live." Rashi's intent, I believe, is to say that everyone is entitled to feel like a Tzaddik at certain moments in one's life. The Tzedakah
act can fill the person with that feeling, and then, (hopefully) future acts,
personality changes, and purer intentions will emerge later on in his or her
way of life.

One final word. Talmudic relationships are often expressed by the terms
"Rav- רב = teacher", "Talmid- תלמיד = student", "Chaver- חבר = colleague
or friend", and "Talmid-Chaver- תלמיד־חבר = a student who has become
a friend." One particular passage in the section called Massechet Kallah
reports Rabbi Tarfon as having referred to Rabbi Akiva as Rabbi Ve'Alufi
"My teacher and my Mitzvah hero". The context is a Tzedakah story, and
Rabbi Akiva had acted out some Tzedakah deeds which impressed Rabbi
Tarfon. *Aluf* would imply more than just "Mentor", more, as I said, like
a "Mitzvah hero". A nice Talmudic touch.

Sometimes terms overlap; at certain times they contain a greater intensity than at other times, but the general sense and usage becomes clearer
the more we encounter the terms. Reading more and more of the texts
and listening to the stories will help clarify the shades of meaning.

POVERTY:
The linguistic rule of thumb goes that the greater number and variety

of terms for certain objects or concepts in a language, the more sensitivity to and interest in that object or concept. The usual examples include "such-and-such number of words for snow in Eskimo languages," "12,438 terms for camel in Arabic," and the like. We have taken note of that with the four roots in Hebrew for "humiliation". One more statement from ancient Jewish literature illustrates a certain concern in Jewish thinking:

> There are seven terms for the poor.
> (Leviticus Rabba 34:6, Margoliot 4:782)

The text then lists the seven terms, explaining their connotations: one who is crushed, one who is without possessions, one who sees all kinds of good things around but cannot afford to buy them, one who is lowly, and so on down the list. It was a good reminder in ancient times, and a good one for today, that poverty and poor people are not monolithic, not a category, but individuals with individual reasons and circumstances for being poor, and different responses and capabilities to cope with their situation.

IN SUMMATION:

The Tzedakah world has numerous frames of reference, and the key to each matrix is a grasp of the terms interacting, contrasting, and elucidating one another. As a poet, I believe that the more we attune ourselves to the terminology and catch-phrases of our modern world, and then compare and contrast them to the Talmudic-Rabbinic language, the more able we will be to function with a distinctly Jewish pattern of Tzedakah — of doing that which is just, right, decent, and compassionate.

OCCUPATION: MITZVAHS

I will break the suspense. When my readers finish this article, I want them all to think, "My occupation is:

1. Life-saver
2. Dignity-restorer
3. Everyday-miracle-worker
4. Mitzvah-magician
5. Hope-giver
6. Solution-maker
7. Tool-user-for-Mitzvahs
8. Soul-repairer
9. Broken-body-fixer
10. Mitzvah-power-hungry-person."

Now we can study the text:

"Open the Gates of Righteousness for me." *(Psalm 118:19)*
[At the Time of Judgment] in the Future World
everyone will be asked,
"What was your occupation?"
If the person answers,
"I used to feed the hungry,"
they will say to him,
"This is God's gate;
you, who fed the hungry, may enter."
. . .
"I used to give water to those who were thirsty," —
they will say to him,
"This is God's gate;
you, who gave water to those who were thirsty, may enter."
. . .
"I used to clothe the naked,"
they will say to him,
"This is God's gate,
you, who clothed the naked, may enter."
. . .
and similarly with those who raised orphans,
and who performed the Mitzvah of Tzedakah,
and who performed acts of caring, lovingkindness.

David said,
"I have done all of these;
let all the gates open for me."
That is why the verse says,
"Open the Gates of Righteousness for me,
I shall enter them, thanking the Lord."
Midrash on Psalms 118:17 Buber p. 486

I first learned this text one Shabbat morning at my synagogue. My rabbi, Rabbi Matthew Simon, used it in one of his sermons, and I was stunned. I had been working with the subject of the text for a long time, but did not have a specific passage to clarify it. So much has happened, so many discussions based on the text, since then. I would now offer some comments to help relate it to the overall context of Tzedakah:

1. The text essentially draws a distinction between "making a living" and "occupation". All of the answers to the question relate to Tzedakah; none mention business, crafts, professions. This Midrash indicates that, *no matter how a person makes a living, his or her occupation is Tzedakah.*

2. King David, at least according to this text, does not wish to·be remembered for being King, for conquering Jerusalem, for writing the Book of Psalms, but rather for the fact that he was involved in a variety of Tzedakah work. A rather striking assertion, (A comparison to present-day heads of state would be interesting.)

3. A person's means of making a living *can,* most certainly, be tied into the occupation of Tzedakah. Bookkeepers and lawyers can do work for free (anyone can), merchants can donate goods to those in need, a car mechanic (such as my friend, Dean Kertesz) can repair automobiles of people who are in shaky financial situations and who desperately need the car in good shape to make their living. He can do it at cost, or free.

Perhaps the most extreme and prominent example is Bob Geldof (now Sir Bob Geldof), singer in the rock group "The Boomtown Rats". By all accounts, the group was wild, doing bizarre things such as releasing live rats into the audience at concerts. And yet, Geldof, Sir Bob, used all his connections and talents and put together Live Aid and Band Aid, raising many millions of dollars for Tzedakah.

4. The idea that everyone's occupation is Tzedakah is a great equalizer, with the potential to minimize rampant egotism, jealousies, false criteria of relative status — all because of the exalted goals of Tzedakah, the Life-Force, the Good Act, the Right Thing To Do. Thus, the surgeon and the teacher, the firefighter and secretary, clarinetist and stock trader — no matter the job — have this in common: immense Mitzvah potential and power to save lives, restore dignity, repair souls, etc.

5. How you make a living demands certain talents. The occupation of Mitzvahs may need the same talents, or a whole range of different ones. For some, Mitzvah work comes from their hobby talents, or their skills-at-leisure (swimmers, swimmers who teach life saving; baseball players, baseball players who are Big Brothers and Big Sisters, taking disadvantaged kids out for a leisurely game). Some talents are just sitting there, unconnected to making a living, hobbies, or leisure . . . waiting to be harnessed to Tzedakah work. Some of those talents include: loving, caring, parenting, smiling, bear-hugging, making up games, daydreaming, memorizing long lists of names, numbers, or things, etc. Each has its place in the array of Mitzvah occupations.

Prime example: Janet Marchese of White Plains, NY, after adopting a child with Down's Syndrome (demanding unique talents), helped place another 300 such children in adoptive homes.

6. In the context of raising children: it would seem that if a child does not know by age 16 what he or she wants to do for a living, that is fair enough. However, by that age, he or she should be fully aware of what his or her occupation in life is: Mitzvahs.

7. We should not confuse the Internal Revenue Service. . . .When it comes to fill out our tax forms, and the form has a blank space for occupation, do *not* write "Mitzvahs" or "Tzedakah." *They* want to know how you make a living.

8. Ultimately the quality and nature of an individual's Tzedakah work depends on genetic make-up, soul-texture, stamina. Some do more, some less, for a wide variety of reasons: little discretionary time, circumstances of health, etc. The wondrous thing is the absolute uniqueness of every person's variations on the theme; everyone lives out the life of Tzedakah differently. In the extreme case, I would reverse a trend in secular society: eccentricities are viewed with curiosity, occasional admiration, and great forgiveness, particularly towards the wealthy, academics, and artists. (Poets get away with a lot of quirks; painters, professors, and millionaires, too.) I would say that even these eccentricities can be channeled into Mitzvah work. Thus, for example, some writers' ability to work at their writing for 24 hours in a row could just as well be put to writing Mitzvah texts. In 1986, I think particularly of Emma Lazarus's poem "The New Colossus" at the base of the Statue of Liberty — this being the year of its repair and re-dedication. A millionaire gourmand's predilection for the finest foods could be transferred over to providing the finest-of-fine Purim, Passover, Rosh HaShana meals for those in need. Examples are everywhere to be found. One final one comes to mind: Jerzy Kosinski, award-winning author, is, by all accounts, a strange individual. And yet, he often goes into hospitals late at night to talk to and read stories to people in pain, lonely, unable to sleep.

In preparing this article, I asked four individuals with specific talents to describe Mitzvah-occupation experiences. These are the people, and the replies to my request:

Reuven Lerner, highschool student, Old Westbury, NY, computer whiz, on ways to apply his Computer Whizkeit to Tzedakah:

Ten Things that a Computer User Can Do.

These being the 1980's, computers have become a part of almost everyone's lives. And computer users — programmers, writers, and many others — have certain skills that can be helpful to others. Here are ten suggestions that you may want to undertake in your community (or suggest to a computer-using friend) to help others with your talent.

1. Many synagogues are starting to computerize their offices nowadays. Why not help them do so, and if they haven't thought about it yet, offer it as a suggestion and yourself as a consultant. Most shuls need the extra efficiency of computers in many areas (e.g. newsletter, members' lists, etc.), but don't have anyone pushing for it. If your local synagogue doesn't need any help, there are many local Jewish organizations which might need assistance.

2. Contact local schools with special education departments. One of the best things that they can do is learn how to program — be it BASIC or LOGO, or for the advanced students, even Pascal. In general, these kids need to feel that they can control something, and computers provide the perfect environment. Graphics usually go over well with this kind of group; see what they're like, and go from there.

3. Try to get a ''Grandparents' Programming Club'' started in your community. There are many older citizens who have no grasp of the new technologies, but could gain much out of learning programming languages. Due to vision and hearing impairments, you'd want to stick with a computer that has a larger screen and/or graphics capabilities (so that you can adjust the screen colors, and with them, the contrast).

4. I know many people who have started collections (be it coins, stamps, or otherwise), and need someone to push them to continue. Through a computerized inventory system, you may want to be this needed partner, and give them that added support.

5. The Jewish community is *desperate* for some good educational software! Team up with a local Hebrew school or Day school, and try and find out what their needs are. If you can provide them with needed games, testmakers, drills, and other such materials, they will be eternally happy.

6. Get together with your synagogue youth group, and form a greeting card company! Armed with either your own or bought software, colored paper (easily available from most computer supply houses), and a mailing list, you can send people birthday, anniversary, and lots of other kinds of cards. Not only do they feel good from this (and why not — it's not often that you get a printed, personalized card!), but it's a way to raise money for your Tzedakah program (say, $1 a card?).

7. Using a modem, create a Jewish bulletin-board system. There are many inexpensive and public-domain packages available, as well as books on how to write your own software. You could have Bible quizzes, singles services, a list of upcoming holidays, and many other functions that could work in a major Jewish community.

8. Around Pesach time, go around with a small vacuum cleaner, screen wipes, disk-drive cleaners, and other such tools, and be a Kosher-for-Passover-Computer-Cleaner! It's a real chore to clean a computer when you don't know exactly what you're doing, but with a little practice and experience, you could be helping out dozens of people! Advertise in the

synagogue newsletter — they usually enjoy publicizing such activities that their members do.

9. Go to your local rabbi and offer to put his sermons on disk. *Every* rabbi has problems finding old sermons; they just take up a lot of room. If you were to put his entire file cabinet on a box full of disks, he'd be eternally grateful. Better yet, teach him how to write his sermons on the word- processor, and when he's done with that, to use his database to create a list of members in the hospital, etc. Rabbis need this information on hand, and any help that they get, they appreciate.

10. There are surely members of your community with computer (and other electronic) equipment which they don't need, but don't know what to do with. Ask around, and collect all of this old (and even broken) equipment. Donate this stuff to a local (or even not-so-local) Tzedakah, where you can then assist in bringing them into the modern age. Most of these Tzedakot need such equipment, but don't have the budget nor the time to set it up.

From Jacob Kabb, Customer Services Coordinator of TMC of Atlanta, a telecommunications firm, in reply to my request for a list of ways someone in telecommunications can apply his work, and encourage his company to be involved in Tzedakah work:

1. Encourage certain days to be reduced rate or free call to selected groups or people (food banks, social agencies, the elderly, single mothers, etc.) on Mother's Day, Valentine's Day, Grandparent's Day, Thanksgiving, etc.

2. Provide certain consultation and free advice to social agencies, poverty groups, service people.

3. Offer educational talks and seminars about the industry to various age groups of kids through high school.

4. Be fair and honest in dealings with colleagues and customers.

5. Encourage co-ops and groups to pool calling habits and to offer the difference in savings to a special cause or needy individual (unnamed).

6. Network with equipment wholesalers to get inexpensive phones to be donated to the poor.

7. Encourage old phones (most of which today are very usable) to be donated to people who need them.

8. Help agencies and needy groups learn about technology and savings, especially in terms of message and data transfer, etc.

9. Encourage a true service ideal in the workplace vs. the lack-of-respect-to-the-customer method.

10. Encourage placing a food hopper for donated food for the food bank in the workplace.

11. Donate dollars in honor of outstanding employee achievement.

12. Research telephone tax laws and educate where the money goes and how it is allocated. Share that information.

13. Encourage the establishment of consumer hotlines to objectively explain current telephone options on the market.

Debra Friedmann, Washington, DC, also known as "Panda the Clown". Trained in psychology and sociology, Debra has had a variety of jobs, including convention planning for major hotels around the United States. She is a clown (one of 3 or 4 I have met) who has been asked by a group called "Washington Special Arts" to do a workshop on clowning for mentally retarded adults. She does magic — a great Mitzvah-tool. (David Copperfield, the world-renowned magician, has developed uniquely successful programs for individuals with physical disabilities as a form of physical therapy — with incredible results.) (Yes, he's Jewish, too.) And, she's a balloon animal maker. In the Fall of 1986 she went to Israel for her sister's wedding, without clown costume, but ready to do some Mitzvah work with balloons. The following is, in her own words, an account of her visit to ALYN Orthopaedic Hospital in Jerusalem:

The smiling eyes filled with energy as I filled my balloons with air. The squeaking sounds of my twisting balloons into shapes of dogs, giraffes and mice added suspense; the children giggled and asked questions.

Yet, this was not a typical group of youngsters. This was *Alyn,* a center for children with severe orthopedic problems. A center that serves as a home, a school, a hug, a total living environment. Alyn offers skills that give people a chance to share and contribute to society. A chance that so many healthy people take for granted.

At first it was so difficult — the wheelchairs — so small — and so many. Yet the children were so relaxed, and it soon became natural to feel comfortable with them. After all, this was the only life that they knew.

While they delighted in my balloons, when I looked into my bag of stickers, flower rings and bracelets I felt almost embarrassed. How could I offer these things for smiles when so many hands were held stiff and gnarled or missing the usual five fingers. But, my mother-in-law urged me on, saying, of course that toy ring will look as lovely on his finger as it does on ours. It did.

The children were so cheerful and loving. The whole atmosphere amazed me. Being an entertainer of children I am very aware of the aura in which I work. There was no question that these kids had been encouraged, challenged and given confidence. The concept of ALYN amazed me. It was bright and the halls filled with the Jerusalem sun. I can't forget the faces and I won't forget ALYN. This center is an example for all of us — showing that good things do happen because of good and caring people.

I wore no usual clown make-up or costume the day I visited ALYN, and

I'm sure that my visit there gave me much more than I could ever give to my small audience.

(Debra is somewhat evangelical, and justifiably so, about the power of clowning, magic, balloon animal making, and related Mitzvah occupations. She assures me much of it is easier than expected, and not very expensive. She is willing to talk with people who are interested in looking into this kind of Mitzvah activity more fully. Debra Friedmann, 4615 Verplanck Pl., NW, Washington, DC 20016.)

Finally, from Garth Potts, Director of the Jewish Federation of Greater Oklahoma City. Garth is a fine artist, and I asked him to tie in his artistic talents with Mitzvah work. His reply:

As per our discussion, the "mitzvot" of using art often is a matter of interpretation; however, here goes:

1. Art therapy is a technique which allows the individual to reach out and describe feelings otherwise locked away from language. I have seen it played out in clay and various 2-D media like paint or crayons. The "client" creates the picture which then either tells the story or becomes the basis for discussion. The "talent" comes from the ability to introduce, direct, and interpret the materials and results.

2. I used various illustrative techniques, including ink, paint, etc., to design a program of Jewish-content graphics at the Vancouver JCC. The program included 3 murals depicting Israeli dance, Noah's ark, and various life cycle and historical symbols plus appropriate Hebrew as well as Hebrew/English office signs throughout.

3. Certainly with weddings, mitzvot can be made with the "calligraphic execution of a ketubah". I would think the designing and making of a wedding dress would also fall into the category.

4. Incorporating artistic capabilities into the teaching of basic life skills, like reading, writing, even swimming, might be stretching the point. While not especially Jewish, motivation through the skillful weaving of visually exciting materials could enhance an otherwise-lethargic learner's ability to comprehend.

I hope this will be helpful.

In Conclusion:

A conversation I thoughh I heard on the CD Metro:

"What is your occupation?"

"Life-saver, dignity-restorer, everyday-miracle-worker, Mitzvah-magician, hope-giver, solution-maker, tool-user-for-Mitzvahs, soul-repairer, broken-body-fixer, Mitzvah-power-hungry-person."

A. One should use one's face, hands, and feet
only to honor one's Creator

(Tosefta Braḥot 4:1)

1. Some ways to use your face for Mitzvahs:
   a. At a house of mourning (*Shiva)*, show how carefully you are listening to the mourners as they speak to you of their sadness.
   b. Keep your eyes scanning the horizon for Mitzvah work still to be done. (Like Abraham, whose tent had openings in each direction, so he could see strangers coming from a distance and welcome them into his home.)
   c. Speak good, gentle words to those who are sick or sick at heart.
   d. Paint your face, clown-style, and entertain in hospitals and institutions.
   e. Have eye contact and maintain eye contact when someone comes as a potential recipient of Tzedakah — if the recipient wants to be seen straight on. If not, then don't — to avoid embarrassment. (A dermatologist told me he had a side door for teen-agers to come into his office if they were too embarrassed because of skin problems to come through the main wating room)
   f. Fill in a dozen more on you own.

2. Your hands:
   a. If you are a home repairperson hobbyist — be on call with local Jewish Family Service agencies to do repairs for people who cannot affort to pay for them.
   b. Write checks to Tzedakah; twist arms to get other to do the same.
   c. Touch the elderly, the weary, the sick — whomever — to minimize their feelings of isolation.
   d. Play football with a latchkey child through a Jewish Big Brothers or Big Sisters program.
   e. Write or type letters for individuals unable to do so for themselves (because of paralysis, foreign-language difficulties, etc.) A major service many Tzedakah agencies perform is helping people fill out government forms to obtain benefits they are entitled to.
   f. Fill in a dozen more of your own.

3. Your feet:
   a. Go shopping for people unable to get out and go on their own.
   b. Take someone out for a stroll who would otherwise stay home. (Project Ezra and Project Dorot, two of New York's one-on-one visiting programs with the elderly, specialize in this Mitzvah.)
   c. Drive people to synagogue and communal events who are otherwise unable or unwilling to come on their own.
   d. Do a UJA-Federation Walkathon or Jogathon.

    e. Walk away from shady, unseemly deals, and walk (or run) towards Tzedakah opportunities. (I am grateful to a teen-ager, a United Synagogue Youth Israel Pilgrim, for the first half of this interpretation.)

    f. Fill in a dozen or more on your own.

4. A related text:

Rabbi Akiva said:

There are 248 positive Mitzvot in the Torah,
corresponding to the number of parts in the human body.
Each and every part of the body shouts to the person,
"Do a Mitzvah through me;
the benefit will be that we will live,
and you will live a long life."

          (Mechilta, Ki Taytzay 2, Buber, p.23)

    a. This text expands on the previous one, opening up possibilities for people to use their shoulders (carrying stones to build a sanctuary) and other body parts for Mitzvah work.

    b. Most marvellously, a special project at the *Einstein medical facility in New York, seems to combine all body parts, the total human machine, to devise a unique Tzedakah project. They have created a program called Helping Hands: Simian Aides for the Disabled. They train capuchin monkeys (the organ-grinder variety) to do a multitude of tasks for quadriplegic individuals. With names like Freeway, Cleo, Henri (short for Henrietta), and Jo, these animals do everything from bringing food from the refrigerator to turning pages of a book. The monkeys have a life expectancy of about 30 years, much longer than the near-analogous seeing-eye dogs for the blind. They are good companions; and a source of great excitement when the human-and-monkey team head out into the outside world, providing added companionship. The article, from *Smithsonian Magazine* (around July or August, 1986) is too filled with exhilarating details to re-tell here. I read hundreds of Tzedakah articles — but this one stood out immediately . . . . a clever idea? More than that, much more. Awesome, revolutionary. Human beings applying their talents to devise such a project. That's *exactly* what Tzedakah is all about. Israel, incidentally, is one of the other countries trying out this program.

    (If I were a Rabbi and wanted to make a sermon out of this, I would say something like, "Now, if we can train monkeys to do Mitzvahs, why can't we train ourselves to do them?")

Helping Hands is moving to Boston, early 1987, and will be associated with the Boston University Medical School: Dr. M.J. Willard, c/o Helping Hands, Department of Rehabilitative Medicine, University Hospital, 75 E. Newton St., Boston, MA 02118.

Sue Strong and her friend, Henrietta.

5. The "face, hands, and feet" text has proven to be an excellent exercise for children, down to the earliest ages. As soon as they can begin to grasp the meaning of Tzedakah, they ought to be exposed to this text. It will undoubtedly expand their understanding in the most real-of-real contexts.

B. The Rabbis said to Rabbi Yehoshua ben Levi:
   The little children have come to the place of Torah study and are explaining things so astounding they were never even said in the time of Joshua

   "*Alef-Bayt* א—ב"stands for "*Elaf Binah-* אלף בינה", learn wisdom and insight.
   "*Gimel-Dalet* ג—ד , *Gemol Dalim* גמול דלים" . . . What is the essence of this Torah-wisdom? To take care of the poor."

   (Shabbat 104a)

   1. We are used to "A is for Apple, B is for Boy, C is for Cat type of learning the alphabet. The Talmudic examples carry a heavy value-force, speaking of how people should act.
   2. "*Bina* בינה" is one of the ancient Hebrew words meaning "wisdom." Torah study is a seeking out of wisdom, and facts and memorization are only tools to reach insights into Menschlich living.
   3. The schoolchildren spell it out more specifically, namely, that

Torah should lead us to Tzedakah, becoming caring people, taking upon ourselves the responsiblity to provide for others.

4. A related text — Rabbi Simla'i sermonized:

The Torah begins and ends with acts of lovingkindess —
It begins with an act of lovingkindness, as it says,
"The Lord made clothing of skins for Adam and his wife, and he clothed them." (Genesis 3:20)
It ends with an act of lovingkindness, as it says,
"And He buried Moses there in the valley." (Deuteronomy 34:6)
(Sotah 14a)

The schoolchildren continue their alphabet exercise, asking about the shapes and relationships of some of the letters, the Gimel and Dalet:

"Why is the leg of the Gimel (the person doing the Mitzvah of Tzedakah) stretched out towards the Dalet (the recipient)? It shows that the Mitzvah person must run to seek out the recipients, (and not wait passively for the opportunities to come by)."

. . . .

"And why is the face of the Dalet (the recipient) turned away from the Gimel (the giver)? To remind the giver that he should do the Mitzvah without causing embarrassment to the recipient."

C. Since the Tribe of Dan was the most populous of all the tribes, they marched last [throughout the forty years' of wandering in the wildnerness.] They were responsible for returning any objects anyone might have lost along the way.
(Jerusalem Talmud, Eruvin 5:1)

1. A most curious Midrash, but not so surprising in the light of the Talmud's interest in the Mitzvah of Hashavat Avaydah — Returning Lost Objects. A number of pages are devoted to it in the section Bava Metzia.
2. Tzedakah reasoning might run something like this: if it is so important, such a sacred task, to return a lost watch or sheep or wallet or piece of clothing to someone, think of how much more important it must be to help return someone's hope, dignity, and sense of well being.
3. Tzedakah not only allows the Mitzvah doer to save lives through food, shelter, and the like, but also allows people to perform this Mitzvah of returning the lost aspects of a person's soul.

D. "Love your neighbor as yourself," *(Leviticus 19:18)* —
Rabbi Akiva says,
"This is a great Torah-principle."

Ben Azzai says,
"This is the story of humanity:
[When God created the first human being,
He created him in the likeness of God] *(Genesis 5:1)*
is an even greater principle.   *Sifra, Kedoshim, on Leviticus 19:18*

1. Rabbi Akiva quotes one of the most well-known verses in the Torah,
    a basic principle of life.
2. Ben Azzai attempts to be more all-encompassing, saying that the
    mere fact of being created by God means everyone shares in the
    Likeness of God.
3. According to Ben Azzai, the shortcoming of Rabbi Akiva's princi-
    ple is: if you do not treat yourself well, you would then not have
    to treat others well. On the other hand, if you recognize the Likeness
    of God in everyone, including yourself, you will more likely be
    aware of how to act, i.e., everyone (including your own self),
    deserves to be treated with Kavod, with respect for human dignity.
4. Ben Azzai would seem to imply that love itself is not sufficient in
    interpersonal relations. If love is taken to mean at times "a feeling
    or a mood of love", this mood or feeling may pass, and with it,
    a desire to love others. The Likeness of God is a permanent, ingrain-
    ed feature—though, always an active principle.
5. Tzedakah, defined as "The right thing to do", fits well into Ben
    Azzai's view. Even when in an unloving mood or frame of mind,
    we are instructed to do Tzedakah, because human beings, *by defini-
    tion, by dint of being created in the Likeness of God,* are entitled
    to be treated appropriately.
6. A powerful related text:
    "There are many with me." (Psalm 55:19)
    And who are they?
    They are the angels who watch over people.
    Rabbi Yehoshua ben Levi said:
    An entourage of angels always walks in front of people,
    with messengers calling out.
    And what do they say?
    "Make way for the image of the Holy One, blessed be He!"
                        (Deuteronomy Rabba, Re'eh 4)
7. And another:
    [At the time of Creation,] only one human being was created . . .
    in order to illustrate the greatness of the Holy One, blessed be He:
    When human beings mint coins, they all look alike, but the King
    of kings of kings, the Holy One, blessed be He, "minted" all
    human beings from the same die as the first one, and yet, not a
    single one resembles another.   *(Mishna Sanhedrin 4, end)*

E. Rava said to Rafram bar Papa:
    Please tell us some of the good things Rav Huna used to do.

    He said to him:
    I do not remember things from his youth,
    but I do remember things from his old age . . . .
    [One of the things he used to do was] —
    whenever he was about to sit down and eat,
    he would open his door and say,
    "Whoever needs to, may come in and eat."

                                                        (Ta'anit 20b)

    1. When the editors of the Talmud, Ravina and Rav Ashi, made their
        final selections as to what would be excluded and what would re-
        main, why did they pick this ever-so-brief vignette?
    2. I believe they wanted to raise the issue of the value of human be-
        ings. They wanted to remind us what things people do that are wor-
        thy to be remembered.
    3. Recalling that some historical figures are remembered as great
        generals, others as Robber Barons, and still others as eccentric
        millionaires, we, as Jews, are being reminded that Mitzvah deeds
        are the most important things we can do, the most worthy of be-
        ing recalled among friends and for future generations.
    4. Of all the things Rav Huna had done in his life, Rafram bar Papa
        chose to recall that he personified the Mitzvah of Hospitality, open-
        ing his doors for the hungry not only on Passover, as was the custom
        according the the Haggadah, but every time he was having a meal.
    5. Now, centuries later, in the late 20th Century, we find that, indeed,
        this was a worthy choice — reading the story gives us an uplifted
        feeling, a sense of purpose and a touch of warmth.

F. As the fetus emerges into the world . . .
    [becoming a human being], . . .
    it is made to take an oath.
    And what is that oath?
    "Be righteous . . . ."
                                                        (Niddah 31b)

    1. In Yiddish we would say Zei a Mensch — "Be a Mensch."
    2. One can imagine this poor kid, barely a few seconds old, having
        to commit himself or herself solemnly to all that "Mensch" implies
        — decency, caring, compassion, Tzedakah. (Jewish tradition does
        teach after all, that a child's education should begin early . . . . but
        this is really very early!
    3. And yet, the meaning is very powerful: we enter life with a com-
        mitment to live up to certain high standards, to have a sense of values
        that stands for kindness over cruelty, gentleness over harshness,

caring rather than hardheartedness. This Talmudic view contrasts strongly with the view that we owe nothing to anyone, that our lives are our own to live solely as we see fit, and if we want to waste it or throw it away, it's nobody's concern but our own.

4. For fifteen years or more I have been going back to the this text, over and over agian, reviewing it with students and friends and teachers. In my angry moments, I remind parents that the oath does not say anything about Nobel Prizes or status-titles. In my kinder moments, I explain to them, and to myself, that it is just one more Talmudic reminder of just why we are born and what we are to do with this thing called Life.

G. Our teachers have said:
Once, while Moses, our Teacher, was tending Yitro's sheep, one of the sheep ran away. Moses ran after it until it reached a small, shaded place. There the lamb came across a pool of water and began to drink. As Moses approached the lamb, he said, "I did not know you ran away because you were thirsty. You are so exhausted!" He then put the lamb on his shoulders and carried him back.
The Holy One, blessed be He, said, "Since you tend the sheep of human beings with such overwhelming love — by your life, I swear you shall be the shepherd of My sheep, Israel."

(Exodus, Rabba 2:2)

1. God chooses Moses to lead the Jewish people first and foremost because he is a caring person.
2. The text makes clear that Moses cared for *every individual sheep.*
3. Moses is willing to admit that he had not been sensitive enough, saying, "I did not know . . . you were thirsty" — another important quality of Jewish leadership.
4. Most striking of all is Moses literally carrying the sheep back on his shoulders. Leaders must extend and exert themselves to the utmost for their constituents, the sheep they care for.
5. It is not surprising, therefore, that many Jewish leaders were originally shepherds: Abraham, King David, and Rabbi Akiva, for example.
6. Leaders of small Hebrew Free Loan Societies are particularly known for extending themselves beyond what is normally expected, as are many, many case workers in Jewish Family Service agencies, stretching themselves physically, emotionally, and sometimes with their own financial resources to take care of others. In all sectors of Jewish work you find these shepherds who will carry the people with their own arms, though the shoulders might ache, and the body and mind be exhausted.
7. Binyamin HaTzaddik, supervisor of a local Tzedakah fund in the time of the Talmud did just that: when a woman and seven children needed assistance and the money had run out — he fed them out of his own money. *(Bava Batra 11a)*

H .   Rabbi Yishmael said:

One who wishes to acquire wisdom should study the way money
works, for there is no greater area of Torah-study than this. It is like
an everflowing stream. And one who wishes to study money matters should apprentice oneself to Rabbi Shimon ben Nannes.

(Bava Batra 175b)

1. We usually associate the idea of wisdom with philosophy, theology,
psychology, history, literature, and similar subjects. The Talmudic sages
had a more realistic, down-to-earth approach: generally understanding
"wisdom" to mean Menschlich thinking, insight as to how to live an upright,
compassionate life, they concentrated on money matters. People interact
with money so frequently, paying, receiving, donating, worrying about it,
that they felt this would be a much better criterion for gaining an understanding of wisdom.

2. The Hebrew term for "the way money works" is   דיני ממונות...
a Talmudic term encompassing most of Civil Law...torts, damages, con-
tracts, property, inheritance, theft, robbery, a multitude of chapters on how
people relate to each other when it comes to possessions and commitments.
Much of it is a study of how people can avoid trampling on others or being trampled on by others, and what redress there might be in the event
of conflict. That kind of day-to-day wisdom is of primary concern to the
Jewish way of life.

3. By studying people's attachments to money and things, the Rabbis
are saying, we can grasp the nature of the human being more fully.

4. The final phrase — "apprentice oneself to Rabbi Shimon ben Nan-
nas" — would indicate that in such often-complex and intricate matters,
it is wise to have a financial advisor. Not in the sense of an investment banker
or accountant, but one who can help people make ultimate sense of people-
and-money, both in the broad, philosophical sense, and in the everyday
occurrences of people's actions and transactions.

5. A related, more generalized text would be;

Rabbi Yossi says:
Respect other people's money
as much as you do your own.

(Sayings of the Fathers 2:17)

Most interestingly, there is a text almost identical to Rabbi Yossi's statement . . . .only one word is different, and I am certain that when people
heard the one phrase, they also heard the echo of the other:

Rabbi Eliezer says:
Respect other people's dignity
as much as you do your own.

(Sayings of the Fathers 2:15)

6. Yet another text quotes Rabbi Yochanan as saying,
   "All the parts of the body depend on the heart,
   and the heart depends on the pocket."
   Jerusalem Talmud, Terumot 8:4)

Again, most realistically, the Rabbis understand that our actions and our moods are often determined by our concerns with money. They were not Ivory Tower thinkers; they lived among the people, came from the people, worked with them, shared their common experiences, and knew how much other people's lives — and their own — were tied to money.

7. One additional text —
   Rabbi Ila'i said:
   A person may be known by three things —
   by his cup, by his pocket, and by his anger.
   And some say:
   by his laughter.
   (Eruvin 65b)

The same theme . . . watching how a person uses his or her money, how he or she acquires it, what they buy with it, and how much they give away, offers a more accurate view of the nature of the person.

I. Rabbi Yehoshua ben Levi said:

If you are alone on a journey, you should occupy yourself with Torah
. . . .
If you have a headache, you should occupy yourself with Torah . . . .
If you have a sore throat, you should occupy yourself with Torah . . . .
If you have a pain in your bones, you should occupy yourself with
Torah . . . .
If your entire body is in pain, you should occupy yourself with Torah

. . . .
(Eruvin 54a)

1. There are many reasons to study Torah, besides for the pure purpose of Torah study itself.
2. If we study Torah as a lead-in to Tzedakah work, this text might yield the following interpretations:

If you are alone on a journey, study Torah because Torah-leading-to-Tzedakah connects you to other people. Life-as-a-journey is not solitary or lonely because there is constant companionship through Tzedakah.

If you have a headache, study Torah because Torah-leading-to-Tzedakah will (a) help make you forget your own personal aches and (b) will serve as a cure for the headaches caused by the immensity of suffering in the world. Tzedakah can heal the suffering of others, and alleviate the headache you felt through your sympathy.

And so on, down the list.
The last phrase is the starkest —
If your entire body is in pain, you should study Torah-leading-to-

Tzedakah . . . . there are so many stories of people debilitated by serious illness, or even near death, who feel less pain because they continue their Tzedakah work. Their lives continue, full of meaning, full of vigor beyond the doctors' expectations, because of Tzedakah. We have all heard stories about such people, or seen them in action ourselves. There must be some Great Truth in this text and in their lives.

J.   Rabbi Yehuda used to say:
     There are ten strong things in the world —

     . . . .

     Death is harder than all of them,
     but Tzedakah saves from death, as it is written,
     "And Tzedakah saves from death." *(Proverbs 10:2)*

                                                  (Bava Batra 10a)

   1.   By food, by clothing, by shelter, by medical research and the like, the recipient is physically saved from death.
   2.   Our Tzedakah deeds live on long after us, not only in buildings or institutes or lectures that bear the names of those who funded them, but in the stories people tell after us, long after we are no longer alive. And by people learning from a pattern of Tzedakah embodied in our actions, who take upon themselves to live their lives in similar fashion.
   3.   People are saved from a living death:
       a . The recipient regains self-dignity, a sense that he or she is cared for and believed in as a human being.
       b . The giver lives purposefully by doing Tzedakah, rarely, if ever, feeling worthless.
       c . The Talmud compares being poor to being dead. The recipient is saved from poverty = death, and the giver is saved from the impoverishment of a shallow life. Maimonides expresses this most eloquently:

            There is no greater or more glorious joy
            than to bring happiness to the hearts of the poor,
            orphans, widows and strangers.
            One who brings joy to the hearts of these disadvantaged
            individuals resembles God . . . .
                                        (Mishna Torah, Laws of Megillah 2:17)

K.   It was taught in the name of Rabbi Yehoshua:
     The poor person [standing at the door] does more for the householder than the householder does for the poor person.

                                                  (Leviticus Rabba 34:8)

1. The Mitzvah doer feels good, fulfilled, uplifted, a sense of joy from doing the Mitzvah deed.
2. The feeling of fulfillment stems from feeling that the Mitzvah person is living up to his or her image — the Image of God.
3. The Mitzvah doer gains a sense of self-worth.
4. The Mitzvah doer feels connected, part of the lives of others, and feels important, that his or her life matters to others. Any psychologist will explain that being needed is a basic principle of mental health. Loneliness fades.
5. Because of the variety of Mitzvahs waiting to be done, it may take a very quick or seemingly minor Mitzvah to demonstrate how little it takes to show how much human beings matter to each other.
6. The recipient of the Mitzvah gains the food, fed with dignity, or the clothes, or whatever, a sense of physical well-being, as well as the sense that people care, that no one is alone.
7. I am not sure whether or not the person doing the Mitzvah gains more than the recipient — they just emerge from the Mitzvah moment gaining different things.
8. People doing Mitzvahs don't do Tzedakah necessarily to gain all these benefits. These perks come with the "package", naturally, if the Mitzvah person is open to feel them.
9. Many have remarked that "the poor person standing at the door" gives the Mitzvah person an *opportunity* to do Mitzvot. I have noticed in a number of places in conversation with people that there are many who seek places to put their Mitzvah energies and Tzedakah money, but can't seem to find the right ones, the ones that will match with the specific tenor of their personalities. There are mis-matches: one who is unhappy working with elderly people, sometimes shifts his or her energies and money to children. Others may enjoy funding scholarships to Jewish camps after trying other projects that did not satisfy their own needs. Some give up, or are about to give up, after a few distressing encounters with Tzedakah that is out of tune with their personalities. *Ultimately,* the needs of the recipient are paramount, and within certain bounds, our own needs should not be the primary consideration. How these bounds are defined — I leave that for lengthy discussions in each specific Tzedakah situation.

L."Do not rob the poor because he is poor." *(Proverbs 22:22)*

Our Rabbis have taught:

What is this verse speaking about?

If the person is poor, what could he possibly be robbing him of? Rather, the verse must be speaking of the Gifts to the Poor that the Torah requires the person to give — the Gleanings, Forgotten Sheaves of grain, and Corners of the Field, and the Poor Person's Tithe.

The Holy One, blessed be He, issued a warning that a person should not
rob him of these gifts which are rightfully his because he is poor.
His poverty is as much as he can handle.
Is it not enough that the wealthy person is comfortable, and the poor person is in pain — and yet he would steal from him what the Holy One, blessed
be He, gave to him?!

(Numbers Rabba 5:2)

1.   This text will make no sense to the person who considers himself
     or herself "self-made".
2.   Jewish tradition considers that a certain portion of our income never
     really belongs to us — it always belongs to other people, i.e., the
     poor.
3.   The glory of the Jewish way of giving is that we are privileged to
     decide how to distribute our Tzedakah money, that, as Jews, we
     have a thing in our lives called a Tzedakah Fund. We are the guar-
     dians of the money, the supervisors, the trustees and executors, and
     can apply our human wisdom to provide for others. Not doing so,
     at least in the opinion of the Rabbis, was tantamount to stealing what
     rightfully belongs to others. It may sound harsh, but it makes sense
     within the Talmudic mode of thinking.

4.   A related text:
     Rabbi Elazar of Bartota said,
     "Give Him what is His,
     for you and whatever is yours is His."

(Sayings of the Fathers 3:8)

Briefly put, all is ultimately God's property — including our own selves.
We get to keep most of the possessions during our lifetimes — the 80-90%,
but the rest, being God's, has be to re-apportioned. And we are to serve
as the agents for that Mitzvah of Tzedakah.

M.   All those years the Jews were in the desert, they carried two containers
     with them—one of the dead [containing the bones of Joseph], and one
     of the living [containing the Ten Commandments and the broken pieces
     of the first tablets]—and they were carried side-by-side.
     Passers-by would ask, "What is the nature of these two containers?"
     The Jews replied, "One is for the dead, and one is for the Intimate
     Presence of God."
     "And what right does this dead individual have to be carried so close-
     ly to God's Intimate Presence?"
     The Jews replied, "The person whose body lies in the one container
     embodied all the words written on the Tablets lying in the other
     container."

(Sotah 13a-b)

1. The Talmud refers to Joseph as "Yosef HaTzaddik–Joseph the Righteous One".
2. When people study the life of Joseph in Genesis Chapters 37-50, the impression is hardly that he was a Tzaddik. We have stories of his causing trouble with his brothers, his flashiness, some high-handedness when wielding power . . . a number of personality deficiencies.
3. Still, the Talmud calls him *Tzaddik* — and the Midrash quoted above says he embodied (literally, *Kiyyem* — "Lived") all the words of the Torah.
4. Over the centuries, commentators have struggled with the apparent difficulties between the Biblical account and the Talmudic-Midrashic understanding of this person.
5. My only solution is this: Joseph saved the entire Egyptian people from starvation in the great seven-year famine. I would imagine that, for that alone, he is entitled to be called *Tzaddik*.

FEEDING THE HUNGRY

This section uses a variety of materials to examine the issue of hunger, hungry people, and Jewish responses to it: an article, outline and reactions to The Tzedakah Habit, a food project, a summary of MAZON's activities, and letters and stories from various individuals doing Tzedakah work in this area in their own communities.

The media and the reality have flooded us with images and statistics about hungry people, in America, in Canada, in Africa, everywhere. Numbers fly back and forth between the U.S. government and hunger experts (usually strongly contradicting each other); individuals like Kenny Rogers, the country-Western singer, raises 2,000,000 pounds of food in less than a year during his concerts; a woman in the Washington area seeks out the Jewish hungry and homeless to help raise consciousness and to get more done about the problem, and at least three recently-established national Jewish organizations are dealing Jewishly with the problem-and-reality, some exclusively devoted to it, others giving grants among other projects they fund (besides the Jewish Federations' extensive work): MAZON-A Jewish Response to Hunger, the Jewish Fund for Justice in Washington, and the American Jewish World Service in Boston. Food banks are everywhere, and a sprinking of Kosher food banks are making their presence known (The Ark, Chicago; Sova, Los Angeles, etc.) There are many instances of responses and Jewish responses. One eye-opening experience stands out in my mind: At the meeting of the Board of MAZON in the Spring of 1986, Dr. Larry Brown, an expert on hunger from Harvard, explained that it would take only $4-6 billion, channeled through existing government programs, to relieve an incredibly high percentage of American hungry individual's immediate needs. I had come to the board meeting convinced that grass roots programs, could compensate for government withdrawal of funds. After Brown's speech, I understood that it has to be a two-pronged attack, both the People at their Mitzvah work, and lobbying and pressure on the government to re-orient its policies.

But all of the above statistics and arguments and responses are too broad, too far-reaching as a starting point for this section of the book. As is my custom, I have to begin with a story, to return to something I can see with my own sense of seeing:

The story unfolds in Jerusalem; it is a story of chickens. One of the Mitzvah people I have known for many years explains a custom of his family and its origins . . . Once, my friend's wife had relatives visiting them from the States. The Jerusalem family was very cordial and generous with their time and hospitality. At the end of the visit, one of the wife's relatives gave her $100. The wife was thrown off-balance by this gesture, but accepted the money, not wanting to make the American relative uncomfortable. And still, the wife was uncomfortable, unable to accept money for the Mitzvah of Hachnassat Orchim - hospitality. So she went to their butcher and said, "For every chicken we get for Shabbat, provide another for someone who wouldn't have a decent Shabbat meal. Do it anonymously, of course."

From this came the idea for The Tzedakah Habit, and a growing awareness in myself, and among many friends, that something not only *ought to be done* for hungry people, but that, indeed, something *can be done.*

TUNA FISH AND THE TZEDAKAH HABIT

Before leaving for the Soviet Union 11 years ago, I remember asking my friend, Rabbi Jonathan Porath, "How many kinds of salad dressing do they have in Russia?" With a surprised look and a bit of *rachmoniss* for my ignorance of the ways of the Soviets, he expounded on a thorough list of differences between the two cultures — cars and lack of cars, unicolored and multicolored buildings, phonebooks everywhere and phonebooks nowhere, food products we take for granted that would bring high prices on a black market over there. Electrical appliances, *tchatchkas* and grocery store items on the two lists were worlds apart.

I thought of that conversation recently: I was buying cat food. I could have picked Meow Mix or Tender Vittles or any one of three or four shelves' worth in the A&P or Krogers. Cans, tins, bags full of goodies for my friend's household pets, Shleppe and Laya. We Americans *do* want the best for our pets, or so the media assure us.

Shleppe, by the way, is a tortoiseshell with a many-toned meow. She is notorious for picking up weird things and taking them to far and secret places (such as a shankbone one Passover). Thus her name. "Laya" is short for "Himalayan," long-haired like Persian but with points like a Siamese. That is the primary etiology of her name, though it is clear that her owner intended overtones of Princess Laya from *Star Wars,* and also one of our four foremothers. They are normal cats, sometimes nudnicky, sometimes obsessively affectionate, and nearly always on the look-out for a nosh.

That's where the mitzvah-lesson comes into the story. (I had already been warned by the *Talmud* to be on the lookout for mitzvahs-through-animals. One passage — on page 100b of the section *Eruvin* — specifically mentions cats.)

It was nosh-time, and Shleppe and Laya heard the sound of the electric can opener and came sprinting over the furniture to their bowls. I was serving a container of cat-tuna. Cat-tuna costs less than half the price of the least expensive variety of human-tuna, and its smell is tolerable, though a little strong. As I forked out a little into each of their bowls, I began to consider the specific differences between cat-tuna and human-tuna . . . probably nothing more than the fact that whatever is left over from the good parts for people goes into the cans for the cats. I flashed on bizarre pictures of miscellaneous body parts thrown into a huge grinder and other humongous machines, steel giants stuffing it all into containers for felines around the free world. Still — nightmarish as it might be — it is, nonetheless, tuna.

Just like in the commercials, the cats did a good job of gobbling it down.

While I watched, the revelation struck. I recalled a story of someone involved in a food project for elderly poor Jews in New York, how he and others had discovered some people eating dog food. Now the message came

Shleppe and Laya.

through more clearly, and I asked myself, "Just what would it take to reduce me — what financial straits and human despair — would bring me to eat Shleppe and Laya's kind of tuna?" It was an unpleasant vision, frightening, a thought that recurred time and again as I read article upon article about food distribution to the poor and soup kitchens, and as I opened more and more cans for the cats in the house.

It happened again, while shopping. My friend and I had decided that whenever we'd go grocery shopping, we'd always buy at least one item for *Tzedakah:* a can of fruit or vegetables, soups, whatever. We'd let them accumulate and then take them to some food project. Once, standing by the shelves, I tried to figure out how many loaves of bread one five-pound bag of flour could make, and how long it could keep me alive if that were absolutely all there was left to eat in the house. Again, it was frightening, particularly since I know that no one can understand hunger unless he or she has been through it personally. I was doing secondhand author-thinking, and even though I had been horrified by other writings on the subject, particularly Knut Hamsun's novel, *Hunger,* I knew my imaginings in no way approximated the reality.

Since that time with Shleppe and Laya a few months ago, I have discussed this project with a number of friends, all of whom seem enthusiastic about it. A Dallas Federation group has recently adopted the grocery buying as an adjunct to its regular programs. They call it "The Tzedakah Habit" — and it is no more or less than that: go shopping, buy an item or two for *Tzedakah,* stockpile it, then distribute it either personally or through an appropriate agency.

The media are full of news items about food projects: Cook for a Friend, Grow for a Friend, outdated foodstuffs from stores delivered to foodbanks, restaurants giving over their surpluses or cooking a little extra, even a restaurant in Tel Aviv that has certain hours where all the food is free for any poor people who need it. I now realize that I have been collecting stories about this kind of mitzvah for about a year — ever since I visited The Ark's food pantry in Chicago: coffee, flour, canned goods, all manner of foods for the down-and-out of the Jewish community. It was a visit that impressed me greatly, but not until I watched Shleppe and Laya did the extension of such a project come to mind — The Tzedakah Habit.

My friends and I do not believe this will solve all the problems of hunger in America. As we talk about The Tzedakah Habit, though, we believe there are modest implications which are important to consider:

1. In the face of the massiveness of hungry thousands, individuals may feel helpless. "There is nothing I can do to change that," they would say. The Tzedakah Habit negates that: *Some* one, *some* few will benefit. Of that there is no doubt at all.

2. Since everyone shops frequently, The Tzedakah Habit will serve as a constant reminder of our obligations to perform the mitzvah of *Tzedakah.*

3. Food-buying "feels" different from check-writing alone. It is an important supplement to *Tzedakah* work that takes the form of money.

For families with children of all ages, it is an ideal way to inculcate the reality of *Tzedakah.* If a four-year-old or 16-year-old goes with a parent to the store and is offered the opportunity — at frequent intervals — to make the *Tzedakah* selection, I imagine that years down the line the Jewish community will not have to struggle so mightily to sensitize many of its members to this mitzvah. It will be deeply ingrained in their way of living. Furthermore, the family is tied together that much more strongly: a special shelf in the house would be set aside for the food-for-others, the food would be delivered to recipients or an agency such as the Jewish Family Service by the family-as-a-unit, the accumulating insights from the project could be discussed at the dinner table. By taking a little time and making a little room week after week, for years, the benefits to the givers would be immense. So says the Midrash: "The poor person does more for the homeowner then the homeowner does for the poor person." *(Leviticus Rabba 34:8)*

Now I am feeding the cats again, considering the texture, the smell, the color of cat-tuna. Even when I am away from them, I can still see and smell the fish. It haunts me how Shleppe and Laya's dinner could be my own, maybe, or is, indeed, the daily fare of many people.

It's not a new idea, The Tzedakah Habit. Not at all. The Midrash tells us that "Rabbi Tanhum would always buy two pieces of meat and two portions of vegetables, even though he needed only one for himself. One was for him, and one was for the poor." *(Ecclesiastes Rabba 7:30)* To whatever extent we may choose, it appears that the time is right to follow his example.

THE TZEDAKAH HABIT

(As Outlined By the Women's Division of the Jewish Federation of Greater Dallas)

Rabbi Tanhum, though he needed only one portion of meat for himself, would buy two: one bunch of vegetables, he would buy two — one for the poor and one for himself.

(Midrash Kobelet Rabba 7:30)

1. The purpose of this project is to buy an extra item when you grocery shop, collect the items over a period of time and then bring your collection to Jewish Family Service, who will distribute the food and sundry items to persons in need.

2. Plan to bring your collected food and sundry items to a SHARING PARTY at Jewish Family Service on Sunday, July 10, 1:00-3:00 p.m. (More details will follow). Children and families are invited.

3. Please use the following categories as a guide for your shopping. (Do not buy anything that requires refrigeration or can go stale or spoil.) It may be helpful to buy one item from each category on a rotating basis in order to collect an assortment:
    a. *staples* (such as noodles, rice, cereal, etc.)
    b. *canned goods* (fruits, vegetables, tuna fish, etc.)
    c. *beverages* (juices, soft drinks)
    d. *personal sundries* (shampoo, toothpaste, bar soap, etc.)
    e. *paper goods* (kleenex, toilet paper, napkins, etc.)
    f. *household cleaning items* (Tide, Comet, etc.)

Upon three things the world is based: upon the Torah, upon service, and upon acts of loving kindness.

(Sayings of the Fathers)

It is our hope that the "Tzedakah Habit" will involve your families and children and enhance their understanding of compassion and giving.

Special Suggestions

1. Explain the grocery shopping project to your children.
2. If your children go shopping with you, let them help pick out the Tzedakah item.
3. Encourage your children to decorate boxes or bags to hold the Tzedakah foodstuffs.
4. Designate a special place in your pantry or kitchen to store the Tzedakah groceries.
5. Bring your children and families to the Sharing Party on July 10!!!

A letter from a friend, describing the effect of The Tzedakah Habit on her daughter:

I wanted you to know that we have taken up your suggestion of buying a grocery item each week to put aside for someone in need. Esther (5 1/2) has really caught the spirit of it, wanting, when she is with me, to choose the item that day. "It has to be something I like," she says. And she's decorating the carton we're storing the goods in.

Harriet Hoffman, Assistant Campaign Director of the Dallas Federation, was a real pioneer in the project now known as The Tzedakah Habit (one of her groups gave it the name). She and some of her groups adopted it as a group project, not being satisfied with just suggesting the idea to the members. As a follow-up, the Federation sent out the following evaluation questions:

1. Did you enjoy taking part in this Service Project?
2. In what way did your children participate?
3. Would you be willing to work on the Tzedakah Project again?
4. (Optional) What is the approximate monetary value of your items?
5. Suggestions & Comments:

July 10, 1983, they also had a Tzedakah Sharing Party, when the participants had a chance to talk over their experiences. On the invitation there was a line, "Bring your decorated bags and boxes for display." A real enthusiasm, a joint venture centered on hard-and-fast Mitzvah work.

And two similar items from Dallas:

1. The Beatlemania evening for the Younger Set group of the Federation — price of admission included one non-perishable food item.
2. The New Dimensions group of the Federation — one of their programs. Admission — $5.00/person plus one non-perishable food item or

one toy. Food for the food bank of Jewish Family Service. Toys for children in the Rosh Ha'Ayin community in Israel, Dallas's Project Renewal twin city.

From Rabbi Gray Greene, Congregation Bnai Jacob, Longmeadow, MA:

Dear Danny,

I finally finished *Massechet Chagiga* [a section of the Talmud] and had a Siyyum-celebration last night. I'm sure you've seen these *Midrashim* I have highlighted before; nevertheless, I'm drawing them to your attention. It was a very nice *Siyyum*. Judy and I charged a price of admission — one canned food item to be donated to a local food bank. My friends responded generously. We wanted to couple study with action. Besides, it fit in well with the message — a person's table serves as atonement for one's deeds.

A copy of a letter from Chaim Lauer, Assistant Executive Vice President of United Jewish Appeal-Federation of Greater Washington, to congregational rabbis, June 13, 1985:

> To: Synagogue Rabbis
> From: Chaim Lauer
> Re: Helping the Homeless

I would appreciate your input on an idea.

Recently, food was left over after a catered Federation affair. The hostess suggested that instead of throwing it out, we would accomplish a Mitzvah by making the food available to one of the many institutions that are feeding the homeless or housing battered women. Although it was late at night, we were able to deliver the food to one of these organizations. Their response was almost heart-rending.

More recently, Danny Siegel and I were discussing the issue of the homeless and the needy. It struck us that perhaps there may be a way to systematize or institutionalize this simple approach to helping those in need.

Do you think that your synagogue would be interested in sharing leftover food commodities with the more needy of our community? It would often entail packing and delivering the food.

It strikes me that this is a wonderful way of combining many Mitzvot, including *Gemilut Chasadim* and *Bal Tashchit*. Furthermore, it is a productive way of joining the general community in expressing our concern for all the needy in our area.

If reaction to this idea is positive, I will circulate a listing of all the local services dealing with the homeless, abused women, and other kinds of shelters.

I appreciate your getting back to me on this as soon as possible. I thank you, in advance, for your cooperation and consideration.

(POSTSCRIPT): There was sufficient response from the rabbis for Lauer to continue the process by sending out a 60-page descriptive listing of appropriate locales and agencies for the homeless, hungry, and spouse-abused in the Washington area to each of the rabbis.

A letter from Jane Berkey, Director of Planning, United Jewish Federation of Greater Pittsburgh, responding to my inquiry about a Kosher food bank and hungry Jews in her area of the country:

In response to your question as to whether we have a Kosher food pantry in Pittsburgh - we do not.

Like many cities,we have had difficulty obtaining hard data regarding the hungry in our community. We do know that the many food pantries and kitchens are being used to capacity. That, coupled with the continuing high rate of unemployment in Western Pennsylvania, really sufficiently validates the need, at least for me.

As to hungry Jews, our Jewish Family and Childrens Service has had very few requests for food. Our recent survey returns also did not indicate food as a high-need item. I guess this means one of several things. There are no hungry Jews here (unlikely), Jews have not sought "Jewish help" in this area (probably true), hungry Jews are receiving help through the network of Pantries and Kitchens in the general community (most likely the case).

We do provide a kosher meal site as well as a kosher meals-on-wheels program. Participation in both of these has grown over the last few years, probably as a result of a growing elderly population and the difficulties of stretching a fixed-income budget.

Finally, up until now participation by Jewish organizations and synagogues in providing goods to food pantries has been rather fragmented. Our local chapter of American Jewish Committee has expressed an interest in educating participants and helping to coordinate their efforts. We are cooperating with them in this effort.

I'll keep you posted.

MAZON

In the April, 1985, issue of *Moment Magazine,* the editor, Leonard Fein, made a relatively simple suggestion: for catered affairs, the Mitzvah-party-giver should add 3% to the cost and use the money to feed the hungry. Shortly thereafter, by November, 1985, MAZON (meaning "food") was indeed gaining momentum, feeding Jewish and non-Jewish poor alike, reaching the synagogues and Jewish institutions at the far stretches of the land, bringing in Mitzvah-money from catered affairs, non-catered affairs, and other moments in people's lives when they simply want to feed people. Bar and Bat Mitzvahs, weddings, anniversaries, and other Simchas in many places are taking on a different tone, a more Mitzvah-oriented character.

Fein estimates about $500,000,000 is spent annually on catered Jewish affairs in North America; 3% of that would be $15,000,000 more money available to feed the hungry. Those are staggering figures from such a simple idea; certainly not enough to feed every hungry person everywhere — that takes too many billions to count. And yet, $15,000,000 — who would have every thought there was so much Tzedakah potential from such a simple practice?

I became a MAZON board member in 1986, in the infant days of the organization. My first board meeting (MAZON's second) left me impressed and moved: dedicated people from every aspect of Jewish society — religious, non-religious, wealthy and moderate-incomed, young, old, laypeople and Rabbis — all with the same concern . . . . and a passionate feeling that they are pioneers, rolling up their sleeves to help the "early days" of labor lay a foundation for blossoming and blooming victories on this ugly, scarred battlefield of hunger.

From a conversation with Irving Cramer, Executive Director, September 9, 1986:

75 synagogues are MAZON partners.

150 synagogues are participants in the program.

75 - the second half - are moving towards full partnership.

The 1986 Yom Kippur Project:

1. Suggested texts for sermons were sent to rabbis around the country, asking them to speak about hunger annd MAZON and Yom Kippur mourning.
2. Requests came in for 41,000 brochures.
3. 200 Rabbis would speak on MAZON
4. They would request that individuals and families give to MAZON the value of the food they had not eaten on Yom Kippur. Thus:
   A. If only 50 family-units/synagogue respond,
   B. If the 50 give $20/family unit = $1,000.
   C. 200 synagogues × $1,000 = $200,000 to relieve the trials and pain of hunger.
   D. Estimated cost of the program: $7,500.
       If $200,000 comes in, that's 3.75% overhead.
       If only $100,000 comes in, that's still only 7.5% overhead, a very reasonable figure.

From another conversation with Cramer, November 5, 1986:

1. Estimates are that 500-600 rabbis took part in the Yom Kippur project.

2. MAZON recently received a check for $1823 from The National Federation of Temple Youth (NFTY), the Reform movement's youth group. The 1986 NFTY Board voted to charge an additional 3% for its conclaves, Kallot, and institutes, the proceeds of which go to MAZON, potentially a sizable sum of Tzedakah money.

MAZON recommends that other youth groups do the same, and adult organizations might want to follow their lead.

As is true with so many Tzedakah organizations, the letters accompanying the checks are often supremely moving, and Cramer indicates that MAZON is receiving its fair share of such messages. The idea has certainly struck a sympathetic chord with many Jews.

MAZON, Inc. 2288 Westwood Blvd., #200, Los Angeles, CA 90064, 213-470-7769, ATTN: Irving Cramer.

A list of MAZON's first round of grants is to be found in Appendix C to this book.

A letter from Rabbi Jack Moline, Congregation B'nai Israel, Danbury, CT, to Leonard Fein and Ted Mann, of MAZON:

I get about a billion requests every year to dedicate sermons during the Days of Awe to genuine, worthy causes. Just this year, I've already heard from Israel about tourism, Rabbinic Cabinet about Soviet Jewry, the Jewish Theological Seminary about the Centennial, the Shalom Center about nuclear disarmament, and various PAC-men about everything from Khaddafi to Robertson. Add to this our own local dayschool, Federation, ecumenical group, coalition for the homeless. Add to this my own prison ministry, my yearning to address each year some condition of my and my congregants' souls, the rising intermarriage incidence in the community, and, coincidentally, the initiation of our synagogue's building fund campaign. All this in 4 or 5 sermons!

When I got your letter I said, "Great — another one," and put it in "the pile".

And then, just now, I read it.

I'll make time and I'll make room, and I'll do it not as an afterthought or creative reading, but in lieu of our usual Torah study.

I have a practice of not eating lunch on Friday so as to better enjoy Shabbas dinner. It is Friday afternoon as I write this, and I am hungry and thirsty. Tonight my meal will be savored in gratitude more so than ever. I have two daughters under the age of five. That 20,000 of their playmates will have died between my morning coffee and my Kiddush wine for lack of access to the bounty of The God Who Feeds and Sustains Everyone — I cannot ignore it.

You have opened my eyes yet a bit wider to this tragedy, in such a way that it has become not just another in the parade of problems which clamor for a corner of my conscience, but as a personal priority, a mandate for anyone who would seek to uphold the Mitzvot.

I thank you for being my rabbis.

From Rabbi Melvin Glazer, The Jewish Center, Princeton, NJ:

. . . . Other activities here at The Jewish center have given me great joy over the High Holiday season. I asked my people to bring a can of food to Kol Nidre services, to be donated to our local Crisis Ministry Food Bank. They responded magnificently, and we collected over 700 pounds of food at that service.

In addition, I asked my people to sponsor me in a Hunger Walk which will take place in several weeks. I suggested that it would be nice if we could send a check for $1,000.00 from The Jewish Center to the Christian Ministry. To my great surprise, two days after Yom Kippur I was contacted by a member of the Board of Directors and was told that he had made phone calls to every Board member and that I was being sponsored in the amount of $2,000.00 by the Board. Needless to say, I was overwhelmed and ecstatic, and see all these as beginnings of much work in the Tzedakah field.

From Rabbi Marc Wilson, Temple Israel, Charlotte, NC. In his previous congregation, Shearith Isarel, Atlanta, Rabbi Wilson established a shelter for the homeless:

Dear Danny,
    Two quick Tzedakah notes before the holidays:
    1. Temple Israel collected over a ton (!) of non-perishable food as admission for each member for Kol Nidre services. The food is being distributed through the Jewish Family Service and a local church agency, Loaves and Fishes. As our "Food Basket" is an ongoing project, I believe that the Kol Nidre Drive will be a stimulant for keeping it filled throughout the year.
    2. We have made the commitment to start a Winter Shelter for Homeless Mothers and Children. We will be renovating one of the houses owned by the Synagogue and will be able to accomodate three or four women and their children. We should be opening in mid-December, and we already have 80 volunteers who have offered to work in various capacities. If you know of any "Malachim-Angels" who would like to help fund the project, please point them my way.

From Barbara Diamond, an old friend from USY youth group days in Arlington, VA, now living in Los Angeles:

A very special thing happened today, and I wanted to share it with you as it may be of interest for the Tzedakah fund. As always, we went to our Kosher butcher to get our meat this evening, and Mrs. _____, the owner, began to tell us of people who are literally starving in the Orthodox Jewish community of Los Angeles. We simply sat there in utter disbelief, but she showed me that there is a group of Rabbis and community members who are supporting through their efforts 39 families who are on a starvation level in our community. The main project is to provide a Shabbat meal for them, but in fact, the food delivered is enough to support their family for a week. It is delivered not as a charity, but in the spirit of Shabbat . . . These are not just elderly Jews, but young, out-of-work people, many of whom have many children to feed. They have found merchants of Kosher food who will extend them almost unlimited credit, until G-d willing, they will be able to pay them back. Our butcher appears to be up to about $5,000 in the hole . . . and they are just wonderful people . . . they are not complaining. They are survivors of the Holocaust themselves with numbers on their arms, and they look at all of this with a beautiful heart. They even supply the food at or below cost to help out the organization. The group is getting no major funding from any organization. They simply try to get people to contribute what they can.

From Suzanne Gladney, immigration lawyer, religious school chair-person and Temple Tzedakah committee activist, The Temple, Congregation B'nai Jehudah, Kansas City, MO:

Things are continuing here with Sanctuary (our congregation and one other are seriously discussing what we should do); with the shelter for the homeless (our annual blanket and coat drive was joined by another congregation); ninth grade class went to the shelter to paint some rooms, and a group of the students went "dumpster dipping" to search for thrown-away food.

We go to the city produce market starting around 12:00 p.m. They close up around 1:30-2:00 and start dumping old items they think are too "bad", but are still usable. A corps of volunteers goes to the shelter around 3:00 and starts processing the collected produce to retard spoilage — cutting up and putting in plastic bags for use during the week.

I think it was a real eye-opener for the students when they found nearly $1,000 worth of food in the dumpsters in one afternoon and brought it back to the shelter.

In another letter from Suzanne, a few months later:

The kids are still talking about the dumpster dipping experience. If you want one that will really stick in their minds for a long time, this is certainly it. And, the "flak" from the parents goes away so quickly!

Champagne:

A group of Catholic laypersons in Boston delivers food to the hungry. One of the items in the package is a bottle of champagne — a brilliant stroke!

Some of the recipients are so delighted they say, "Do you mind if we start with the champagne?" (No — not an alcoholic . . . . just thrilled to feel like someone special.) "I can't wait to tell my friends."

I learned this principle from little children. When they talk about the "Tzedakah Habit" — buying an extra item at the store whenever you go grocery shopping, an item of food for Tzedakah — they say they'd buy candy or cookies, besides the normal things they'd buy. They may not know about high protein foods, nutrition, sugar shock, but they do know what a nice touch is, what makes you feel good.

Jerry Silverman, religious school and public school teacher in Philadelphia:

Dear Danny

Thanks for your note. No, we're not in touch with Trevor, but I'll discuss it with the principal.

As for the seniors, we brought small cans of juice to the David Neuman Center at 6600 Bustleton Avenue. Many Russian immigrants now live in that area and are in need of food. More importantly, elderly widows and widowers come for music, a low-cost lunch, and used clothing. For the most unfortunate, a self-service food closet is available for people to simply take what they need, and the juice was for this purpose.

You might want to be reminded of what I did in the low-income high school where I teach geometry. To demonstrate the derivation of *Pi*, I asked the students to bring in any kind of canned food or drink. We measured the circumference, divided by the diameter, and, no matter what sized can, the answer was always approximately 3.14. The 50 cans were then donated to some needy families of the school.

From a bunch of letters sent to me from Frank Ferrell, Trevor's father, working to feed and shelter the hungry and homeless of Philadelphia:

I found out about your organization from the Jewish Center of Princeton. I would like to donate $50.00 from the gifts I have received from my Bar Mitzvah to your organization because it is interesting to see a young man do so well in taking care of many homeless people.

. . . A couple of weeks ago, Danny Siegel spoke to our Hebrew School. He introduced your book, and, consequently, I bought the book so that my 9-year-old Hebrew students could read it.

You are an inspiration to all of us, children and adults alike. I hope that in some small way my class will be able to emulate your acts of faith.

Please accept this small contribution to help you in your endeavors

After much research and a lot of phone calls, a Tzedakah problem is solved:

1. Everywhere I go, people are distressed at how much food is thrown out after catered events. The most recent story comes from Anita Bogus, Chairperson of the Marlboro, NJ, Jewish Center Tzedakah Committee. She reports that one bat mitzvah kid was distressed, very distressed, to see enough food to feed 200 people thrown out by the caterer.

2. By chance, my Western Clipper, Trude Holzmann of Denver, sent me an article from a Denver paper about how some Jewish organizations in New York have solved the problem and are passing on massive amounts of wonderful food from events to the hungry.

3. I call Helise Lieberman at the office at JACY (Jewish Association for College Youth) on some other business and ask her to check out various phone numbers for me. One number I want, mentioned in the article, is for the Metropolitan New York Council on Jewish Poverty. She not only gets me the number, but gives me a personal contact (Andy Frank, Metropolitan Council on Jewish Poverty, 9 Murray St., 4th Floor E., NY, NY 10007, 212-267- 9500.)

4. Andy gives some background, and points me to the ultimate experts:
City Harvest
11 John St.
New York, NY 10038-4075　　　　　　212-349-4004

I speak to Helen Verduin Palit, the director. It becomes immediately evident that they not only have all the expertise, but also the materials, forms, releases, and, best of all, a magnificent program that works in New York (and they have helped set it up in other cities). That day, she indicates, they were feeding 7,000 people full meals at a cost of 25¢/person. She anticipated every question I had, particularly the one that keeps getting thrown back at me: fear of being sued if someone is hurt from tainted food. Besides telling me about Good Samaritan Laws in 40 states, she gives me more details about this, and other objections people might have.

The problem is solvable — that is clear. City Harvest is very careful to point out that people interested in getting hot and cold food to the hungry should consult with them and follow the procedures carefully. And I tell her that in the book, and on the road, I will hand out the number freely, urging people to call, to save some of the tons and tons of food that winds up in the garbage, edible, sometimes gourmet, food, which would benefit many thousands of hungry people.

The problem is solved.

THREE ORGANIZATIONS I THOUGHT MY READERS MIGHT LIKE TO KNOW ABOUT

I. YAD SARA

You see, there's this railroad car in Jerusalem....it's more than a mile from the end of the tracks. It's only a block away from the downtown triangle of Ben Yehuda-King George-and-Jaffa, just off the sidewalk on HaNevi'im St.

There's a story behind this coach, the extra car from Rakevet Yisrael, the Israeli railroads:

One day, Uri Lupoliansky is in his office at Yad Sara (he, the founder and director), wondering how he is going to get more space for the Jerusalem branch. He decides to call the Israeli railroads to find out if they happen to have a spare railroad car. As it happens, they do — in Haifa. Uri wonders whether or not they would be interested in donating it to Yad Sara. As it happens, they would be interested, though they would need to fix it up a little.

So Rakevet Yisrael fixes it up, rides it down to Jerusalem, to the end of the line, more than a mile from where it is needed. So the mayor closes the streets in the middle of some night, and huge cranes (their use donated, no doubt) haul this Big Thing over to the place it is needed on HaNevi'im St....the new main branch of Yad Sara in Jerusalem.

That's how things work with Yad Sara.

I had to start with the story, because Yad Sara is one of those places that sounds just too good to be true, through it's true. As of August, 1986:

1. Yad Sara is only 10 years old and has 50 branches all over Israel, 3400 volunteers (less than a dozen salaried people), and
2. Nearly uncountable thousands of pieces of medical equipment which are lent out for free (to be truthful: there is a nominal, very nominal deposit).

What also sounds too good to be true is how simple it is: you take thousands of volunteers and many more thousands of pieces of equipment and place them in convenient locations around your country and then you just lend them out.

Look - I've been there 50 times. I used to be suspicious: how can it really work? How can it grow so quickly? How can every kind of Israeli get so involved — as lenders and borrowers — Jew, Arab, Christian, religious, non-religious, young, old? How do they get along so well?

There are two important facts that will flesh out something about this Magic Kingdom:

1. Medical care in the hospitals in Israel is considered very advanced. It is the home care which was lagging, and Yad Sara has stepped in to compensate with incredible speed, skill, and dedication.

2. In the world of Tzedakah, the experts and non-experts always assume that healthcare projects are well-funded. People are obsessed with being

well, frightened of disease, terrified of dying in misery or alone. I used to think that, of all the Tzedakah projects I have been involved with, Yad Sara had the least money-worries. Not so. Just down the block from the railroad, in the national office of Yad Sara, Uri and I have talked this over again and again.

Yad Sara has too many adjunct projects to mention: projects for the elderly, repair shop, manufacturing of walkers and canes, mobile ambulance-supply vehicles, laundry service for incontinent individuals, etc. It is too much to explain; it stretches the imagination of anyone who hasn't seen Yad Sara.

So I will concentrate on medical equipment. I have had this fantasy that Uri will say to me, "I need $250,000 for 89 hospital beds, 123 wheelchairs, 46 oxygen machines, 71 air mattresses,..." and I will just sit down and write him a check. That's a bit in the future. In the meantime, I am publishing a shopping list they sent me. Here is a chance for people to buy a specific stake in someone's life. It is, of course, only a partial list:

ITEM	QUANTITY NEEDED	PRICE
Hospital beds	50	$700
Hearing aids	60	$250
Neurogard pain-relieving device	50	$250
DEVO-44 oxygen machine	??	$1,600
Oxygen tank (including accessories)	200	$280
*Wheelchair - chair for child and/or removable railings and footrests	50	$350
*Standard wheelchair	20	$220-450
*Motorized wheelchair	20	$2,500-4,000
Suction pump	30	$280
Patient lift	30	$870
Resuscitation mask	80	$185

This list may be out of date; there may be other, less expensive equipment they need, or more expensive, according to your personal Tzedakah preferences. The best thing to do is write to Uri, tell him the extent of your Tzedakah budget, and ask him what he needs most for that amount of money. Write: Uri Lupoliansky, c/o Yad Sara, 43 HaNevi'im St., Jerusalem, or call 02-244-047.

Contributions are tax-deductible in the United States through: American Friends of Yad Sara, 1 Parker Plaza, Ft. Lee, NJ, 07024, ATTN: Mr. Charles Bendheim, 201-944-6020.

For Canadian contributors — consult with Uri concerning tax-deductibility.

I thought my friends would like to know about this place, these people.

---

*By a rough estimate in the summer of 1986, Yad Sara had about 8,000 wheelchairs at their disposal — more than the entire Israeli army keeps in stock for times of emergency. And still, they don't have enough.

II. THE NATIONAL YIDDISH BOOK CENTER

Sometimes it sounds like a fairytale. Sometimes it is of such propor-
tions you think of myths, or even fishermen coming home bragging about
just how long the fish was, how much it weighed. In actuality, it is a myth-
in-the-making, something that will be discussed many, many years into the
future.

A 23-year-old kid, frustrated that he couldn't get his hands on certain
Yiddish books for some of his courses, this kid, this Aaron Lansky, began
to knock on doors in Montreal to find those books. Now. at the ripe age
of 31, his National Yiddish Book Center (at the ripe age of 6) constitutes
the largest collection of Yiddish books in the world, 600,000 volumes. In
a warehouse in Holyoke, MA, a gigantic storehouse of Yiddish.

In his early, dreamy days about the project, Lansky estimated there
might be about 75,000 books to gather. Wrong! They are still coming in
at the rate of 1,000 a week.

Aaron Lansky is a classic *Ziesser* — a sweet kid. (I can call him "kid",
being already a sage, well-wearing 42 years old.) It would take many
paragraphs to describe my first meeting with him at the 1986 Conference
for Alternatives in Jewish Education, but this article is about his work, not
his prophetic vision.

I will list some statistics and facts — rough estimates, based on articles
and related literature as of late September, 1986 — soon to be very outdated:

1. About 15,000 people are members, at membership fees of $25 and
   up.
2. The annual budget has grown to about $500,000.
3. Students, scholars, and university libraries in 20 countries on 5 con-
   tinents have received books from the Center — over 15,000 books.
4. Six interns worked sorting and shelving books in the summer of
   1986, two others during the Fall, and probably more during the rest
   of the year. This aspect of the program will inevitably expand.
5. Inquiries from scholars and universities pour in from everywhere.
6. 2,000 people applied for 45 places in their Summer Program in Yiddish Culture week-long seminar, 1985.
7. After limiting the 1986 summer program to Jewish leaders, 65 individuals participated.
8. 85,000 pieces of out-of-print Yiddish music were added to the
   Center's stacks in 1986, the result of a massive, treasured find in
   a Brooklyn garage.
9. 200 people around North America are "Zamlers" — book-gatherers,
   helping to pick up, ship, and deliver the books to the Center.
10. The office is in Amherst, MA, about 20 minutes down the road from
    the central annex. The annex has 18,000 square feet of storage space.
11. It is estimated that only about one per cent of Yiddish literature
    has been translated into English. One of the Center's projects is to
    commission more translations.
12. On the 5th anniversary of the Center, 2,500 people gathered at the
    annex to celebrate the occasion.

13. About 60 colleges and universities offer Yiddish courses, a number that can be expected to grow under the influence of the Center.
14. 5 full-time and 7 part-time people work there (counting the cleaning lady, according to my confidential source).
15. Another project: *Der Nayer Hoyzfraynt* — The New Yiddish Home Companion. This will be a series of recordings of great Yiddish literature.
16. Among others, the following have donated collections of books: William Uris, father of Leon Uris, and the late Marjorie Guthrie, Woody Guthrie's mother, who donated her own mother's (Eliza Greenblatt's) collection. Many other names we might recognize could be added, I am sure.

My Yiddish is so-so. I understand more than I can speak, I can listen to the Torah reading in Hebrew while I follow in a Yiddish translation, or work my way through a Sholom Aleichem or Peretz story if I have ready access to the English. It is my practice to avoid borscht-belt Yiddish crudenesses, and I try to stick to a higher Yiddish, the Yiddish that reflects the warmth, depth, and breadth of this thousand-year old aspect of Jewish culture. That's a bit of my background.

And now, having met Lansky, I just keep thinking about all of the garbage cans, dumpsters, and Jewish burial sites that have been robbed of their prey — these books. I keep thinking of the people — survivors, refugees Yiddishists, socialists, lovers-of-Yiddish — who brought these books from Europe, or bought them here, books from printing presses in North America, South America, wherever, and how one ''kid'' has saved them and is making use of them on a scale inconceivable to anyone on God's earth a mere ten years ago.

This is neither a museum nor a memorial to the dead, but rather a most astoundingly vital attempt to breathe life into the books and all the memories they contain, a unique link to our past, and a vision of the future only a person who is mad — or a ''kid'' — could imagine.

I thought my readers would like to know about this place.

The National Yiddish Book Center, c/o Aaron Lansky, POB 969, Old East St. School, Amherst, MA 01004, 413-256-1241. You may inquire as to the names of Zamlers in your community, or you may decide to become a Zamler, contributor, or just plain fanatic for the Center.

III. THE A.H.F.L.

A *Chevra* (from the Hebrew "Chaver" — "Friend") can be any one of a number of things:
   It can be your friends.
   It can be people you associate with.
   It can be people you love to discuss Torah and Mitzvahs with, and to *do* Mitzvahs with.
   It can be society-in-general.
   It can be any association of people.

One of my very favorite Chevras is the AHFL — The Association of Hebrew Free Loan Societies. In 1984 I stumbled across their group at a convention, and then in 1985 and 1986 I was given the opportunity to share some Torah with them at their annual conventions.

What a Chevra it is! Over twenty groups scattered throughout the United States and Canada with a single purpose: lending out Tzedakah money at no interest — a *very* ancient Jewish practice, extending back into Biblical times. There's Denver and Phoenix and San Francisco and New York and Toronto and Cleveland and San Antonio....so many, though not enough.

There are young people and older people involved.

There are recently-founded societies, recently-revived societies, and societies that have functioned for a hundred years running.

There are those that interview the borrower extensively, and at least one that barely checks out the background; some who have one co-signer, some more, some none; some who have a perfect pay-back record, and others who lose money here and there from defaults and don't really mind. At least one or two have expressed the feeling that, "If you aren't losing some money, you aren't a successful free loan society."

There are those that lend out hundreds of thousands of dollars a year, and some a few hundred dollars; some give student loans, and others do not, and the same with business loans.

Some have paperwork down to the barest minimum, and others only one bare notch above the barest minimum.

Some of the presidents of the societies are descendants of free-loaners; and some are brand-new to this kind of Mitzvah work.

What they have in common is this:

1. They all believe that someone in need should not be further beaten down by being asked for interest payments.

2. They all minimize bureaucracy and maximize Menschlichkeit.

3. They all see themselves as continuing in an immensely long and grand chain of tradition.

4. They all love their work and believe it has a sublime element, unique and uplifting, of considerable significance in their own personal lives.

5. They push themselves when the funds are low to find more, on the spot if necessary, with phone calls, often with money from their own pockets.

6. They do the utmost humanly possible to preserve the borrower's dignity.

7. They have a rhapsodic, even prophetic, tinge to their speech, speaking in the grandest, broadest terms of "humanity", "caring", "concern", and, of course, "Tzedakah".

When I study Torah with them, I ask, "How many of you have saved someone's life?" And the universal, spontaneous, and immediate answer is obvious — all hands raised, quickly, without hesitation.

When I study Torah with them, I ask, "How many of you have played a part in getting someone to regain his or her self-dignity?'' The same spontaneous answer — all hands raised, quickly, without hesitation.

That's my kind of Chevra!

Oh, they re humble, unassuming....even as they disagree on policies and methods of free-loaning, there is always kindness, understanding, respect, a certain honorableness in their voices.

When our ancestors came to these shores, more often than not one of the first things they established was a Gemillut Chessed Fund, or Gemach — a free loan society, so that the future of the community would be assured, because the businesses, households, and individual lives had a certain unique kind of security. This approach is still valid today, whether it be personal loans, student loans, loans for a car, a business, a bail-out from debt, an unpaid and unpayable phone bill or utility bill, whatever. Security with dignity.

I thought my readers might want to know about this Chevra.

Those wishing to inquire about free loan societies in their local communities may call or write AHFL, 703 Market St. # 445, San Francisco 94103, 415-982-3177, Julius Blackman, President; or Henry Leopold, Co-President, AHFL, c/o Hebrew Free Loan Association of Detroit, 21550 W. 12 Mile Rd., Southfield, MI 48076, 313-356-5292.

THE ZIV TZEDAKAH FUND
ANNUAL REPORT

April 1, 1986 ‡

I. TO THE FRIENDS OF ZIV, שלום וברכה - SHALOM U'VERACHA!

The following is our annual report for the period of April 1, 1985, to March 31, 1986. We continue to grow: we have given away $60,140.00, and there are now about 2500 people on the mailing list. In addition, I am happy to report once again that more and more religious school children and bar and bat mitzvah young adults are contributing. One particular young man raised $1,638.00 for Ma'on LaTinok, $1032.00 for Life Line for the Old, and $1,091.00 for a third Tzedakah project, asking those who were invited to make out checks to those specific places. While we were not directly involved in his bar mitzvah Tzedakah work, we are delighted that our report found its way into his field of interest. We are astounded (pleasantly so) at the awesome power of the younger generation to inspire us all.

(* = people, places, and projects previously funded by Ziv.)

II. ZIV'S SPECIAL PROJECT: HADASSAH LEVI'S WORK WITH RETARDED CHILDREN THROUGH ''MA'ON LATINOK''- מעון לתינוק ($16,600.00)

*Hadassah Levi continues to provide extraordinary care for her nearly forty children with Down's Syndrome. Raised since infancy under her inspired supervision, they are now six, seven, eight, and nine years old, strong, healthy (many of them in school)—all offered a joyous present and promising future through her efforts.

Hadassah has received authorization to raise a total of 100 children with Down's Syndrome, and there are many infants in hospitals and institutions whom she is ready to take under her care. Throughout the past year she has been seeking out and negotiating for a new place. Despite these efforts, our latest reports indicate that nothing has been finalized. Many times it seemed a move was imminent, but ultimately none of the possibilities worked out. At the moment she is negotiating for another place, but, again, it is uncertain whether or not this location will be hers either.

I am sorry to have to leave the developments hanging, as I know there are many of you who have been waiting for word. I, therefore, suggest the following if you are planning to visit by yourself or with a group—contact Hadassah first at her home. All instructions are listed below. Contributions should go to the Ma'on according to the instructions, listed below also.

---

‡Over the course of time, some of the addresses and phone numbers in this report will become out of date.

We are pleased to report that many individuals contribute to Hadassah Levi's work directly, in particular the United Synagogue Youth Tikun Olam project, and Chavurah Tzedakah in Norwalk, CT, which publishes a Ma'on Newsletter. If you would like the newsletter, contact Ellen Donen, 10 Maher Dr., Norwalk, CT, 06850, 203-847-5667.

(Ma'on LaTinok—Contributions: "Yediday Ma'on LaTinok", c/o *Hadassah Levi, 45 Rambam St., Givata'im, Israel [her home address].* Contact Hadassah at home. *Home phone: 03-324-080, or 291-251, ask for beeper #963.* For arranging group tours, call Rabbi Ron Hoffberg, 201-276-9231.) $16,600.00

III. ETHIOPIAN JEWS IN ISRAEL ($1,000.00)

Through our good friend and Tzedakah-advisor on Israel matters, Dr. Eliezer Jaffe, we contributed to the Association of Ethiopian Immigrants, an organization of Ethiopian immigrants working for the smooth settlement of Ethiopians in Israel, and the preservation of their unique cultural character. We believe strongly that much of this work should be done by Ethiopians themselves, and our contribution went for various self-help projects and subsidies for their Amharic (Ethiopian language) newspaper.

(Association of Ethiopian Immigrants, c/o Mekonen Tekele, POB 44921, Haifa, Israel. For further information, contact Dr. Jaffe in Jerusalem, see XI:3.) $1,000.00

IV. RELIEF FOR THE VICTIMS OF THE MEXICAN EARTHQUAKE ($200.00)

When we saw the devastation in Mexico City on the news, we sent a contribution for relief through the American Jewish Joint Distribution Committee. "The Joint" is responsible for relief for Jewish communities throughout the world, doing incredible work, and also serves as an avenue for general disaster relief. (We channeled our funds through them last year for famine relief in Ethiopia.) As of January 2, 1986, The Joint had delivered $600,000.00 to Mexico City for the task of rebuilding the shattered lives of the victims. It is most worthwhile for everyone to learn more about The Joint's work for Jews and non-Jews everywhere.

(*American Jewish Joint Distribution Committee, 711 3rd Avenue, NY, NY 10017, 212-687-6200, ATTN: Dr. Saul Cohen.) $200.00

V. INDIVIDUAL ASSISTANCE ($3,076.00)

Through our various agents, we funded a variety of immediate individual needs in the United States and Israel, including: books for schoolchildren for a Jerusalem family, computer-word processor equipment for a 12-year-old young man with cerebral palsy, a small part of the bill for expensive brain surgery for an Israeli brought to the U.S. for treatment, and other individual needs, some of them emergencies.

Three of our agents have been critical to us in carrying out this work, one of whom wishes to remain anonymous. The other two are:

*Si Levine, 23 Horkania St., Jerusalem, 666-864, our so-called "retired" American in Israel who really does full-time Mitzvah work, helping us for years.

Chuck Pearlstein, 22522 N. Bellwood, Southfield, MI 48034, 313-352-0482, a young friend whom I knew as a USY'er. If you are interested, Chuck can always direct you to individuals where there is an immediate need. In addition, he continues to be very involved with Jewish prisoner projects in Michigan. $3,076.00

VI. INTEREST-FREE LOANS ($800.00)

*1. Gomel L'Ish Chessed- גומל לאיש חסד Interest-Free Loan Society: Once again we contributed to this fine association in Israel. One of the board members is Dr. David Weiss, scientist, lecturer, Torah-scholar, and Mensch, and we are privileged to continue our efforts to make his Mitzvah work possible.

(Gomel L'Ish Chessed, c/o Dr. David Weiss, 56 Ben Maimon St., Jerusalem, 669-363.) $800.00

2. Ziv renewed its membership in the Association of Hebrew Free Loan Societies, an umbrella organization of like-minded groups throughout North America. Contact Julius Blackman, President, AHFL, 703 Market St., Suite 445, San Francisco, CA, 94103, 415-982-3177 about free-loan societies in your community, *and* about starting one if no such group exists. This is a *most* critical Mitzvah activity.

VII. ZIV'S SECOND SPECIAL PROJECT: YAD SARA–יד שרה ($18,550.00)

*Yad Sara's purpose is simple: lending medical supplies to individuals and families free of charge. Now ten years old, Yad Sara expands *very* quickly, under the supervision of Uri Lupoliansky, a modern-day Tzaddik. They have over 60,000 pieces of equipment, over 160 varieties to lend, more than 3,400 volunteers, over 50 lending centers scattered throughout Israel, 8,000 wheelchairs, and a multitude of monitors, pumps, hospital beds, crutches, hearing aids, emergency transmitters for potential heart attack victims, and a laundry service for over 80 people who are partially disabled through incontinence (so they need linens, pajamas, and nightgowns also) — and only 10½ salaried workers. We urge everyone — particularly physicians — to supply equipment for them. Yad Sara will be delighted to send you a "shopping list" of what they need. (The needs are immense.)

Our contribution was used to purchase the following: 20 respiration monitors to help prevent crib death ($540 each), 6 oxygen machines ($900 each), two hospital beds ($700 each), one children's wheelchair ($350), and two Neurogard devices for relief of chronic localized pain ($300 each).

We note the enthusiasm of two synagogues on behalf of Yad Sara — The Marlboro, NJ, Jewish Center, which contributed 4 respiration monitors as a result of a High Holiday appeal I made, and Temple Beth El, Cranford,

NJ, which purchased another 3 monitors, after Rabbi Ron Hoffberg's similar High Holiday sermon.

This is one of those *must* places to visit in Israel (on a par with Ma'on LaTinok and Life Line for the Old). Anyone coming in contact with the Yad Sara people gets a hint of the glory of living Tzedakah work in action.

Uri Lupoliansky, founder and director, rare Jew and human being, makes it all happen.

(Yad Sara, c/o Uri Lupoliansky, 43 HaNevi'im St., Jerusalem, 244-047. Uri's home: 813-777. Contributions to: American Friends of Yad Sara, 1 Parker Plaza, Ft. Lee, NJ, 07024, 201-944-6020 $18,550.00

VII. FOR THE ELDERLY ($3,000.00)

*1. Life Line for the Old-Yad LaKashish- יד לקשיש : Historically, this was the first place I ever visited for Tzedakah connections over 15 years ago, long before Ziv was founded. It continues to grow, though hard-pressed financially. There are 13 workshops for the elderly, who come from their homes to make gorgeous items — Challah covers, Tallaysim, toys, metal Mezuzot, ceramic items, clothing — a multitude of products made by the Elders of Jerusalem, in addition to the book-bindery where they repair the schoolchildren's books for all of the schools of Jerusalem, their Meals on Wheels, and other projects, now including a small dining hall for lunches for many of the Life Lineniks. They also employ young and old physically, emotionally, and mentally disabled individuals. Myriam Mendilow's dream!

This will be my 11th consecutive summer bringing the United Synagogue Youth Israel Pilgrimage teen-agers to Life Line (bringing our total to over 6,000 young people), and the effect is magical, for both young and old. When you are in Israel, if you have time for no other Tzedakah-oriented visit, go to Life Line.

We contributed towards a central heating unit for a needlework workshop and materials for another workshop, where the teacher, Anat, has trained the Elders to produce marvellous needlepoint, crocheted, knitted, and woven products.

We repeat from last year: *Our Jewish communities in North America could learn a great deal by sending experts, observers, Jews of every kind, to watch this project in action, and to set up similar Life Lines over here.* Myriam Mendilow amazes!

For synagogue and other group tours, contact Rabbi Ron Hoffberg, 201-276-9231.

(Life Line for the Old, 14 Shivtei Yisrael St., Jerusalem, 287-829, ATTN: Myriam Mendilow. Contributions: American Friends of Life Line for the Old, c/o Florence Schiffman, Treasurer, 1500 Palisade Ave., Fort Lee, NJ 07024.) $850.00

2. Israel Levin Senior Center, Venice, CA: Famous because of the book *Number Our Days,* and the Oscar-winning movie of the same name, this is an activities center in the Los Angeles area providing many acitivities for the elderly of the neighborhood. We contributed towards purchase of wool for their Toys for Tots program whereby over 50 elderly people come to

make toys for children which they distribute to hospitals and other institutions.

(Israel Levin Center, 201 Ocean Front Walk, Venice, Ca 90291, 213-392-3362, ATTN: Karen Horowich.) $100.00

3. Three New York-based projects: (עזרה, דורות, הצילו)

* A. Project Ezra: continually dazzling, providing for the Jews of the Lower East Side. We contributed towards High Holiday and Purim food, transportation for the elderly to cemeteries before the holidays, cost of a wheelchair-accessible van for disabled individuals for outings, and electric bill subsidies for the Stanton St. Synagogue. A *must* place to visit when in New York. Misha and the Ezra people will arrange to take you around.

(Project Ezra, c/o Misha Avramoff, 197 E. Broadway, Room U-3, New York, NY, 10012, 212-982-3700 or 982-4124.) $1,050.00

* B. Project DOROT: Serving the elderly Jews of the upper West Side, and the homeless Jews of New York with their 16-bed shelter. In less than two years they have had more than 190 people come into the shelter, *with more than 65% of them permanently re-settled off of the streets,* a staggering figure, a sublime Mitzvah-achievement. Those concerned about homeless individuals would do well to consult DOROT on their successes.

Our contributions went for Channukah food packages and other holiday needs — food, transportation, and similar needs.

Shaul F'taya, of blessed memory, founder of Chazon F'taya.

(DOROT, c/o Judy Ribnick [one of Ziv's former Tzedakah apprentices], 262 W. 91st St., NY, NY 10024, 212-769-2850.) $400.00

* C. Hatzilu: The Jews in need from Brooklyn, the Bronx, and Long Island are reached by this very caring organization of volunteers - with a personal touch. Our contribution went for Passover food packages.

(Hatzilu, c/o Al Cohen, 38 Gainsville Dr., Plainview, NY 11803, 516-349-7063 or 536-0290.) $150.00

[Note: while it is true that the preponderant number of Jews living at or below the poverty line are elderly, those individuals now referred to as "The New Jewish Poor" include many younger people — people who have lost jobs, single-parent families, some individuals with psychological difficulties, and many others for whatever other reasons. They are coming to agencies everywhere. Seminars and study groups and studies are good and important. Visiting agencies and projects where Great Things are happening is even more important.]

* 4. Melabev- מלבב :This is a series of four day care centers for elderly individuals with debilitating mental disorders. They do wonderful work, again, with a very caring, personal touch. We subsidized the purchase of materials for their activities. Melabev was the recipient of Israel's National Gerontology Association Award in 1984. Those who have a particular interest in individuals with Alzheimer's disease may wish to be in touch with Melabev. (Melabev, POB 293, Jerusalem, 285-661, ATTN: Phyllis Jesselson.) $350.00

5. Ezrat Avot- עזרת עבות : A center for the elderly—particularly Yemenites—in Jerusalem, providing hot meals, activities, free loans, opportunity for the elderly to study Torah, and other projects. David Morris, our agent in Israel was most impressed with their work, and I hope to visit this summer. (Ezrat Avot, 7 Tarmav St., POB 5063, 287-984, ATTN: Naomi Sharabi.) $100.00

IX. SPECIAL EDUCATION PROJECTS AND WORK WITH EXCEPTIONAL PEOPLE ($8,700.00)

* 1. The work of Rabbi Leib Heber: Rabbi Heber visits a number of institutions in Pittsburgh and Western Pennsylvania where there are retarded and mentally and psychologically disabled Jews. His project for many years, the Rabbi has The Magic Touch, bringing the warmth and beauty of Judaism to those he visits, often for the holidays, providing celebrations and a sense of Simcha-joy to all of them. He is loved by those he visits and all those who work with him, the personification of Menschlichkeit. Our contribution went for High Holiday, Purim, and Passover food, and other needs.

(Rabbi Leib Heber, c/o Western Pennsylvania Auxiliary for Exceptional People, 281 Sharon Dr., Pittsburgh, PA 15221, 412-421-1757.) $450.00

* 2. Yad Ezra- יד עזרה Sewing Workshop: Yad Ezra's network of Tzedakah projects grows each year — workshops for the mentally and emotionally disabled people, free food deliveries for Shabbat and holidays, discount supermarkets for the financially distressed, free dental clinic, day care center, Yeshiva for individuals with emotional problems seeking stabili-

ty — the vision-brought-to-reality of Reb Osher Freund and his many, many volunteers. (Many such projects are the result of one visionary — Mendilow, Levi, Lupoliansky, "Tzedakah-geniuses" if you will, though they would generally admit only to having a simple idea which then took off. So, when visiting the projects, it is important to meet the Visionaries.)

As in the past, we contributed to their sewing workshop, where, in a warm, caring atmosphere, many people whose lives may have been torn or shattered begin to find peace, meaning, and the ability to re-integrate into society. They make dresses, Challah and Matzah covers, and other items, wonderful as gifts.

I have said many times: what is normally considered "all that anyone can possibly do" is really much less than that, once we are exposed to these incredible — and real — Tzedakah projects and people. The sewing workshop is on 4 Kineret St., a small side street, open Sunday-Thursday till noon. Jerusalem - of course. Go out of your way to find it.

(Yad Ezra, [main headquarters,] 15 HaRav Sorotzkin St., POB 7199, Jerusalem, ATTN: Shmuel Katz. Phone 526-133. Shmuel's home: 817-767.)
$1,000.00

* 3. ALYN- אלי"ן = נכים ילדים לעזרה אגודה Orthopaedic Hospital and Rehabilitation Center: ALYN is a first-class operation offering long-term resident care for physically disabled children from disadvantaged homes. There is no institutional "feel" anywhere in the place. Our contributions go into a special fund providing for former ALYNniks who are now living independently outside of the hospital. Our friend, Brenda Hirsch, linked us to the following Mitzvah work: dental work for one individual, helping to underwrite the ALYNniks smash-hit performance of "Beauty and the Beast", and assistance in purchasing a special van for one of the ALYNniks who is getting her driver's license, despite being in a wheelchair. (Part of the cost of the van is paid for by the Israel National Insurance.)

(ALYN, corner Olsvenger and Shmaryahu Levin Sts., POB 9117, Kiryat HaYovel, Jerusalem, ATTN: Brenda Hirsch. Contributions: ALYN-American Society for Crippled Children in Israel, 19 W. 44th St., Suite 1418, NY, NY 10036, 212-869-0369.) $1,000.00

* 4. Chazon F'taya- פתייה חזון : This expanding series of workshops provides work and job training for mentally and emotionally disabled individuals. Despite extreme financial difficulties and government cutbacks, it is still functioning nicely. Simcha Ovadia-F'taya and her son, Yehuda, do marvellous work making it happen. Our contribution went for projects and equipment they desparately needed.

(Chazon F'taya, c/o Simcha Ovadia-F'taya, POB 6070, Jerusalem, 814-454. Street address: 6 Shimon Chacham St., another small side street, but worth seeking out.) $5,000.00

* 5. Irene Gaster Hostel for Retarded Adults: Now moved to a new facility at 102 Chevron St., Jerusalem, the hostel continues to provide wonderful resident and non-resident care and activities for retarded adults. Our contributions went for a vacation trip to the Galilee and training sessions for the women residents in make-up and self-help beauty skills.

(Note: The hostel is now under the aegis of AKIM-Jerusalem [not the *same as the national organization with whom we are not in touch].* Correspondence to Curt Arnson, c/o AKIM-Jerusalem, 42 Gaza St., Jerusalem, 631-728. Contributions: *AKIM-Jerusalem,* indicating it is for the Gaster Hostel. Send those checks to Curt Arnson.) $500.00

* 6. Curt Arnson (see #5 above) also indicated that the Hettena Day Care Center in Jerusalem for the retarded needed funds to keep operating in August. $500.00

7. Friends of the Home for Young Disabled in Gonen (Jerusalem): Through one of our friends at the Gaster Hostel, we were told this project needed additional funds to keep its physical therapy program operating.

(Friends of the Home for Young Disabled in Gonen, San Simon, Jerusalem, 668-517, ATTN: Dr. Baruch Ophir.) $250.00

My friend Marci with one of the children of Hadassah Levi's Ma'on LaTinok.
(Photo taken a few years ago.)

X. PROJECTS FOR THE HUNGRY AND HOMELESS ($1,100.00)

* 1. B'nai B'rith Project Hope, Washington, DC: B'nai B'rith's annual Passover food package delivery project. This is our annual $500.00 contribution. Many cities have such projects, through B'nai B'rith, synagogues and other groups.

(B'nai B'rith Project Hope, c/o Len Elenowitz, 8801 Post Oak Rd., Potomac, MD 20854, 301-983-1345, night; day, 261-1402 X 2945.) $500.00

* 2. Martha's Table: Veronica Maz's superb front-line project for the hungry — particularly children — and the homeless in Washington, DC.

Chaim, bookbinder at the Life Line for the Old.

Mr. Wolf, bookbinder at the Life Line for the Old. Mr Wolf
worked there into his '90's.

Our contribution went for Thanksgiving food for their annual special dinner.

(Martha's Table, 2124 14th St., NW, Washington, DC 20009, 202-328-6608, ATTN: Veronica Maz.) $100.00

* 3. Trevor's campaign for the Homeless: Trevor Ferrell is the young man — now 13 — you have read about and seen in the news. He, with his father's help and the assistance of many volunteers, not only delivers food and blankets to Philadelphia's homeless, but also now runs a shelter, Trevor's Place. (They have branches in Oklahoma, York, PA, and Buffalo). I had the opportunity to meet Trevor this Winter, an unassuming individual, and I add my own sense of admiration and amazement to the thousands of others who believe in his work.

(Trevor's Campaign for the Homeless, c/o Trevor Ferrell, 120 W. Lancaster Ave., Ardmore, PA 19003, 215-649-6400. Ask about getting the book about him.) $150.00

* 4. Christian Service Program, Shreveport, LA: Sister Margaret McCaffrey, one of the Righteous Ones, continues her front-line work with food, shelter, job assistance, and other critical projects for the benefit of a large number of individuals in Shreveport. I was introduced to her a few years ago by a Jewish women's group, and hope to get back to see her at work.

(Christian Service Program, POB 21, Shreveport, LA 71161, 318-221-4539.) $350.00

Note: Other outstanding projects in this area of Mitzvah work:

A. The Ark: The best of the best — long-standing paradigm of immediate, personal-touch care for the hungry and homeless Jews of Chicago. 2341 W. Devon Ave., Chicago IL 60659, 312-973-1000, Rabbi Louis Lazovsky, Director.

B. Kosher food bank in Los Angeles: SOVA, 3007 Santa Monica Bvld., Santa Monica, CA 90404, 213-453-4606. Fine work!

C. Food pantry in the synagogue: Congregation Tifereth Israel, 3219 Sheridan Blvd., Lincoln, NE, 68502, 402-423-8569. Contact Rabbi Ian Jacknis.

D. Women's shelter in the synagogue: Congregation Shearith Israel, 1180 University Drive, NE, Atlanta, GA 30306, 404-873-1743. A 10-bed shelter under the supervision of congregants. Chairpeople: Helen Spiegel and Sara Duke.

E. For information on the national situation of the homeless: Rabbi Martin Siegel, The Meeting House, Robert Oliver Place, Columbia, MD 21045, 301-730-6044.

F. MAZON: As a result of Leonard (Leibel) Fein's articles in *Moment Magazine,* a Jewish organization set up to deal with the issues of and help try to solve hunger in American was formed. Leibel, the editor of *Moment,* proposed a 3% voluntary tax on all catered Jewish affairs. The organization, MAZON, now exits: 2288 Westwood Blvd., Suite #200, Los Angeles, CA 90064, 213-470-7769, ATTN: Irving Cramer. MAZON has great potential and your inquiries are most welcome.

David Morris, Ziv Tzedakah Fund agent in Israel, horsing around in the pool
with one of the members of the Irene Gaster Hostel for Retarded Adults.

XI. MISCELLANEOUS PROJECTS AND MITZVAH PEOPLE ($2,700.00)

*1. The Rabbanit Bracha Kapach: Sort of a Mitzvah Wonder Woman,
the Rabbanit continues to dazzle with her clothing projects, wedding dresses
for brides unable to purchase their own, Passover food project
קמחא דפסחא, מעות חטין , camping scholarships for disadvantaged children,
and her ability to be an everyday problem-solver for people in her
neighborhood and all around Jerusalem. Our contribution was for Passover
food supplies and miscellaneous needs for individuals and families.

(The Rabbanit Bracha Kapach, 12 Lod St., Jerusalem, 249-296. Contributions made out to "The Rabbanit Bracha Kapach/Moreshet Beit
Tayman". Meet her!) $1,550.00

*2. Beit Tzipporah Battered Women's Shelter-Isha L'Isha-אשה לאשה:
We continue to support this much-needed and newly-refurbished shelter
for battered women in Jerusalem. (There are four such shelters in Israel.)
It is a very moving place to visit, people helping others re-discover their
self-dignity. Our contribution was for a washing machine and other
necessities.

(For information, write Isha L'Isha, POB 10403, Jerusalem, or to Joan
Hooper, 62 Shimoni St., Jerusalem. Phone 639-740. Checks made out to
"Woman to Woman" or to the New Israel Fund - see below, XV:2)$950.00

[Note: We remain in touch with two other women's-oriented groups

— The Linda Feldman Rape Crisis Center, POB 158, Jerusalem, 245-554, ATTN: Ronny Perlman, and Mitzvah-The League for Family Rights, a divorce mediation group of individuals doing very important, fine work. Mitzvah: c/o Lynn Sharon, POB 3186, 6 Shatz St., Jerusalem, 226-339.]

*3.   Zahavi- זהב״י = זכויות המשפחה ברוכת ילדים: An excellent organization providing services for large families - four children or more. We give them $200.00 annually, towards a family's reference library for school-aged children, one of their major projects. Dr. Eliezer Jaffe was our original contact, and remains our advisor.

(Zahavi-Jerusalem Association for Rights of Large Families, c/o Dr. Eliezer Jaffe, 1 Metudela St., Jerusalem, 690-744. Jaffe at home: 637-450. Contributions through P.E.F.-Israel Endowment Funds, see below, XV:2.)
$200.00

The author in one of his favorite places—the courtyard of Life Line for the Old, talking to a group of USY Israel Pilgrims.

XII. AS ALWAYS, TREES ($14.00)

We planted two trees this year, one in honor of Ziv's contributors, and one in memory of the parent of one of Ziv's good friends who had passed away. It is always a rare experience planting trees with your own hands. $14.00

XIII. ZIV AGENT-EDUCATOR IN ISRAEL, DAVID MORRIS ($4,400.00)

David Morris, ''Our Man In Israel'', does wonders for us. More and more people are introduced to our projects through his seminars and tours, and much of our Israel-related work would be impossible without him. A real success story, from "Kid in St. Petersburg, Florida" to "Mitzvah Man in Israel." We wish him a Yasher Koach - יישר כוחך - more strength to continue the Mitzvah work.

David will continue working for us this coming year. We would like to engage him for 11 months at $4,650.00 *AS IS OUR PRACTICE, WE TAKE NO FUNDS FOR HIS WORK FROM OUR GENERAL BUDGET. ONLY CONTRIBUTIONS THAT COME IN SPECIFICALLY RECOMMENDED FOR HIS WORK WILL BE USED. Each year it is a tight situation, so if you wish to support this aspect of our work, please indicate as such when contributing.*

For tours and other information from David, contact him at Pinchas Rozenne St. 7/6, Ramat Sharett, Jerusalem, phone: 430-902. (Different phone number than last year. Ah, Israel! Right after we published last year's report, they changed the number.) $4,400.00

XIV. SUMMARY OF ZIV FINANCIAL ACTIVITIES

	4/13/81- 3/31/85	4/1/85- 3/31/86	Total to Date
Allocations (including Ziv agent- educators and apprentices)	$185,607.50*	$60,140.00	$245,747.50
Expenses (including last year's mailing and printing, but not this one)	$3,714.32	$942.98	$4,657.30

*This figure represents $750.00 more than reported last year. We accidentally omitted a $750.00 contribution to Ma'on Latinok, which is now included.

XV. ADDITIONAL MISCELLANEOUS INFORMATION

1. This report was prepared with the help of the Montgomery County Mental Health Association and the students of the Temple Beth Ami religious school, Rockville, MD. We are grateful to them for all of their assistance, and for the money they save us, which allows us to give more to the projects and people on this report.

2. P.E.F. Israel Endowment Funds, c/o Sidney Musher, 342 Madison Ave., Suite 1010, NY, NY 10173, 212-599-1260. New Israel Fund, c/o Jonathan Jacoby, 111 W. 40th St., Suite 2600, NY, NY 10018, 212-302-0066. (For contributions to Isha L'Isha and Zahavi. Write for information about their Mitzvah work.)

3. If you want to set up a synagogue Tzedakah Committee, contact the people from the Marlboro, NJ, Jewish Center, a synagogue whose members have accomplished great things: Arnold and Anita Bogus, Chairpeople, 5 Union Hill Rd., Morganville, NJ 07751, 201-536-3358 (home), 421-1777 (Anita's office). Marc Sternfeld, a previous chairperson, is available for talks to help you set up such a committee in your synagogue. Call 212-703-8098 (office).

4. Mitzvah programming for college students: Marci Fox, one of our finest Tzedakah assistants is in charge of Mitzvah projects for 8 campuses in the Los Angeles area — a smashing success. if you want ideas and infor-

mation, call Marci at 213-208-6639 (Hillel), 213-207-4876 (home). Write: Marci Fox, c/o LAHC, 900 Hilgard Ave., Los Angeles, CA 90024.

5. Dysautonomia: A number of people have asked about the Dysautonomia Foundation. Contact Lenore Rosemen, Dysautonomia Foundation, 370 Lexington Ave., NY, NY 10017, 212-889-5222.

XVI. CONTRIBUTIONS NOW AND ZIV'S FUTURE

These are guidelines and other points to allow our work to continue by alleviating my work load:

1. I will return to Israel again this summer, around June 18th. If you wish to contribute, do not send checks to me, but rather to:

Bena Siegel, Treasurer
Ziv Tzedakah Fund
11818 Trail Ridge Drive
Potomac, MD 20854.

We had over $32,000 last summer. I would like to match or exceed that this time around, if possible.

2. No earmarked funds, please. *The only exception is if you wish to recommend a contribution towards David Morris's work.*

3. Our policy remains as always: all contributions received from now until I leave for Israel will be used in Israel during this summer. After that, we will use the funds for Israel, the United States, and other places.

4. No earmarked or recommended funds after the summer either, please. All contributions (except for Morris) will be allocated at the discretion of the Board and myself, though you may contribute directly to your favorite projects, of course.

5. Our Board's policy continues, as in the past: ZIV IS NOT ACCEPTING REQUESTS FOR FUNDING OF NEW PROJECTS AND INDIVIDUAL WORK. New projects listed on this report are the result of our own initative. *Please,* we have been overwhelmed with requests, and we simply cannot handle all the work. Please.

I continue, and will continue to do talks and seminars for synagogues, teachers, JCC's, Federation and UJA groups, for laypeople and professionals. People everywhere are responding nicely to our work, and it is very exhilirating for me. Everywhere I go, I meet great, dedicated people.

The Chevra- חברה - the network of Mitzvah people - grows and grows. We have begun to feel an effect in many communities and schools, and, of course, on the many recipients of our Tzedakah work. It is always a privilege to be your Shaliach- שליח -Messenger. I am touched by your confidence in me, and grateful.

Yishar Kochachem - יישר כוחכם - more strength to all of you.

Danny Siegel, Chairman

יעקב יהודה בן יצחק זעליג הלוי ויהודית

תם ונשלם שבח לאל בורה עולם

A HODGEPODGE OF STATISTICS

There's this old joke about a guy who always takes the train back and forth between New York and Los Angeles because he's afraid to fly . . . . he once heard the odds on a bomb being on the plane, and it was too risky. It's too long to tell, and jokes rarely work in print, but the gist of it is that people can twist statistics this way and that and prove what they want, fudging numbers here and there, analyzing, correlating, and interpreting as they see fit. And besides, the media is always inundating the public with numbers and polls and surveys.

Taking all that into account, I would still list, with some comments, a haphazard collection of statistics. And yet, even though so many statistics can be warped, they are useful thought-provokers, even while we keep in the back of our mind that they may not always represent the truest of true realities. This is just sort of a free-form listing, each considered in the light of the issue and reality of Tzedakah:

1. Martha's Table, a project to feed hungry people, with a particular stress on children, reports from Washington, DC, that in 1985:
   A. over 600,000 sandwiches were served
   B. over 22,000 meals served from another project, "Kid's Kitchen"
   C. Between February 1985 and August 1986, elderly volunteers made 18,906 sandwiches for the hungry. (Age range of the elders 70-94.)

2. Bread for the City, also a Washington project for the hungry and homeless, in its latest annual accountings estimates:
   A. over 150 tons of food distributed
   B. over 40,000 pieces of clothing distributed
   C. to more than 23,000 clients.

3. The Ark in Chicago, Jewish work with hungry, poor, and homeless individuals, provides the following annual estimates:
   A. 3500 food baskets
   B. 20,000 hot Kosher "Meals on Wheels"
   C. over 2200 medical and dental appointments and over 900 prescriptions (doctor's time is donated; because of laboratory work, there is some cost on dental work, people pay some fee — they have to feel they are doing some of this for themselves; prescriptions are discounted, if obtained from a pharmacy, free if from the Ark's donated supply.)
   D. 100 homeless served through a variety of services.

4. Trevor's Place, the shelter run by Trevor Ferrell and staff in Philadelphia — the 14-year-old, Trevor, the one honored by the President, honored by so many:
   A. 80% of those who come to Trevor's Place have made the transition to more permanent housing, and 80% have found jobs

B. 165,000 meals served to Philadelphia's street people by Trevor's food campaign, every night for 2 ½ years, never missing a night. Never.

5. Project Dorot's shelter serving homeless Jews on the Upper West Side of New York — over 65% now re-settled in more permanent housing.

6. The Lord's Place Family Shelter, Boynton Beach, FL, Brother Joe Ranieri's Project (he and Trevor know each other): over 90% successfully transferred to permanent living situations.

7. Yad Ezrah's array of Mitzvah projects in Israel — started by one person, Reb Osher Freund (like so many of these projects) — facts and figures from 1984-85:
   A. 6000 are full members at Yad Ezrah's five supermarkets.
   B. 800 very poor receive free weekly food packages.
   C. 2800 screened families received all Passover needs free of charge.
   D. 107 are enrolled at Yad Ezrah's four workshops for individuals with mental disabilities.
   E. 84 students are enrolled at Yad Ezrah's educational department - Ohr Yerushalayim, students with special needs.
   F. 518 free grants were given to poor brides.
   G. 62 weddings were catered for the poor at Yad Ezrah's Kitchen for the Poor.
   H. 9873 patients were treated at Yad Ezrah's Dental Clinic at 50% discount to free of charge.
   I. 500 children from poor families are enrolled at Yad Ezrah's network of seven Day-Care Centers.
   J. 6500 tons of surplus fruits and vegetables were distributed to the poor free of charge.
   K. 1500 Free Loans amounting to $190,000 were granted to the needy.

8. Myra Gold, 1986 Women's Division Campaign Chairperson, Associated Jewish Charities of Baltimore, reported some statistics about the Tzedakah needs of Baltimore's Jewish community at a program I was at, October 8, 1986:
   A. 8% of Baltimore's Jewish households earn less than $10,000 a year
   B. 12% of Jewish adults were unemployed and looked for work during the last 3 years
   C. 17% of the population is over 65, 6% over 75
   D. 47% of all children's cases at Jewish Family Service involve parental separation
   E. 65% of Jewish households are widowed, divorced, childless, or never married.

9. From New York Magazine, October 13, 1986, their big issue called "Doing Good" — all places and projects are in New York:
   A. City Harvest matches surplus food and hungry people — in nearly four years distributed enough food to provide 3,500,000 meals.

B. Coalition for the Homeless estimates:
1. 60,000 homeless in the city, 10-11,000 of whom are children
2. an estimated 100,000 "on the brink of homelessness".
C. CSS/RSVP/NYC (Community Service Society/Retired Senior Volunteer Program/New York City) places volunteers over the age of 60:
1. 700 such RSVP groups exist around the country
2. New York has 10,000 volunteers, 800 locations
(Comment: How come I never heard of them before?)
D. Literacy Volunteers of New York, teaching people to read —
1. estimates 1-1,500,000 functional illiterates in New York City
2. over 600 a year learn to read through this group
(Comment: Depressing or exhilarating? Do we say, "We'll never beat the odds"? 600 out of 1-1,500,000!)
E. Gay Men's Health Crisis, since 1981:
1. has helped 1,450 people with AIDS
2. 140 new individuals come in every month.
F. From the article, "Our Ladies of Charity", about society women and their involvement in Tzedakah parties and balls:
1. a group called JOB (Just One Break) raised $335,000 for disabled individuals — from one event
2. the New York chapter of the Juvenile Diabetes Foundation raised $500,000 — from one dinner at the Pierre Hotel
3. the centennial gala for the Metropolitan Opera raised $1,200,000 — from that one event
4. the New York Hospital cabaret two years ago raised over $1,000,000 — from one event.
(Comment: Awesome numbers. The article and the phenomenon are wonderful, ambivalent, big BIG fund-raisers. I just can't quite get a grip on how I feel, though it is clear that when you're that rich, many people can get off the hook and self-indulge. And yet, it's wonderful to see how much, in some circles, Tzedakah is a part of the rules of their society.)
G. Alan Greenberg, chairman of Bear Stearns, the Wall Street financial investment firm, with his executive committee, made it a *requirement* for the managing directors to give away a percentage of their salaries and bonuses. Some sectors of the firm are buzzing with Tzedakah activity:
1. Man of the Year for UJA's Wall Street division, the dinner honoring him raised $13,000,000
2. Bear Stearns is
A. United Way's largest donor on Wall St. per capita
B. UJA's largest per capita donor in the country
3. $3,800,000 contributed by 130 Jewish staff members to UJA-Federation. The word gets around.
(Comment: There's really no pattern . . . you have poor and middle-income people who give, and others who don't. You

have rich people who don't give, and others who do. Universally, though, Greenberg proves how much difference one person makes. "Imagine," the skeptical might say, "All that Tzedakah on Wall Street!"

10. From a Yankelovich, Skelly and White survey for the Rockefeller Brothers Fund, 1985:
    A. 89% of Americans reported giving an average of $650 (2.4% of their income) to Tzedakah
    B. 35-49 year-olds gave an average of $910
    C. donors with incomes below $10,000 gave an average of 3% of their incomes
    D. donors making more than $50,000 gave an average of 2.9%
    E. givers aged 30-34 gave an average $500, 1.6% of income
    F. people who attend religious services once a week gave an average of $990
    G. people who never attend average $300
    H. volunteers average $850 in monetary giving
    I. non-volunteers average $510
    J. those who pledged to church or synagogue based on actual dollars gave an average $880
    K. those who pledged according to a proportion of their income averaged $1,210
    L. 38% said they were not giving enough to Tzedakah
    M. 51% of those who support volunteering did not themselves volunteer in 1984.
       (Comments: There is enough material here for a dozen analyses. Yuppies do not fare well in the survey. That's nothing new, but we always feel better when there are numbers to back it up. This would be a good text for religious school children to study.)

11. From an editorial in the *St. Petersburg Times* (Florida), August 18, 1986, a review of a survey of more than a thousand college students:
    A. two-thirds said that they want to make "a good deal of money"
       (Comment: Nothing wrong in that, in and of itself. Think of the people at Bear Stearns.)
    B. 59% agree with the statement that "It's not what you know, it's whom you know that helps you get ahead."
       (Comment: We are beginning to get ourselves in trouble.)
    C. 34% think it is important to be a millionaire before the age of 35
       (Comment: Now we're in *real* trouble.)

12. The Real Hodgepodge — some items that don't fit anywhere else:
    A. The Jewish National Fund (JNF) has planted 170,000,000 trees in the last 85 years
       (Comment: Most of us already know that . . . We get trees in the mail, we plant for occasions. Everyone has a tree planted for him or her in Israel . . . well, almost everyone.)

  B. Only 7% of all the lawyers in Texas did any *pro bono* work in 1981.

    (Comment: This was in a survey I read in *Texas Magazine* which a doctor had lying around his office while I was waiting to get a sore arm treated.)

  C. From Mark Talisman, Director, Washington Office of the Council of Jewish Federations:

    1. 7% of the Jews give 94% of the money to UJA-Federation

      (Comment: Talisman suspects that the figures are more disproportionate in the recent past, since those 7-94% statistics came out.)

    2. for every unit of housing for the elderly we open, 27 more people want space.

13. Jewish Education Service of North America (JESNA) Spring, 1986 newsletter, "Trends", reporting statistics on Jewish education — a special area of interest for Tzedakah work, to see how many students are available at all for Tzedakah education:

  A. Nationally - "About 41% of the eligible students enrolled in a Jewish school *at any one time*"

  B. Nationally - age 13-15, 35% are enrolled

  C. Nationally - age 16-17, 12% are enrolled

    (Comment: There are numerous assessments and analyses of these figures — they don't take into account informal education like youth groups, etc. Still, in all, not a pleasant picture.)

14. Executive Summary of "A Demographic Study of the Jewish Community of Greater Washington, 1983, two statistics . . . one educational, one about Tzedakah:

  A. About 57% of the 6-13 age group is currently enrolled in some kind of Jewish education; age 14-17 = 15%

  B. 34% of the community's households makes no contributions to any Jewish organization (31%-Chicago, 35%-Los Angeles, Rochester-21%)

After compiling this list of statistics, so many things come to mind: Who can interpret which statistics best? What trends do they *really* indicate if any? Do I know, despite the impressive numbers in some of the first lists, do I know they are doing their work efficiently, with a minimum of waste? (I do know some of the projects; others I have only read about, which isn't always enough.) How do I keep from getting obsessed with numbers?

What is clear is that the figures and charts suggest many fruitful areas to examine. They can help people find new perspectives, as long as we keep remembering that the 18,906 sandwiches made by the elderly for Martha's table are real food, made by the hands of aged individuals who still remain involved in Tzedakah. The studies and surveys are tools, very useful tools when handled correctly. Beyond the numbers, though, are the people, the Mitzvahs . . . always.

WANTED: FIVE MILLIONAIRES OR MULTI-MILLIONAIRES WITH VISION

(Five Projects in Need of Big Funding)

BY WAY OF INTRODUCTION

My dreams often dance with ideas for Tzedakah projects, usually to the extent of a few hundred or a few thousand dollars here or there. Now, for a short while, at least, I thought I would make up a few new dreams, in technicolor, with loud, full orchestras playing in the background. For just a bit, I wanted to think big.

I think things clicked when I saw a newspaper article a few years ago abot some big executive from some big firm like Coca Cola leaving the sum of $100,000,000 to Emory University. At that time I thought, "My, what an idea . . . . to have $100,000,000 to distribute." But that figure is even beyond the "beyond the wildest stretches to distribute." So I have toned down the numbers considerably to somewhat less than $1,000,000.

The following proposals are invitations, serious ones. I am not writing tongue-in-cheek. In this particular article I am not looking for small contributors — not for these projects — though by far, most of my Tzedakah work involves $18 contributions, 25, 50, $23.97 from a religious school Those concerns will remain the same, those activities will not change. This is just a side project. I am seeking lump sums, simply laid out at the disposal of the project co-ordinators. Therefore, only millionaires need apply.

These barebones proposals are based on the following assumptions:

1. This money is, indeed, available.

2. Many generous people are seeking ways to make an impact on the Jewish people and the Jewish community.

3. These projects are relatively easy to set up — easier than we might think at first glance.

4. Big Money is being discovered all the time — sometimes for extremely worthwhile projects, sometimes for ideas which border on the senseless and the silly. (Perhaps the community should establish a Proxmire-like Jewish Golden Fleece award of their own.)

5. Some of these projects can begin as early as next Fall or Winter, Spring or Summer.

6. An appropriate tax-exempt status is available for each project.

7. In some cases, established structures are already available which could integrate these projects into their frameworks.

8. It is time to make some new breakthroughs, smaller perhaps than the founding of an array of Jewish camps years ago or the establishment of Brandeis University, but, still, some of these have the potential of developing into larger projects.

Then let us begin.

PROJECT I: ONE FULL-TIME ADULT EDUCATION TEACHER

Funding: $60,000 salary, $10,000 expenses.

Description: One teacher to teach adult education in one city. That's all. No administration, no principalship. Just teaching.

Comments: As far as my experience extends, I know of no town or city in North America that pays a Menschlich wage solely for an adult eduation teacher. The job of full-time teacher of adults (= Big People) is an unknown concept in almost every locale I have visited. People bow their heads reverently, beat their chests, and apologize when I raise the issue. Most local adult education courses are four or six or eight lectures a semester, and that's all.

At a $60,000 salary, there would be no difficulty in finding an appropriately talented and exciting teacher. (Indeed, some of my friends, maestros and maestras of the classroom, have expressed interest when I mention the project.) Some would gladly leave their present jobs to assume such a responsibility.

If done properly, adult education on a sophisticated and mature level can leave a staggering effect. For example, Rabbi Harold Stern of Bnai Emunah in Skokie, Illinois, has conducted a weekly Bible study class for well over twenty years. I was fortunate to substitute for him one morning — a snowy winter morning in Chicago, and 35 women still came out. The class was high-powered, intense, challenging. I envy them the material they have covered over the years.

Multiply that effect in different places or more times a week in one location.

And the ultimate irony is that, according to Jewish tradition, adult education is *more* important than the education of the children. The Talmud addresses this issue, Maimonides rules on it, the Shulchan Aruch Code of Jewish Law concludes as follows:

> If a parent needed to study Torah, and the parent had a child who also needed to study, but there was not enough money available in the family budget for both, if both have equal learning capabilities, then the parent takes precedence. (Yoreh De'ah 245:2)

Why the modern Jewish community has not acted on this, I do not know. Perhaps Project I will be an appropriate preliminary step. Furthermore, it would be nice — besides funding this one teacher — if hundreds of Children of the Sixties would use their old anti-war tactics (demonstrations, sit-ins, placards) to demand their more-than-equal rights for their own Jewish educations. Together, these two thrusts could produce some enviable results.

PROJECT II: SCHOLARSHIPS FOR HIGH-POWERED PROGRAMS

Funding: $100,000

Description: The giving of one hundred $1000 scholarships towards a life-changing Jewish experiential and learning program.

Comments: My experience for eleven years with the United Synagogue Youth Israel Pilgrimage has shown me very clearly that a summer in Israel with USY leaves a lasting impression on the great majority of the participants. Many of the experiences will carry over for the rest of the participants' Jewish lives.

Costs have soared. Pilgrimage now costs about $2400 or more for the six weeks in Israel.

The scholarships would be given on the basis of need. I, personally, have a network of friends who would *quietly* seek out the appropriate teen-agers. I believe that wide publicity should be avoided at all costs and that the monies should be distributed without fanfare and undue publicity. Otherwise politics of all kinds and pressures of every variety will surely rear their ugly heads.

One third of all the 5500+ USY kids I have met during these summers admits that he or she knows at least one other teen-ager who would have gone had there been more scholarship money available. Even if only half of this number turns out to be "the kids who are really ready for the experience," there is still room — plenty of room — for one hundred scholarships.

The same kind of program could apply for Ramah Camps, BBYO's Kallah and ILTC summer camps, the Reform Movement's camps, or any solidly Jewishly-oriented Jewish camp or summer program in Israel or North America.

Now, if someone wanted to give $500,000 — $100,00 for USY Pilgrimage, .$100,000 for Ramah, $100,000 for Camp Olin-Sang-Ruby, $100,000 for Kallah and ILTC, and so on — I doubt that any objections would be raised.

Whenever I speak, I keep running into these former "kids". About fifteen former USY Israel Pilgrimage participants went one Winter on the UJA Student Mission to Israel, future involved leaders of the Jewish community. Others are in Jewish studies programs around the country, people in the process of assuming their roles.

PROJECT III: A BOOKMOBILE

Funding: $150,000 the first year, $40,000 each for the next six years.

Description: A giant travelling Jewish bookstore on wheels to make the rounds of Jewish communities throughout North America, selling books and offering programs of intense cultural content.

Comments: Many years back, my friend, David Shneyer, proposed such a project for the United Synagogue of America. For about six years, that oganization had such a bookmobile. I drove it one year: 16,000 miles, 136 stops in nine months, to campuses, synagogues, JCC's from Maine to Florida and out to California and back. Back then, the truck cost $29,000 and would now cost about $100,000. The machinery worked for about six or seven years until it just lay down and died. In those years, though, it served a very great need in the Jewish community. It is still needed.

Everywhere I go, people still ask me, "Whatever happened to the Bookmobile?" The need was felt not only in the boondocks of Jewish America, but also in the big cities. People responded: adults, Hebrew school kids, teachers . . . . it was a unique phenomenon that should not have passed from the American Jewish scene.

Here, too, as in the case of the scholarships, established structures are available, waiting just to apply a sum of money to start it all over again.

PROJECT IV: BUYING HADASSAH LEVI A PERMANENT HOME FOR THE CHILDREN AND INFANTS WITH DOWN'S SYNDROME SHE IS RAISING IN ISRAEL

Funding: $1,000,000-5,000,000

Description: In the mid-seventies, Hadassah Levi gathered nearly 40 infants with Down's Sydrome and has been raising them ever since. Each had been left behind in the hospitals. A new home will allow her to take in at least 60 more infants who have been waiting for her for well over a year as she has struggled to find a new place.

Comments: Even though government subsidies will cover a portion of the expenses once she takes in the new infants, the burden will be enormous. Ideally she should own a place. There are two options; a building or an agricultural village. For a number of years, Hadassah has owned 50 acres of land and has planned out, with architects' drawings, the idea of having a village-type structure for her children. Lack of money has held this up, though she still speaks of it.

Hadassah is a living saint, bound by a solemn personal vow to give these children a full life, an exciting life.

I have nothing to lose by writing this proposal. There may actually be someone out there ready to step in and make this happen. I have known Hadassah for a decade. She is one-in-a-generation.

PROJECT V: A NORTH AMERICAN TZEDAKAH RESOURCE CENTER:

Funding: $200,000

Description: A director (with secretary) to provide materials, speakers, and insights into involving people in the Mitzvah of Tzedakah.

Comments: People are available for such a position. Establishing an office and assembling the materials would be relatively easy as much research in this area has already been done by interested parties.

The ultimate goal of getting more and more people involved in their local Tzedakah work, or UJA, or JNF, or the local old-age home, or Passover food-package project could be more easily reached if there were a central agency of this type. Their accumulated knowledge and experience could be passed on to others seeking such information.

One prime example: once, when I was in Portland, Oregon, a soon-to-be-formed Tzedakah collective asked me to speak to them. The people were seeking more information about the Jewish way of giving, where to give, how to give, how to function as a collective. I could supply a few reference names and some materials, but the job would have been less haphazard had there been a central agency.

Another prime example: a young man wanted to start a crafts project in a local home for the aged. With a Tzedakah Resource Center, its would be readily available, phone numbers, reference people, ideas — all prepared for such an eventuality.

More such prime examples crop up every day.

Thousands of Hebrew school children and Sunday school children and day school children and Yeshiva students could enter Jewish life better prepared for this Mitzvah, through assistance to teachers and bureaus of Jewish Education.

Some agencies provide some of these services already: Federations, UJA, some bureaus of Jewish education, and others, but there is no all-encompassing Tzedakah resource agency.

All those people not yet enjoying the Mitzvah fo Tzedakah!

CONCLUSION:

I feel better, refreshed. I have gotten it out of my system.
Serious inquiries only, please. To me c/o Town House Press.
Only Millionaires need apply.

BAR AND BAT MITZVAH (AND OTHER JEWISH LIFE EVENTS) AND TZEDAKAH

Part I: An Invitation, Jewish Collectibles

I used to collect all kinds of things: baseball cards, model airplanes, football cards, coins, more baseball cards, miniature license plates, stamps, more football cards, pennants from places I had visited, letters from friends. When my parents sold our big house, the house of my childhood, and moved to an apartment, I think some of the collections went by the wayside. Part of my childhood disappeared with those things, and I think my parents were telling me to begin to grow up and start collecting new things.

It took me many years to decide on other collectibles and their variations. I collect books, and I still keep some old letters (perhaps fifty or a hundred a year), but as I look around my apartment, I see there's not much else I have accumulated over the past decade. I suppose it is my fear of moving again. I have moved so many times, and it always begins with the hundred and thirty and more cartons of books, and then the dishes and wall hangings, and the few pieces of furniture.

So I don't collect so many things any more.

There is a prize collection, though, that has grown in the past year, some documents that now number about 150, a beginning of sorts—invitations. I collect invitations, mostly from bar and bat mitzvahs, though some include other important life-transition events. They have this in common: all of them are connected to Tzedakah in some way.

I think it is best to preface this Study in Modern Collectibles with the negative. Some time in the beginning of March, 1982, the Miami Herald had an article entitled, "Bat Mitzvah Party To Be Like One Big Shopping Spree." The medium-length piece describes how one mother considered exactly what theme would be most appropriate for her daughter's bat mitzvah party. Her conclusion was that since her daughter loved shopping, she would write dozens of letters to department stores from Miami to New York, asking the stores to contribute something towards the party. The trappings of the event included posters, balloons, hatboxes and the like from the various stores. For eight months the mother worked at this project, and with help (three men working five hours), the party room at the California Club disco was indeed a sight to behold. I will spare us the details of the menu, but Pamela Noel, the columnist, very wisely noted that "she will go through bat mitzvah ceremonies at . . . the night before the party."

I am certain a thousand sermons could be written about this article, the misplaced efforts the unbalanced relationship between the ceremony and the festivities. It reminds us of the bar mitzvah in the Orange Bowl and the ceremony I heard of for someone's pet, something like a "Bow Mitzvah," in honor of the dog

The Ultimate was achieved, apparently, in September of 1986, when a family from Westchester, NY, rented out the QEII, complete with full crew of 1,000 for an all-night bash-to-end-all-bashes. I will again spare us the details of the menu, entertainment, and gowns worn by the mother, mentioning only that the rabbi stated, "In a home that has everything, (the parents) stress to their children that which gives us purpose in life." Cost: about $500,000.

Returning to the piece in the Miami Herald, the reporter describes a bar mitzvah that same week-end at another shul in Miami, at Beth Torah, a congregation I know well, I used to teach there, have admired the rabbi, Max Lipschitz, for years, learned many kinds of uplifting Torah from him. There, at "B.T.", Stephen Feldstein was sharing his bar mitzvah with 13-year-old Misha Smeliansky, who lives in Moscow. I would have expected no less at Beth Torah.

I did not manage to get a copy of Stephen's bar mitzvah invitation, but I have gathered others. Whenever I do a lecture,I ask people if they have invitations mentioning "Twinning", or similar generous gestures— some efforts to fight off the enormous egocentricity of the bar and bat mitzvahs that emphasize the partying and hyper-adulation of the child—leaving behind the broader significances of becoming a Jewish adult. I have often met the bar and bat mitzvah emerging-adults themselves, the ones who have "Twinned". Each exchanges letters with his or her Soviet Jewish counterpart, a child in a refusenik family, struggling to leave the choking life in Russia. I can't tell you for certain whether or not the "Twins" over here beat the hell out of their siblings three times a week, or whether or not they are recalcitrant students in school. But I can tell from what many describe to me that the Twinning has had a very great impact on them.

Another negative note, in the midst of all this enthusiasm: when I ask fifteen, sixteen and seventeen year-olds if they think bar and bat mitzvah kids would like to give away some of their money to Tzedakah there are mixed reactions. On two separate occasions I have heard the following— "'No. they would not. They worked hard for it; they earned the money. They deserve to keep it." I am appalled. Bar and bat mitzvah has become a job in some places, like a job as a high tech computer specialist, or a psychiatric social worker. A person works, gets paid, keeps the wages and spends it as he or she pleases.

I heard it the second time just recently, which is the main motivation for writing this article.

But let us return to the positive, good feelings:

1. Joshua Sidney Koch of Des Plaines, Illinois, shared his bar mitzvah with Aleksandr Pekar of Moscow.

2. Jayson Howard Mogilner of Homewood,Illinois, shared his with Vladimir Fradkin, and at the same synagogue, Marc Diamant Machtiger shared his with Efraim Rosenstein.

Efraim Rosenstein—I knew I had heard that name somewhere before. I looked through old copies of Moment Magazine and discovered that David King, son of Rabbi Bernard King and Mrs. Barbara King of Newport Beach,

California, also shared his bar mitzvah with the same young man in Moscow. I wonder how many letters Efraim and his friends have received from all over the world. I think, "Wouldn't it be nice if there were some giant reunion in Jerusalem, once Efraim and his friends get out, when they will have the opportunity to sing and dance with all their twins." I don't think that the former chief of the KGB, the late Yuri Andropov, was particularly interested in these reunions, but still maybe, somehow, some day.

I haven't finished my list:

3. Rachel Schwartz shared her bat mitzvah at Adas Israel in Washington, DC, with Geula Kopelovas.

4. Hannah Katz of Highland Park, Illinois, twinned with Nelly Stetsenko of Kazakhstan. (I know Hannah's parents. I am not surprised that the invitation reads, "It will be my privilege to spiritually share my Bat Mitzvah with . . .")

5. Deborah Rulnick, daughter of Rabbi Arthur and Mrs. Adrienne Rulnick of Pittsfield, Massachussets, shared her bar mitzvah with Olga Kogan of Leningrad. (The twinning certificate reads, "May the day come soon when the Bat Mitzvah "twin" Olga Kogan will be redeemed and when she together with Deborah Rulnick will be called up to the Torah in the midst of a grateful and joyous congregation." Amen.)

6. Rachel Ann Galanter of Madison, Wisconsin, shared with Anna Lissiker of Cherovtsy, USSR.

7. Eric Michael Goldberg of Elkins Park, Pennsylvania, shared with Leonid Kleiman of the Ukraine.

8. Jennifer Greenberg of Flanders, New Jersey, twinned with Janna Kazanevich, who is referred to in the invitation as her "Soviet Sister".

9. One more—Andrew Stuart Levy of Beverly, Massachusetts, shared with Alexander Magazanik of Moscow. (I have more, but nine is a good start.)

Number Nine is particularly interesting. The outside of the invitation simply says, "Bar Mitzvah" in Hebrew, and then has the two names of the twins. There are pictures around the names: The Statue of Liberty, the Kremlin, and Jerusalem. The other invitations run the gamut, simple to fancy to very fancy, but they all have that one item in common—a reaching out by the child-becoming-adult, a connection with the real responsibilities of being Jewish.

Incidentally, I sometimes get letters along with the invitations. Robin Isserles of Port Jefferson Station, New York, asked me for information about one of my poems about Soviet Jews. She was sharing with Inna Dubranskaya and wanted to use the poem as part of her speech explaining the struggles of Soviet Jews to the congregation. A couple of months after the bat mitzvah (I couldn't attend), I met Robin. I felt very good.

I have thought many times about whether or not I would use the real names of the bar and bat mitzvah people. It might give the appearances that I was thanking them for Mitzvahs. It might embarrass them, single them out, label them as "good-goodies. " I hope they will forgive me . . . they know that I am not giving them medals or the like, but rather simply offering to others, through their example, what might become the general practice.

(In the remainder of the article, I decided to change or omit some names—as we move one step further into this study of sharing. It is the best compromise I could manage.)

A couple of years ago, a friend gave me another invitation to a bar mitzvah, in Waterbury, Connecticut. It dates from 1973, and it consists of two pieces: the invitation, and a similarly-styled smaller piece of paper that reads—

Michael has expressed a desire to share the joy of his bar mitzvah with those less fortunate than he.

In lieu of personal gifts, we have established a fund for various charitable organizations in his honor.

If you would like to participate in this fund, we invite you to do so by sending your gifts to:

Michael Carnofsky Torah Fund. . .

And recently, I received another one from Southfield, Michigan, where the bar mitzvah person says—

It would make me very happy if you choose to honor my special day by contributing to your favorite charity.

Another favorite of mine (one I share wherever I speak) is from Anaheim, California. The young bat mitzvah woman, Marcia Levin, is twinning with Anna Shtein. Furthermore, the speech she gave was all about Tzedakah, and in addition, I received a personal letter. The young woman wrote that she had subsidized a half scholarship for camp for a Soviet Jewish immigrant's child. She also included a check for my Tzedakah Fund. And she also explained that her younger sister, Meryl, whose bat mitzvah would take place on May 4, 1985, was already beginning to raise $3,000 in an attempt, somehow, to get one Jew out of Ethiopia. (The older sister, the recently bat mitzvahed one, contributed $206.00 for that project.) (I don't care, really, if they do or do not shout at each other, or take swats at each other in sisterly fights. That I leave to the psychologists, For the Mitzvah of Tzedakah, though, they work together.)

I needed a "Wow-experience" like that in my life.

And, I felt a little left out. Despite being raised in a generous home filled with the spirit and reality of Tzedakah, somewhere along the way everyone forgot to tell me about this opportunity. June 29, 1957, passed (a hot day in June, a long morning in shul), and I was shortchanged. (No criticism of my parents intended.) Perhaps that is why I am collecting these invitations. . .so others won't miss the chance.

I have another astounding document from the younger generation: a "Tzedakah Fund Report" from Chicago, issued by a bat-mitzvah girl. It details $727.00 in allocations—money given to her to distribute in Israel, plus 15% of the cash gifts from the bat mitzvah. Contributions included Alyn Orthopaedic Hospital in Jerusalem, Life Line for the Old (also in Jerusalem), Yad VaShem, Hadassah Levi's home in Ramat Gan for infants with Down's Syndrome, and other worthy projects.

Part II of the report explains that another $2,250.00 was contributed in addition, by others in her honor to four places in Israel.

Part III lists six more places which received contributions in her honor, amounts unspecified.

Part V has a pie-graph of the allocations according to categories: care for the elderly, medical research and care, education, and children's orthopedic rehabilition.

And Part VI says it all:

It makes me very happy to know that, as a result of my Bat Mitzvah, over $3,000 was contributed to make a better life for people now and in the future: to learn from the past to provide assistance for the elderly, the handicapped, and the needy, so that they may lead productive lives; and to invest in the future through education and medical research.

Wow!

(I would have included another report from Winnipeg, but it hasn't arrived yet. The young woman who is sending it to me put all her bat mitzvah money into a fund from which she has $300 a year interest to distribute to Tzedakah.)

Wow!

There's a million possibilities out there to fight the "Bat Mitzvah Party To Be Like One Big Shopping Spree" Syndrome. If some people want to give it all away, that is fine. If some people want to take a portion of their gifts and gift money and give these away, that is fine. (One rabbi, Rabbi Andrew Sacks, had a high rate of success in personal discussions with the children and their parents. Something like thirteen out of fourteen or fourteen out of fifteen expressed the desire to give away either $100 or ten per cent.) If they want to twin that is fine. And if they want to take the flowers left over from the party to a hospital the day after it is over, or to the local old age home, wonderful.

Only let us hope that some of these become *standard practice* rather than the occasional exception. Let us hope that the "kid" will speak from the gut on The Great Day—eliminating the trivia of most bar and bat mitzvah speeches and getting down to the real issue—Growing Up, becoming a responsible member of the Jewish community. It's all right to *shep nachas.* We can be proud if it is a cousin or son or daughter or nephew, or some relative of a friend. But we ought to be proud because they are doing what is expected of them. A giant hug is certainly appropriate at such moments.

One final, devastating negative: a woman told be that she had inquired among family and friends about this idea of asking people to give to Tzedakah in honor of her child, rather than giving gifts. There was so much bad feedback they had to cancel the project. Many relatives and friends said they would not give to Tzedakah in place of a present.

And one last lunge at Our Times: among my other treasures are a birth announcement from the Washington area, an adult bat mitzvah from Newport Beach, California, a wedding invitation from the Boston area, a 25th wedding anniversary party from Birmingham, Alabama, a 40th from New Jersey, and an informal card for someone's 50th birthday party in New Jersey.

All of them say in one way or another "Honor us by contributing to Tzedakah."

Pick an event, any event—start with birth, baby-naming, bris, or bar or bat mitzvah. All of them are available events. You can even share a party; have them throw a celebration in Israel on the same day as yours; at Life Line for the Old or ALYN or Magen or ILAN or AKIM or ILANOT or Hadassah Hospital or move the party from your home to the local independent housing for the elderly or home for the aged. Or, when shopping for food for the party, add a few cans and packs of the goodies for some food project in your local town, dropping them off on the way back home from the store. Or be a MAZON partner.

There's a million ways to do it. We really owe it to ourselves at these great junctures to pick one, any one, and just do it.

Part II: Updates and Further Developments

Since writing an article about bar and bat mitzvah events and Tzedakah, my files have grown. My collection of invitations is now probably officially The Largest Private Bar and Bat Mitzvah Invitation Collection in North America. (I will write to Guinness book of World Records sometime.) They generally fall into three categories with a fourth, loosely related: (1) people twinning with Soviet Jews, (2) people mentioning Tzedakah projects in their invitation, (3) off-center, off balance, over-garish, poor-tasty or troublingly super-materialistic invitations, (4) invitations to other Jewish life events that mention Tzedakah.

Reviewing them—my prize collection—I see such an array of meanings; on the one hand those who are entering Jewish adulthood as a giver, not as a taker, and on the other, documents expressing an emphasis on self-consumption, egomania, a love of things. My friend, David Tulin, instructed me in this matter: Tzedakah for young people *empowers* them. I had never thought of it that way—we are allowing them to flex their Mitzvah muscles, to feel important in the highest sense, life-saving, vital, of great worth on this earth. Starting them off early, on the right foot. That's on the Mitzvah side. A roughly estimated example would be (from the pure Tzedakah money aspect) something like this:

Assume 2,000 synagogues of any reasonable size in North America.
Assume about 1,000 bar and bat mitzvahs a week.
Assume a 30-week bar/bat mitzvah season.
Assume $1,000/kid in gift money.
Assume 10% = $100/kid to Tzedakah.

1,000 X 30 X $100 = $3,000,000 per year in Tzedakah money from bar and bat mitzvahs. (I think the estimate is low.)

That's the money, not taking into account the time, effort, energy, and talents if the kinderlach do *gemillut chassadim* — active volunteer type of work. That is a most significant contribution to Tikun Olam—fixing up the world, in pure quantity of money and people-hours. And such a contrast to the apparent hollowness of the content of some of the invitations, bespeaking Achievement for Achievement's Sake (and it's adjunct "Good Grades for the Sake of Good Grades"), a showiness, a superficiality. I even asked, through an ad in Moment Magazine for people to send me invitations, and some people who wrote me were so embarrassed, they sent them anonymously or made me promise not to mention who sent them—lest their friends, the designer-and-senders of those invitations find out. Those who mailed them to me felt saddened, uncomfortable. None of them (nor myself) felt self-righteous; just troubled by it all.

Again, surveying the material, and reviewing conversations with audiences during my talks, we should keep in mind a couple of additional items:

1. Post-bar/bat mitzvah teen-agers, particularly, and adults, may feel uncomfortable suggesting Tzedakah projects to bar/bat mitzvah kids if they themselves do not do the same (as I did not). I have found that an open confession that they themselves missed a great opportunity, and expressing a sense of jealousy that the new crop of bar/bat mitzvah kids does have this opportunity, helps to clear the air from both sides. In all events, it is not hypocritical to advocate this program, even if the speaker did not personally do it. (Some adult bar/bat mitzvah individuals are making up for lost time and opportunities by making it a part of ther belated celebrations.)

2. There seem to be pockets in the rabbinate and congregational life where bar/bat mitzvah Tzedakah projects are prominent in the educational program. There are many more than the following, but these four bear mention:
    A. Rabbi Bernard King, Shir HaMa'alot Harbor Reform Temple, Newport Beach CA (mentioned in parts I and III of this set of articles)
    B. Rabbi Andrew Sacks, formerly of Congregation Beth Am Israel, Penn Valley, PA (mentioned in Part II)
    C. My good friend, Rabbi Dan Grossman communicated to me that similarly great things are happening at Temple Sinai, Dresher, PA
    D. Rabbi Melvin Glazer, The Jewish Center, Princeton, NJ.

I will begin reviewing some of the gems with a few items from Rabbi Glazer in Princeton.

1. One child contributed to Project Ezra, helping elderly, poor Jews on the Lower East Side of New York.
2. One child, who herself has a form of cancer, contributed to the Department of Pediatric Oncology at Hadassah Hospital.
3. One child— sending $200. to Hadassah Levi in Israel for her work with children with Down's Syndrome, wrote this note:

Dear Hadassah Levi and Friends at Ma'on LaTinok,

My name is Rebecca Meyer. I'm 13 years old, and my bat mitzvah was on December 21st, 1985. I got your name through the Ziv Tzedakah Fund. I decided that for my Bat Mitzvah it would be nice to take 10% of the money I received and send it to a charity in Israel. Included is the check. I'm very happy to be able to contribute to your good cause. I will keep sending money. This is just the beginning!

Your New Friend—Rebecca

4. Translation of a letter from Yitzchak, who owns and operates a restaurant on 48 Montefiore St. in Tel Aviv, Mitbach Yitzchak, where anyone can eat, whether or not they can pay. On Shabbat, food is served only for the non-paying customers in need:

Honored Rabbi,

First of all, I gratefully acknowledge receipt of the wonderful gift you sent on behalf of one of your students, Seth Meisel, who understood the meaning of the Mitzvah "Share your bread with the hungry". [Isaiah 58:7]

The Tzedakah work certainly continues every day, and when a sum such as this arrives, everything turns more festive, and a Shabbat evening takes on a different atmosphere for 15 people.

I will be very happy if the day will come when you can visit along with this child so that he can see who these people are who benefit from his Tzedakah work.

Now from the general stack of selected treasures:

1. Following up on Meryl Levin's attempt to raise $3,000 to help free an Ethiopian Jew (mentioned in Part I of this article) — she succeeded, exceeding her goal — part of it raised from a Trivial Pursuit tournament which added to her funds. I saw the Older Sister, Marcia, and Meryl, in Israel subsequent to their B'not Mitzvah events, shared some Tzedakah touring with them, then saw them at home in California. Their mother, by the way, is Rabbi King's educational director at Shir HaMa'alot in Newport Beach.
2. Picking up on work for Ethiopian Jews, Adinah Miller, daughter of Rabbi Clifford and Deborah Miller of New Jersey, wrote a poem in her invitation indicating that she would appreciate contributions for Ethiopian Jews instead of presents. She raised $3,000.
3. Temple Sinai, Dresher, PA: Karen Laveson did a food collection campaign, complete with flyers, posters, and speeches. Over 100 pounds of food raised. Beneficiaries: the homeless of Philadelphia, through the efforts of Trevor Ferrell, the (now already) 14-year-old who feeds, clothes, and houses the street people.
4. Michael Minkus, Highland Park, IL, included the following insert in his invitation, reproduced in his own handwriting:
Dear Family and Friends,

Instead of remembering my Bar-Mitzvah with a gift, I would rather you honor me by giving Tzedakah (a charitable donation) to one of the following very special institution. I will be happy to forward any donations you wish to make:

[He then lists three places, including Ma'on LaTinok a home for children with Down's Syndrome in Israel.] Total Tzedakah money raised — $3,761.

5. Insert, also in a young handwriting, for an invitation: Traditionally people honor the Bar Mitzvah with gifts. You would honor me by sending a check to the ARK, a Jewish charity which has great need now.

Sincerely, Andy

[The ARK does front-line first-class Mitzvah work with Jewish homeless, hungry, and poor in Chicago.] Contributions: $3,500. Parents matched it with another $3,500. Total to the ARK: $7,000.

6. Part of the text of Moshe Ranan Engelhart's invitation to a Melave Malka — a Saturday night celebration following his Shabbat Bar Mitzvah: You can join us in a special Mitzvah as we share our Simcha — Please bring a donation of canned kosher food for the Ark food pantry. There will also be a collection rack for winter coats which are no longer worn. The donated coats will be distributed to people in need of them. Nizkeh L'Mitzvot [May we be privileged to do Mitzvahs together]. Results: 150 food items; 80 overcoats.

7. Judah Gould, son of Allan and Merle Gould, close, close friends from Toronto. Allan is the co-author of my book of Jewish humor (or I am his co-author), friends since USY Israel Pilgrimage 1961. I have known Judah since he was born, so this has particular significance to me: Outside cover of the invitation, a 20-line Midrash from Rabbinic literature [Midrash Psalms 118:17] about feeding the hungry, raising orphans, clothing those in need, doing Tzedakah. Inside, an announcement that he is twinning, and the following: To honour Judah on his becoming a Bar Mitzvah, a donation to the Ziv Tzedakah Foundation* would be very much appreciated. Ziv distributes funds to elderly and disabled jews and other individuals and projects with specific needs in Canada and Israel.

* (Ziv Tzedakah Foundation is my separate Canadian Fund, distinct from Ziv Tzedakah Fund, the American project. Merle Gould is a board member of the Canadian fund.)

8. Text of a card on the tables at the reception of Melissa Greenberg, Highland Park, IL. Instead of floral centerpieces, there were food baskets:

"He Who Has Fed Strangers May Have Fed Angels"

My family and I are thankful we are able to celebrate my Bat Mitzvah with you. We are thankful we have enough to eat today and every day. However, we know there are people who never have enough to eat. Monday, my family and I will deliver these food baskets to the "ARK." There, the food will be distributed to needy families. Sharing our happiness with you and our good fortune with others makes this day even more special for me and my family.

Melissa

9. Cards on the tables of the reception for Leah Braun's bat mitzvah, Danbury, CT:

> In lieu of flowers, a donation is being made to the Ziv Tzedakah Fund, in honor of the friends and family of Leah Braun.

Portions of the letter Leah wrote to me:

Dear Mr. Siegel,

> When I became a Bat Mitzvah, as my first act of Tzedakah, I decided to give a donation to the Ziv Tzedakah Fund instead of having flowers on the tables. I heard about the Fund from my Rabbi, Jack Moline, at Congregation B'nai Israel. I didn't feel that this was a personal donation from me, so I've also given some money from my Bat Mitzvah presents. In my Bat Mitzvah speech, I read from the book *Between Dust and Dance* about Tzedakah and what it means. It made me realize that it is important to give Tzedakah, even when you're sad, depressed, or don't feel that you have to...

Sincerely,
Leah Braun

10. Text of cards on tables at Joshua Gruenberg's reception, New Rochelle, NY. (Josh is the son of Jack and Sandy Gruenberg, longtime friends.)

> At Joshua's request, the funds which would have been required for a floral centerpiece on each table are being sent to Danny Siegel's *Ziv Tzedakah Fund* the charity of his choice. Josh is also setting aside 10 percent of the gift money for Tzedakah.

11. Text of a letter to the Rabbanit Kapach, Super-Mitzvah-Woman of Jerusalem [my translation]:

> God has been gracious to us, and two weeks ago we celebrated the Bar Mitzvah of our son, Shlomo.
> Shlomo wanted to set aside a tenth of his monetary gifts, and to send you 15,000 Skekels.* We add 15,000 Skekels of our own, and request that you make some other child happy, one who has reached the age of Mitzvot, but is in need. May God grant you the privilege of more Mitzvot.

Miriam Shteiner

*[Since the note is not dated, and since the value of the Old Shekel varied greatly from month to month and was eventually replaced with the New Israeli Shekel (1000 old = 1 new), it is difficult to calculate how much 15,000 was worth. I am certain it was a significant sum.]

12. Some facts from a *Toronto Star* article, February 7, 1985:
    Julie Tator became a bat mitzvah at Temple Emanu-El in Willowdale,

Ontario. She donated her bat mitzvah gift money — more than $5,000 to purchase an incubator for a local children's hospital.

The Temple requires the pre-bar-and bat mitzvah children to do a year of volunteer work, and Julie worked at that hospital.

The article says Julie admitted it wasn't easy giving it away (it could have gone towards a car or college education), and that the idea wasn't too popular with friends her age.

But she doesn't regret having done it. Previously, her two brothers also gave away their bar mitzvah gift money, about $3,000 each.

13. THE BIG TIME — from a Jerusalem Post article:

Maurizio Piazza Sed's father at one time needed emergency surgery when he had been in Israel. The family, Jews from Rome, had a special attachment to this realm of Tzedakah. Maurizio himself has an orthopedic problem, having had surgery many times.

Maurizio contributed his bar mitzvah gift money — $19,000 — to Hadassah-Hebrew University Medical Center's orthopedic department. 19,000. Wow!

14. A xerox of a thank-you note sent by a retarded adult I met on one of my road trips:

Dear

Thank you for my Bar Mitzvah present.

Love, Jon

[Complete with personal drawing.]

15. Last stanza of a poem written by Lisea Lyons of St. Petersburg, FL, for her Soviet twin:

The most beautiful Bat Mitzvah gift to me,
Would be to see Ann and her family fearless and free.

[I have a couple of other personal poems written by the "kids", and about a half dozen of their speeches, each one more moving than the next. One speaks of her twin, after outlining the saga of her own family's leaving Russia at the turn of the century for the safe shores of the United States.

The back side of a brief talk from one of them indicates that there was no Kiddush — they gave the money for children's books for the library instead. The content of the D'var Torah — the short Torah-talk — had a nice twist, suggesting a variation on a well-known line, "Do unto others as you'd want them to do unto you, but knowing they might not be able to."

Another speech concludes with a heavy quote from The Diary of Anne Frank about giving.

And there is an article for a synagogue bulletin by the father of one bar mitzvah child — one of the most eloquent statements of sharing these events with others I have seen. I suspect though I cannot confirm it, it is the same one above, No. 5.]

16. There are a number of personal notes from the "kids" with a check enclosed to Ziv. Nice touches, much-needed money, good, eloquent

words from the next generation.

17. Interesting note from the Shabbat announcement booklet of Beth Emet, Evanston, IL:

    The candlesticks which remain unlit on the bimah each week were given to the synagogue by Michelle Sari Kaye on the occasion of her bat mitzvah to serve as a constant reminder of these Jews in the Soviet Union who are not allowed to light Shabbat candles as a free expression of their faith.

18. Kleinhandlers — I don't know where they are from — for the daughter's ·bat mitzvah gave books for the library in their Project Renewal twin neighborhood in Israel.

    For the son's bar mitzvah, they planted a tree for each guest.

    David Grossman, Congregation Solel, Highland Park, IL, similarly planted a tree for the guests and family members.

    I have another, of the same type, which I can't find — trees planted by the parents.

    Steven Kustin of New York remembered planting a tree in a JNF forest when he was in Israel as a child. For his bar mitzvah, he wrote in the invitation:

    Steven requests that gifts be sent to the Jewish National Fund for trees to be planted in Israel in memory of his mother, Ellen Gail Kustin.

19. Some bar and bat mitzvah kids from Chicago purchased books, which they used as centerpieces, then donated them to the Solomon Schechter Day School library.

20. Other bar and bat mitzvah kids suggested contributions to: one of the day school's funds, the synagogue or one the local hospices in Jacksonville, Hebrew University, a Children's Therapy Group Foundation in the Kansas City area, UJA Isreal Emergency Fund, Project Renewal, and others. One family from Skokie, IL, had nearly 20 organizations and groups they were contributing to, and on each table was a note explaining what the various groups did in the way of Tzedakah work. There is a favorite of mine, a variation on the above: I am not sure where Jeremy Epstein is from, but I think it is somewhere in the Washington area. His bar mitzvah invitation is laid out like a page of Talmud!

    He requested contributions which would go for sports equipment in Israel. As it turned out, the more than $1,500 that was raised was used to buy 3 special wheelchairs so that Israeli athletes would participate in the Special Olympics.

21. A couple of more notes on twinning:

    Many people enclosed postcards to be mailed to either the twin or to Soviet officials requesting the release of the Refusenik family.

    One bat mitzvah kid sent me copies of letters she had gotten back from her twin. (So few letters get through.)

    One sent me a copy of a letter that begins,

Dear Jeff,
I already in Israel...
I think about you at the time of my Bar Mitzvah...

Your friend, Yakov

One student at Akiba Academy in Philadelphia came up to me after my talk and, in a distinctly Russian accent, said, "I was twinned with." I was stunned. Some program—(not a bar/bat mitzvah program but rather one for older students) had linked up with her while she was still in Russia waiting to get out. And, though incredible to me, here she was standing, talking to me at a Jewish day school in Philadelphia.

One other student at Akiba, Joshua Shapiro, did a nationwide newsletter for fellow bar/bat matzvah aged kids who were twinning. Earlier that week, when I was in Milwaukee, I had heard about him from the father of a bar mitzvah kid who had twinned, and who got the newsletter. Their Soviet twin got out.

22. Two items from schools:

Temple Beth Jacob, Redwood City, CA, has an 11-page packet for the bar/bat mitzvah child; partly examination, partly information-gathering, partly consciousness-raising, it includes, of course, Tzedakah and other Mitzvah suggestions.

Sandy Gruenberg (see No. 10 above) sent me a letter to parents of students at Solomon Schechter Day School of Westchester, NY, wherein they explain that they are encouraging the students to set aside part of their bar/bat mitzvah money for Tzedakah. A superb idea, involving the parents long ahead of the event, through the school. It's part of the Jewish education.

Acharon, Achron Chaviv, saving the best story for last, is an article about Lee Kweller, whose bar mitzvah took place at Congregation Beth Shalom of Pittsburgh. Unable to walk or walk because of cerebral palsy, he nevertheless led services and gave a talk about his Haftorah portion — because of a computer voice synthesizer that was programmed uniquely for his abilities and talents.

BRIEFLY NOTED: SOME INVITATIONS AND SLIGHTLY OFF-KEY ITEMS
I have in the treasure chest of invitations what may be The Largest Bar Mitzvah Invitation in Jewish History (8½" X 8½", envelope 9" X 11", weight: three stamps.)
There's one, complete with three photos of the kid, announcing that he will "star as a Bar Mitzvah" (he's done catalogue and TV work), parties billed as Country Western Party, Bar Mitzvah Fever, and a Super Bowl Bash, the invitation in the form of a football and a request to dress "in your football game attire" ($.73 worth of stamps). And a Racquetball and Hot Tub Party. Also an invitation designed like a Tallis, fringes and all.

Ads catering to the bar/bat mitzvah crowd include, "Clyde's Loves a Bar Mitzvah," employing the work "emmus" in the copy, a linguistic warping, I assume of "emmes," Yiddish from Hebrew "emet" - "Truth," slightly inappropriate. Also, "GIVE A BAR MITZVAH OR A BAT MITZVAH YOUR FRIENDS WILL TALK ABOUT FOR THE NEXT 5,745 YEARS." I wrote to the hotel that was advertising saying, "Jews don't give bar/bat mitzvahs, they attain the privileges and responsibilities of bar/bat mitzvah." I spoke to managers, honchos, responsible individuals, but they were less than impressed.

Newspaper articles: "Eye of The Needle" theme, a child entering the party on a white horse, a "barn mitzvah" with steaks branded with the kid's name, shopping themes, Arabian nights themes, E.T. and Pac-Man themes (already out of style) — who had "themes" in the Old Days? And what hurts the most is I lost the 3rd page of one article. I can't find it anywhere. The sentence before it runs out goes like this, "Over the years, girls increasingly have been bat mitzvahed, where they are called to the *altar* [italics mine] to read from the Torah and Haftorah. Today, says —" and then it poops out, no page 23 to the LA Times View Section 8/20/82. Alef — who knows what juicy tidbit would follow and Bet — I am saddened that Mr. Horowitz, author of the article doesn't know that "altars" were phased out of Jewish life sometime around the date of Tisha B'Av, 70 C.E., when the Temple went up in flames. Either he was thinking of (A) a church (Heaven forfend), or (B) perhaps in some shuls they have re-instituted animal sacrifices as part of a ritual, to give some historical touch to the "theme".

One last kvetchy note on the down side:

A bar mitzvah announcement in the New York Times society section mentions the following closing sentence, "the reception, an extravaganza by current social standards, was thoroughly enjoyed by all guests." That must have been some bash!

OTHER JEWISH LIVE-EVENT UPDATES
The collection grows nicely—Tzedakah tied into:
Birth.
Baby Naming
Birthday party (age 7 or 8) — "Please! It would make me very happy if you would use some of the money that you were going to spend on my present for Tzedakah."
Sweet 16 — for some reason I xeroxed it on the same page as a newspaper article headlined, "A New High: Teens Snort Typing Fluid"...also "no gifts please, Tzedakah instead."
Graduation from Hebrew High School — One of my favorite "kids" — Eddie Pont, Southfield, Michigan.
Religious School Confirmation — Temple Beth Ami, Rockville, MD — donations to Ziv.

Housewarming for an Entering College Freshman — contributions to
  Ma'on LaTinok, the home for children with Down's Syndrome,
  instead of gifts.
Weddings — more and more, and many variations.
Anniversaries — 25th (good friends)
          36th (the couple bought a $560 respiration monitor
          for Yad Sara, to lend to people for free, to prevent
          crib death.)
70th birthday party — "In lieu of flowers, a contribution has been
  made to Life Line for the Old."
50th Anniversary — comes last because the bride and groom were
  past age 70, and because they are my parents, Edythe and Julius
  Siegel. Contributions to Yad Sara for medical equipment and
  Northern Virginia JCC building fund.

That is a nice way to end this marathon catalogue of Tzedakah
documents. And the fact that last night, as I was preparing to begin, I got
an hour-long phone call from New Jersey, parents of a soon-to-be-bar mitzvah young man, who wanted to explore Tzedakah possibilities; how to
state the idea in the invitation, how to decide where to give, what additional options there might be.

There are so many variations and choices: one young woman shared
her bat mitzvah with a 19-year-old woman who has Down's Syndrome,
a resident of a local facility for individuals with developmental disabilities.
(I spoke to the Rabbi. It was one of those great days of high emotion in
the life of the synagogue.) One synagogue used to clasp the bar and bat
mitzvah certificates with a Soviet Jewry bracelet, and some kids go to
jewellers and have a special bracelet made with their twin's name engrav-
ed on it. One synagogue, The Temple, Congregation B'nai Jehudah, in Kansas City gives a unique Tzedakah box to each bar and bat mitzvah celebrant:
individualized artistic Tzedakah money containers designed and executed
by the residents of the Shalom Geriatric Center.

With a little planning and a sense of openness, all these life-events can
take on a deeper meaning, both for those celebrating, and for all who come
to join in the day's activities.

All that needs to be done is to do it.

Part III: An Afternoon with Rabbi King's Kids

Not wishing to sound like the seasoned, weather-beaten old man of
Jewish education, I would still mention that I have been involved in the
field for over twenty years. Over that span of time there are several moments
that so stand out above the others, that I recall them frequently, and feel
compelled to share with others, orally, and in print the ever-so-deep feelings they touched in me.

One such time was an afternoon I spent last year with the pre-present-
and-post bar and bat mitzvah students at Shir HaMa'alot Harbor Reform
Temple in Newport Beach, California, where Rabbi Bernard King has been

Tzedakah boxes made by residents of the Shalom Geriatric Center,
Kansas City, for the Bar and Bat Mitzvah kids of Congregation
B'nai Jehudah.

the rabbi for a number of years. I had known of his efforts for years in the area of involving his bar and bat mitzvah students in Tzedakah projects of all kinds, and I am appending to this article various items from his program and his supplementary efforts to affect the Reform movement in this area.

The afternoon was exquisite: those who had already celebrated the event told me of their Tzedakah projects. Those soon to have them either told me their plans or wanted to discuss certain possibilities they had in mind. As often happens when such an intense session ends, I become hyper, talking and talking, ranting on a high that is, I believe, unique to the experience of Jewish educators and their symbiotic relationship with their students (who are their teachers, of course). What perhaps struck me the most was the fact that it was The Most Natural Thing In The World for them to make Tzedakah a part of their bar or bat mitzvah experience. I think they might have even been thrown off balance a little by how astounded I was as they told me story after story. (Indeed, the day should come, soon, when there is no need to be astounded--when this will be such a normal thing to do in the process of Growing Up Jewish, that we won't keep saying, "Wow!" and "Oh, my!" We'll all just feel good.) Here are just a few of the tales from that afternoon in Newport Beach:

1. One of them was disappointed that he had raised only $225 to aid Ethiopian Jews.
2. One "kid" took a child with cancer to Disneyland, through connections with the "Make a Wish" Foundation. (The temple is not so far from Disneyland.)
3. One bought a lot of food, big bags of it, for hungry people.
4. One was doing volunteer work with retarded individuals.
5. One, after the talk, pulled me aside and wanted to consult. He indicated that his mother works at a battered women's shelter, and that he often visits there to play with the kids. He had noticed that there was a TV there for the mothers, but none for the children, and he wanted to know if I thought it was a good idea for him to take some of his bar mitzvah money to buy them a TV. (How do you keep from hugging such a child?) I told him it was a wonderful idea, and that he should write to me a month before his bar mitzvah because my fund would be interested in contributing $50. Five months later the letter arrived. The check was sent the same day.
6. Another so-called "kid," age 10 or 11, getting an early jump on this work, told me afterwards that the next time I am in Orange County, I should visit the senior center in Irvine. I asked him why. He said he's been there a lot — he goes regularly, and that it's a great place, and that he's already been going there for a year.
7. The difficult part: Twin brothers had decided that their Tzedakah project would be to work for Mothers Against Drunk Driving (M.A.D.D.) Their b'nai mitzvah had been about a year before, and I did not meet them the day I visited; for some reason they were absent. I had a copy

of the announcement of their project, which is unique, stark, powerful. It goes something like this:

A.　Front cover — they say they are working for M.A.D.D., ending with
　　"Everyone of us has a responsibility to help end the tragedy caused
　　by drunk driving."
B.　Inside — two flaps: The Facts and What You can Do, a re-print of
　　Orange County's material about drunk driving. The Facts part stuns
　　you so much, you ask yourself, is this really coming from two "kids"
　　about to become b'nai mitzvah? —

Drunk Drivers Cause More Deaths And Injuries And Destruction
Than Murderers, Thieves And Rapists.

1 out of 2 Americans will be the victim of an alcohol related crash.
Only 1 out of 5 will be the victim of a handgun related crime. The
facts and figures tell the story:

ORANGE COUNTY

125 men, women and children are killed by drunk drivers every
year in Orange County.

And the text then continues for another page and a half. Could we safely
say that, if 100 similar announcements went out in North America that
maybe 23 less people would die on the highways because of drunk driving? It is something to consider. Are these twin brothers, Jason and Joshua
Taussig, responsible for saving the lives of one person, two people, five
people?
The tragedy is, I asked — though perhaps I should not have--if any of them
had had a friend injured in an alcohol-related car crash. Some kids raised
their hands, and one indicated that his friend had died. I rarely weep in
my talks, but I was so choked by sadness, I had to wait till I got hold of
myself.
And this, all this, not long after Rabbi King had had to bury a man in his
earliest twenties, someone he had "bar mitzvahed" years before, who had
been killed in a drunken driving accident: some other driver jumped the
median, smashed into his car, and killed him.

Reflecting on this emotionally charged afternoon in California, and having
called Rabbi King in the middle of writing this piece to clarify some facts,
to re-live the highs, I understand somewhat better his enthusiasm for
Tzedakah in this age group as a vehicle for changing people's lives. I also
have in my collection invitations to the bar mitzvah of two of his children.
They are very telling.
The older son's—David's—indicates that he is twinning with Efrem Rozen-
shtein. (This is mentioned in my first bar mitzvah article.) It also states:

　　According to David's wishes, we ask that in lieu of a gift you bring
　　non-perishable groceries which we will distribute to help settle a Soviet

family. In turn, we will forego a reception and donate these funds to help Soviet Jews in need.

David and we thank you for your blessing and for joining us in the privilege of pursuing *gemilut chasadim,* acts of loving kindness.

The invitation was reproduced in *Moment Magazine,* which no doubt served as a catalyst for others to do similar Mitzvah work.

The middle son's — Neil's — is quite unique, also. Here are some quotes (after the usual announcement of time and place):

Neil will be reading and translating the Torah portion, chanting the Haftorah, teaching and discussing his Tzedakah project.

At Neil's request, in lieu of a reception, we are sponsoring a concert, in Neil's honor, by THE HI HOPES.

This unique musical group is comprised of disabled individuals who spread hope, love and joy through their music.

Please, your presence is Neil's greatest gift.

. . . .

A contribution to a Tzedakah project of your choice would be welcomed. One of Neil's favority programs is:

Project Hope University.

. . . .

Last year when I was out in Newport Beach, Rabbi King and I were enjoying a good *schvitz* at the health club before my talk to congregants in the evening. I asked him to describe what the concert was like. I — even though I am a poet who is supposed to have a command of works — I am not even going to attempt to reproduce his description. "Sublime" is as close as I could get to it, or, to use a popular vernacular term, "Awesome."

POSTSCRIPT

During this morning's phone call to Rabbi King, he mentioned that some of the confirmation class attended the concert. They were groping for ways to bring some relief to the famine-stricken people of Ethiopia. They decided to sponsor a concert by the Hi Hopes themselves, the proceeds to go to the Israeli Abie Natan's project for the Ethiopians.

They raised over $4,000.

Wow!

ONE MORE POSTSCRIPT

When the members of the Hi Hopes heard of the purpose of the confirmation class's project, they refused to accept their honorarium, but instead donated it to the Ethiopian project.

Wow!

Part IV: Bar/Bat Mitzvah: A Tzedakah Project
An Idea Whose Time Has Come

(Excerpts of a letter to his congregation from Rabbi Bernard King.)

The idea: placing the "mitzvah" back into the bar and bat mitzvah. I am urging consideration of this idea for pragmatic as well as spiritual reasons. I am proposing that the major branches of Judaism (Reform, Conservative, Orthodox and Reconstructionist) urge each and every one of their bnai mitzvah to select a tzedakah project as part of the preparation for this important ceremony.

In order to appreciate the bar and bat mitzvah experience, it is helpful to take a much closer look at the heart of the event, a look beyond the occasional aberration of a crassly and lavishly themed reception.

I can recall the hundreds of 13 year olds at whose bar and bat mitzvahs I have officiated. There have been those who stood tall above the reading desk, others barely visible above their prayerbooks...alike, but never the same, each an individual, unique in the history of the human universe.

I recall a boy whose parents had prepared a sit-down luncheon-reception with all the trimmings. One month before the scheduled event, the Yom Kippur War broke out in Israel. Israeli society was shattered into grief by the loss of life and dislocation in the economy. Our 13-year-old prevailed upon his parents to send out a printed card cancelling the reception and asking instead for contributions to be sent to the Israel Emergency Fund.

I still hear the shaking voice of the young boy who made a special appointment to see me to discuss his bar mitzvah, yet one year away. "I want my bar mitzvah to really, really mean something. I have been thinking about this moment ever since I started to learn Hebrew. Please, Rabbi, help me to become the best bar mitzvah I can become." A number of meetings later we decided on a project that would emphasize the "mitzvah" more than the "bar." The child decided to spend his entire summer donating his services at a camp for blind children. He would then report upon his experiences on his bar mitzvah day.

During the last six months one child asked guests to bring non-perishable food for the needy in lieu of gifts, another raised money to save the life of a fellow Jew in Ethiopia, yet another collected toys and clothing for children without parents.

There is much concern in Jewish life today over the question of rites of passage. So often performed with deadening mechanical routine, the religious ritual can become something separate from the living experience. The life passage into and out of puberty will occur, bar mitzvah or not. To allow the religious rite to remain authentically connected to the life passage is the challenge that enables me personally to go on week after week after week...another bar mitzvah, another speech...over and over again. I would rather be spending Shabbat with my own children. I would welcome more space between the pressures of nervous bar mitzvah parents with visiting relatives who have come two weeks early.

Yet the experience here at Shir Ha-Ma'alot - Harbor Reform Temple remains real. For me, the uniqueness of each child removes somewhat the category and leaves the individual.

I am reminded of a story told by Elie Wiesel. It takes place in a concentration camp, possibly Auschwitz. On Simchat Torah, the time following the High Holy Days when our people rejoice in the Torah, an old, old rabbi surrounded by emaciated Jews is prepared to dance. But where in a death camp is a Torah to be found? The rabbi sees a small starving child. The rabbi dances as the inmates sing and clap. The child is the Torah, a living Torah.

It is within this context that I offer the suggestion of adding the Tzedakah Project as a standard part of each and every bat/bat mitzvah experience.

Imagine what this would do for the child involved, the child's family and friends. Think of the self-worth engendered by a child who helps save a life, brings cheer to the infirm, works for the needy, donates time to the physically and mentally disabled, contributes a percentage of her or his financial gifts to a worthy cause. The projects of need are endless and stretch as far as the imagination can reach.

Imagine the enhanced image of the Jew in the general community. Bat/bar mitzvah families would be constantly searching for projects requiring their help. As the Mormons are known for their family night at home and the Quakers for their unstinting commitment to peace, so might the Jewish people become increasingly known for their rite of passage and its noteworthy component of helping others.

The moral power of the Jewish community is potentially enormous. The mechanism is readily at hand. May we together, Reform, Reconstruction, Conservative and Orthodox Jews evolve a way to transform our bnai mitzvah into young Jewish adults who truly reflect the light of the Holy One to the nations as well as to ourselves.

Rabbi Bernard P. King
October 5, 1982

BNAI MITZVAH TZEDAKAH PROJECTS
(by children at Shir Ha-Ma'alot during past four years)

VISITING: Children's hospital wards
                             General hospital ward
                             Hospital for mentally disabled
                             Senior citizen's center
                             Elderly shut-ins
                             Convalescent homes
                             A brain-damaged child

RAISING MONEY FOR:	Neo-natal unit
	Hospital for mentally disabled
	Meir Hospital in Israel
	Hadassah Hospital in Israel
	HI HOPES (musically gifted mentally disabled)
	YIVO
	UJA
	Camp Komaroff scholarship
	Cancer research
	Blind Children's Guild
	Anne Frank Foundation
	American Cancer Society
	Holocaust Memorial, Washington, D.C.
	Council on Soviet Jewry
	March of Dimes
	Ethiopian Jewry
	MADD
	Statue of Liberty restoration
	Orange County Interfaith Shelter
	Amnesty International
TUTORING:	English as a second language
	Adult retarded
	Elementary school student
REHABILITATION:	Helping handicapped children with horseback riding for therapy
ISRAEL SUPPORT:	"Walk for Israel" (Also see VISITING & RAISING MONEY)
HOLOCAUST AWARENESS:	Promoted in public school
OPPRESSED JEWRIES:	Knit slippers for Soviet Jews (Also see RAISING MONEY)
VOLUNTEER WORK:	Orange County Interfaith Shelter
	Shir Ha-Ma'alot/St. Mark work day
	Office work at agency for MS patients
	Anti-drug program at school
	SPECIAL OLYMPICS
	Camp aide: for children with cancer for special education children for the Orange County Jewish day camp
COLLECTING:	Food for Orange County Interfaith Shelter (temple project)
	Clothing for Orange County Interfaith Shelter
	Food for other needy
	Food in fields (gleaning)

ANIMALS: Work with veterinarian
                            Work at animal shelter
                            Contributed to conservation projects

*Resolution Proposal by Rabbi Bernard King to the Central Conference of
American Rabbis convention; endorsed, December, 1982. [The CCAR is
the organization of Reform rabbis]*

Recognizing the need to further inculcate the values of Tzedakah and
Gemilut Chasadism into our Mitzvah experience; and

Recognizing the opportunity to enhance our sense of self-worth as well
as our sense of value not only in ourselves but within the general community as well;

BE IT THEREFORE RESOLVED that the Central Conference of American
Rabbis looks with favor upon the enrichment of the B'nai Mitzvah experience by the addition of a Tzedakah or Gemilut Chasadim project as
a standard part of the B'nai Mitzvah experience.

SOME LATE-BREAKING ITEMS
I HAVE TO PUT HERE
BECAUSE I DIDN'T GET A WORD
PROCESSOR

A story from my friend, Rabbi Peter Mehler, of Milwaukee and Sheboygan, WI:

In Wisconsin the utilities are not allowed to turn off the heat in the homes of poor people. Still, they have a device called a "governor" that keeps the temperature at 55 degrees. So a number of the local ministers and I went out and bought a massive quantity of children's sleeping bags. It's not a total solution, but it brings some relief.

Stories from the Kosher food pantry (the Emergency Food Closet) at the Newman Center, Philadelphia, PA:

Many thanks for the food. I didn't thank the lady enough as I was terribly upset about my ordeal for Tomorrow and Wednesday

Perhaps this is the beginning of better luck for me now, because of your kindness and those of the volunteers

. . . .

We are happy that we were able to help with the Emergency Food Closet. We hope that the items we collected helped those who are less fortunate. You have really helped us learn about Tzedakah and Mitzvot.

Yours Truly,
Mechina II,
United Hebrew Schools, Adath Zion Branch

(Ira Frankel, Michael Grillakis, Carla Iacona, Sherri Kaufman, Rachel Kushner, Mark Ornstein, Jennifer Petrella, Erica Roth)

. . . .

One woman began to cry when she saw that there was toilet paper available at the Food Closet. You can't buy paper goods with Food Stamps.

From Judy Einhorn, Co-ordinator for Emergency Needs at the Newman Center, and Director of Cook for a Friend — a project where individuals and groups cook in their synagagues or homes, package the food, and then the food is delivered by elderly volunteers:

Cook for a friend is unique — it allows individualized specialties to be prepared. It's mostly groups from synagogues and Federation (and a confirmation class from Adath Jeshurun), but there are about 20 individuals besides. There's even a sub-project, "Share a Recipe," where a group invites some of the elderly people out to teach them their particular favorites, and they all cook up a la the recipe.

It all started in 1983, originating as an idea with Vista. Since then, Cook for a Friend has provided 80,000 meals to people who need them delivered to their homes — 425-500 meals weekly to 75-100 people.

Needless to say the personalization of the Mitzvah and the human contact when the food is delivered is of critical importance.

Somewhere in the files I have an article, the gist of which is this:

A bar owner is hauled into court. He has consistently refused entry to a blind woman and her seeing-eye dog. He is abusive both in the bar and in the courtroom, expressing his disgust very graphically with "those people," i.e., people with disabilities.

The woman gets her sweet revenge — the judge comes into the courtroom in a wheelchair.

A summary of a conversation with my friend, Marc Sternfeld, as we walk back home from High Holiday services. He explains:

From 1968-1970 I worked for Grumman on the lunar module (LEM). We were working on computer systems in very pioneering days of the space program. The office was a big trailer — like the 16-wheelers: me, the others, and the computer. (They even put in a bathroom.) The computer's memory was 32K. Nowadays an IBM PC has at least twice the capacity as the huge machine.)

(For two months I let that sink in, then speak to Marc again on the phone. He agrees with me that it would be equally as awesome if people could put their genius to work making Mitzvah projects as efficient...if 6 people could feed as many now as 150 did before or 1,000 before. If people could put all those people-hours and mind-energies to work designing new, more compact ways to accomplish the Mitzvah...)

A scene I recall from the North Shore Jewish Center, Port Jefferson Station, NY, where my friend, Moshe Edelman, is the Rabbi — bags and cartons of food for his food-pantry project, The Rebbe's Tish. It has been functioning for about 5 ½ years, and the enthusiasm and response for the project—contrary to what might be expected—has not abated. I call Rabbi Edelman Thanksgiving morning to review some details, and he reminds me that when they know someone is coming in to pick up food, he will absent himself from the synagogue, so they can gather the food without his knowledge. The Rabbi then tells me more stories from that week:

1. A hundred pounds of potatoes, in five-pound sacks, appears outside his office — from a potato distributor who is a congregant.

2. A congregant works for a firm that gives out Kosher turkeys to its

employees for Thanksgiving — he brings over 4 of the turkeys for The Rebbe's Tish.

3. A person who had left the congregation a year and a half before calls the Rabbi. He had not heard from this man since he left the congregation. He delivers a check for $100 which he wants turned into Thanksgiving food for the needy.

4. The note (with two $20 bills attached) says that the person would like the Rabbi to recite a *Mi Shebayrach* prayer for his mother, who is ill. The money is for The Rebbe's Tish.

5. A $36 check — for Thanksgiving, and if the Rabbi can't find people for Thanksgiving, then for Chanukkah.

6. $50 from a small Lions Club chapter (5 members) — one of the congregants is a member of that chapter. For The Rebbe's Tish.

I begin to realize that if I spent Thanksgiving morning making calls, I could get another 50 pages of stories for the book.

Thanksgiving morning, 1986, a phone conversation with Rabbi Ron Hoffberg, who will be joining my family for Thanksgiving dinner. I call to review with him the details of where I'll meet him at the train station. Rabbi Hoffberg reports:

There's a lot of Tzedakah news on the radio. Harrison Goldin, one of the big politicos in New York had a canned food drive for Thanksgiving — over 70,000 cans were brought in.

News reports also stated that the Salvation Army would be feeding a million and a half people this Thanksgiving in over 1,000 places around the country.

Three more items from the Denver papers, sent to me by Trude Holzmann, who has clipped articles for over a year to help me write this book and refine my talks:

1. Rocky Mountain News, September 3, 1986: Robert Pearson, who turned 99 on September 10th, returned to his woodworking hobby about 6 or 7 years ago. He makes toys which the Metropolitan Association of Retarded Citizens and Disabled American Veterans sell at their thrift shops. The proceeds go to their respective organizations. The cost of the building materials comes from his Social Security check. He makes about 15 toys a month.

2. The Denver Post has a column called "Local Hero." September 29, 1986, they report on Jo Bushnell, who, working six hours a day since 1969, has transcribed printed texts into more than 50,000 Braille pages. She is also one of the best repair people for Braille typewriters. She's fixed over 350 of them sent to her from around the country, and she only charges for the parts — no labor. Ms. Bushnell, age 56, fell into this line of Mitzvah work by accident...Out of curiousity she wrote a letter ordering materials for a correspondence course on transcribing Braille.

3. Other Local Heroes from the column, August 18, 1986: Bob Francois and Barbara Hudson. They run the paint-up/fix-up program in North Aurora, Colorado, fixing up the homes of the poor, elderly, and disabled. About 60 volunteers work in the program — all kinds of people, including people doing community service as part of a court sentencing program.

From a conversation with Rabbi Jan Kaufman, a teacher at the Charles E. Smith Jewish Day School in Rockville, MD. Rabbi Kaufman recalls:

The mother of one of the school's seniors passed away. It didn't feel right that the family should hire *Shomrim,* people to sit with the body overnight, so I spoke with some of the student's classmates. I made a call, and 20 minutes later I received a call back saying they had set up two-hour shifts of students for the entire night. I went down with them for the early shift, to speak with them and get them set up, and to give them some appropriate books to read while they were doing the Mitzvah. The woman in charge of *Tohorah* (ritually washing and preparing the body) asked if any of the girls wanted to be a part of it. A couple of them decided to be a part of this aspect of the Mitzvah work.

All the reactions afterwards — from the students and parents was overwhelmingly positive. For some, it was the most moving thing they had ever done in their lives.

My friend, Kate Kinser, calls Thanksgiving evening from Chicago, after spending time in a women's shelter helping out for the holiday:

Three out of the forty women were Jewish. That's 7½ %, higher than the ratio of Jews to general population in Chicago. (She and I are not about to make a statistical generalization from this one fact, but for those seeking out Jewish homeless people, we should begin by looking in the general community and private shelters).

Three items from The Washington Post — they just keep jumping out from the page:

1. November 19, 1986, pessimistic: a recent survey from the Bureau of Justice Statistics. The report indicates only 18 percent of those convicted of white-collar crimes in 8 states were sent to prison for more than 12 months. (12 months' sentence that is; they didn't track down how much that was reduced for time off for good behavior.) 40 percent of those convicted were not sentenced to jail terms at all.

2. November 27, 1986, optimistic: Colman McCarthy writes an article praising Franciscan priests who run St. Francis Residence on 24th Street in New York for deinstitutionalized mental patients. McCarthy calls the place "a jewel amid a sludge pile," and notes that a second place has opened, and a third on the way, room for 316 people. The project affirms the feeling that deinstitutionalization works when there is follow-up and care, and that, were these places not available, the people would be living on the

street. McCarthy writes a number of nice phrases — "Under the care of three Franciscan priests and a team of nurses, social workers, and psychiatrists, they are assured of what neither money nor medicine can provide: compassion." "When they have a St. Francis Residence, the state mental hospitals aren't needed." Referring to Father Joseph Felice, the director, McCarthy says, Felice "believes that compassion is a proven therapy."

3. November 28, 1986, disgusting: an article by Nancy Lewis. Hillel Daniel Hodes, age 38, PhD in organo-metallic chemistry, was sentenced to the maximum 15 years and fined $125,000 for his attempt to manufacture fentanyl, an unbelievably potent form of a heroin substitute (1,000 times as potent as pure heroin). Street value of his designer drug — $1,000,000,000 — one billion dollars! The presiding justice, U.S. District Judge John H. Pratt, said, "This is a monstrous crime" that "could have been catastrophic." He added that the drug could have killed "thousands of people".

The enormity of the crime caused me to choke, but that isn't what caught my eye originally — it was the criminal's name. "Hillel" — giant of the Jewish people in Talmudic times. "Daniel" — Daniel, as in the Lion's Den, Man of Integrity, Seer, Mensch, Good Jew. As for the family name, some derive if from "Hadassah," meaning a descendant of Hadassah, who was Queen Esther, the one who saved the Jewish people from destruction.

All that Judaism in one person's name, all warped, all turned to devastation and death!

An article I ran across in the files while looking for something else — Esquire Magazine, June 1983, entitled "Getting by on $100,000 a Year" by Andrew Tobias. Tobias describes how people have a hard time squeaking by on this sum, and gives examples of four individuals and their annual budgets. This is an excerpt, zeroing in on the issue of Tzedakah:

1. Case No. 1, investment banker, early thirties, no dependents:

Approximate gross income	$105,000
After-tax income	64,080
Nights out ($150/night, 80 nights)	12,000
Vacation quickies	3,000
Cocaine	3,000
Charity and alma maters	1,500

(Author's note: Tzedakah = ½ cocaine allotment, 1/8 of dates).

2. Case No. 2, commuter, 46, married, two kids at school:

Approximate gross income	90,000
After-tax income	55,430
Tuition, room/board (2 kids)	12,000
Christmas gifts	600
Laundry	600

Cigarettes	500
Haircuts (his)	150
Beauty salon, cosmetics (hers)	500
United Way and other charities	900

3. Case No. 3, real estate developer, recently divorced, 3 kids living with him:

Before-tax income	$125,000
After-tax income	80,000
Maid, four days a week	7,000
"One good family vacation" (Aspen, two weeks, with kids, baby sitter, former wife)	6,000
Charitable contributions	6,500

Sometime in 1986, Ann Landers made mention of a woman in a restaurant, who, because of a disability, had difficulty swallowing. She was in a wheelchair, and her husband wiped away the food as it ran down the sides of her mouth. Someone in the restaurant objected to the scene and complained to the manager (and eventually wrote Ann Landers). When Ms. Landers published the letter, one woman responded positively to it, but a few others felt differently:

1. One reply: Has it occurred to you that everyone at some time in his life experiences sad events and it is not their divine right to burden the general public with their problems?...We are becoming embroiled in everyone's problems all over the world — disease, starvation and dictatorships. No wonder we have turned to drugs, drink and sexual promiscuity.

2. Another: Your response to "Chicago Reader" shows you are not very savvy. Would you believe there are many handicapped people who take great pleasure in flaunting their disability so they can make able-bodied people feel guilty?

3. And part of a third: I have the right when I go out to pay good money for a meal to enjoy it. The sight of a woman in a wheelchair with food running down her chin would make me throw up. I believe my rights should be respected as much as the rights of the person in the wheel chair...maybe even more so, because I am normal and she is not.

4. And finally:...In my opinion, restaurants should have a special section for handicapped people — partially hidden by palms or other greenery so they are not seen by other guests. Slobberers, disabled or not, turn my stomach.

From the Toronto Globe and Mail, November, 1986, a short column "Oh, Canada," subtitled, "Do people give more or less to charity as their income rises?":

Two issues of Tzedakah are discussed — average contributions according to income, and percentage of all Tzedakah contributions given according to income. Here are the results of the Canadian study:

Income bracket (gross)	Average contribution	% of Total Income to Tzedakah
$15,000-20,000	$82	.005-.004
$40,000-50,000	$294	.007-.006
$80,000-90,000	$900	.011-.010
More than $250,000	$6,455	.025
		(of $250,000)

Income bracket (gross)	Percentage of Total Tzedakah Taken In
$15,000-25,000	21% ($314 Million)
$25,000-50,000	39% ($594 Million)
$50,000-100,000	15% ($222 Million)
Over $100,000	11% ($167 Million)

NOVEMBER 11-17, 1986
A MORE-INTENSE-THAN-USUAL WEEK OF
TZEDAKAH WORK

NOVEMBER 11TH

Phyllis Greene, Educational Director of Temple Beth Ami, Rockville, MD, has me in to talk to the 45 Confirmation students. We have $143 of their Tzedakah money at our disposal, and during the evening we collect some more, bringing it to a total of around $190. Starting with a tape of Tzedakah issues by Sally Fox, we have a discussion. Then the fun begins: we begin to get volunteers to do a number of Mitzvah projects, giving each $10-20 to get their projects rolling. I don't remember how much we gave to each specific student, but these are some of the projects:

1. Finding two overcoats from friends, paying to have them dry-cleaned, then delivering them to a shelter.

2. Buying thermal underwear at an Army surplus store and delivering them to a shelter.

3. Buying Tzedakah food and delivering it to the food bank, via the synagogue food barrel.

4. Finding a wedding dress and someone to deliver it to the Rabbinit Kapach in Israel, who will lend it to brides who cannot afford their own. The money is to be contributed in honor of the contributor of the wedding dress.

5. Clowning, magic, and balloon materials — one student is to call our local Jewish clown (Debra Friedmann), learn some tricks, buy materials, and then go visit a pediatrics ward of some hospital to entertain the kids.

6. Money towards another large print prayerbook. (They already have a couple of them.)

7. Buying a Soviet Jewry bracelet to wear, the remainder of the money for Tzedakah food.

8. Buying flowers and visiting the Hebrew Home in Rockville.

9. Buying two trees in Israel (one or both of them in my own honor — I thought it would be nice).

10. Doing some Mitzvah we don't want to know about — anonymous, anywhere the student felt it would be needed.

11. Going to the Hebrew Home, getting a resident to make a Tzedakah box, giving it to a bar or bat mitzvah kid at Beth Ami, and contributing the money in honor of the elderly person who made the box...hoping that it would start a major project.

12. First contribution towards buying a Telecommunications Device for the Deaf (TDD) for UJA-Federation in Washington. (The Board of Jewish Education is already getting one.)

In addition: the synagogue lets me xerox the manuscript of the new book, free of charge; the principal promises to find someone to help work on the glossary of the book and the master listing of all Tzedakah projects; many students sign up for their own Soviet jewry bracelets, and two students want to find kids to read stories to (I refer them to the Shema V'Ezer people who work with exceptional children in the Washington area.)

NOVEMBER 12TH

The first day of my visit to the General Assembly of the Council of Jewish Federations in Chicago. At this annual event I run into so many people I have met in my travels. I will be there till Friday afternoon, and throughout the three days, people tell me stories and more stories. These are some of them:

1. One person tells me he went to Israel and delivered seven wedding dresses to the Rabbanit Kapach.

2. My old friend, Rabbi Steven Glazer of Birmingham, AL, tells me over lunch that his community has actively sought out the Jewish elderly living in non-Jewish old age residences. They have assigned a different Jewish organization to each home to assure that each elder will be visited regularly. He also mentions that the synagogue's youth group, USY, annually cooks turkey dinners at the synagogue and then delivers them to the elderly in one of these homes for Thanksgiving. The teen-agers join them in the meal and provide musical entertainment.

3. Chaim Lauer, Assistant Executive Vice President of UJA-Federation in Washington, DC, tells me the Federation will now provide interpreters for any group of five deaf individuals who wish to attend a Jewish community program. A special Interpreters Fund has been set up...all they have to do is indicate which program they will be at, and an interpreter will be assured.

4. A friend from Cranford, NJ. I remember that she knows sign language, and that she has a friend who has been interpreting in the area at synagogue services. She offers to help, and offers her friend's help if others want to pursue this project. (Laura Rubin, 40 Herning Ave., Cranford, NJ 07016, 201-276-2649; Toby Marx, 6 Makatom Drive., Cranford, NJ, 07016, 201-272-2549.)

That evening, I have the opportunity to discuss Mitzvah heroes with a group of leadership development people. We give out over $100 for Mitzvah projects, similar to the way it was done with the Confirmation class at Beth Ami. I invite them to overpay on my books when they buy them, and the overpayments go back into the Tzedakah fund. We also collect $1.00 from each participant (no more than $1.00) and ask for someone to be our Shaliach-messenger to buy a TDD for the local Federation. We collect about $140-150, and a young man from Tucson volunteers to carry out the Mitzvah, promising to make up the difference if it costs more than what was collected.

NOVEMBER 13TH

More personal conversations, more Tzedakah stories, and a session on interest-free loans, conducted by the Association of Hebrew Free Loan Societies. It is a small session, with perhaps ten or a dozen communities represented. The presentations are loaded, as always, with personal stories of how this person got back on his or her feet as a result of a free loan, or another managed to get a second start because of a free loan society's help. Many stories — my favorite: someone gives one of the societies $10,000 annually and does not want his name published or anyone to find out who he is.

I finish the afternoon and evening with more conversations with friends, more stories, more intensity. It is very exhausting and exhilarating.

NOVEMBER 14TH

A Lunch and Learn at the General Assembly. About 150-200 people. We have a little less than an hour to work on Tzedakah, but it becomes very exciting as people throw out ideas and responses to Talmudic texts. Again, we give out some money for specific projects, and, again, I invite them to overpay on books. At the end of the booksales, there is $140 more in the Tzedakah kitty, and a man comes up to me and says to put something more into the Tzedakah work. He hands me a rolled-up bill, which I look at later. It is a $100 bill. (I had mentioned that someone had done that three years ago at a General Assembly, and I think that this was the same person.) I end my General Assembly with over $200 in Tzedakah left in the Tzedakah pocket, having started with about $140. It seems relatively easy, in a group such as this, to give away a lot of money, and to still come out ahead for the next roadtrip.

I leave the convention to spend Shabbat with friends. At the house, Jeremy, one of the children, mentions that his school is having a canned food drive for hungry people, so we take some of the money to add to what he was going to bring in. At dinner, Kate Kinser, another friend, tells more and more stories about the homeless with whom she has worked. She helps us all delineate the individuals who are in the shelters, removing the categorizations we tend to make of "The Homeless" — reminding us that they are individuals.

NOVEMBER 15TH

Walking home from synagogue with the rabbi, we discuss a mammoth scandal about someone who had contributed $1,000,000 or more to a major Jewish institution and who is now being fined some astronomical millions for irregularities on Wall Street. He invites me in to read the articles. We are appalled, confused by the sheer enormity of the scandal.

After Shabbas, Rabbi Glazer comes out to the house and we relax, and pick up on some of the Tzedakah stories

NOVEMBER 16TH

Back home in Washington, I attend the dedication of the 5th group home for Jewish retarded adults, the Randi and Joel Meisel Home, established through the Jewish Foundation for Group Homes. My sister, Leslye, will be moving in in the next couple of weeks, once the final renovations are done. There are 75 to 100 people there, and all the Tzedakah elements are present: someone who wrote a rather large check to purchase the home, a listing of merchants and companies and other individuals who helped make it all happen through their generosity, moving words from one of the soon-to-be residents of the home, short speeches and words of Torah that speak of "dignity" and "community"...high emotion. It is a gorgeous home, complete with a deck, and cordial neighbors who are most open to having the group home in their part of town. Best of all is the mix of the crowd: the new residents, residents of the other homes, professionals, laypeople, families of residents, and interested people — all there to dedicate this monument to the good things that can happen when people set themselves to Mitzvah work. There is a nice additional touch — the Mezuzah which my parents gave for the house. It is from Yad Sara, the organization in Israel that lends out medical equipment free of charge. It is always pleasant to see two different Mitzvah projects joined together.

Back home I catch up on the mail and continue reading *Annie's Coming Out,* a book my friend, Allan Gould, gave me in Chicago. It is the story of a young woman, Anne McDonald, who had been placed in an institution in Australia who was thought to be retarded, but, through the efforts of one of the people working there, Rosemary Crossley, it is discovered that she is not. The book is co-authored by the two of them, a horrifying and uplifting story. Annie is now living outside the institution, thanks to the efforts of Rosemary. A movie has been made of the story. It is one of those tales everyone should get to know.

The mail contains pictures of the Helping Hands Project for this book (training monkeys to help quadriplegic individuals), letters to Trevor Ferrell with contributions for his work with the Philadelphia homeless that have been sent on to me, a note that Yad Sara tapes have been lost in the mail — all kinds of Tzedakah wonders. The phone machine records some additional messages.

I leaf through some papers and re-discover an article from the Beth Torah bulletin of North Miami Beach: Ivy Routman and her great-grandmother, Mollie Weiss, are due to be joint bat mitzvah celebrants on November 28, 1986. Mrs. Weiss will be 85. The article concludes, "MAZAL TOV to all." Indeed, a MAZAL TOV to them, their family, and friends.

NOVEMBER 17TH

Back at my desk, typing furiously to record all of this while it is still fresh, hoping that people who read about these things will pick up on them and begin to adopt some of these projects for themselves. More phone calls, more contacts, more finishing touches on the book.

This has been an unusual week for me — more intense than normal, though every week brings some sort of contact with Tzedakah work. There has still been time to watch taped re-runs of TV shows I missed while I was on the road, time for a good night's sleep, time to talk to friends and just relax. This is too much to handle every week, but I wish myself, and others, at least one week now and again with as much Mitzvah work whirling around in all directions, settling into the lives of so many people.

A QUESTION ABOUT THE PERSONAL
BENEFITS OF DOING TZEDAKAH

Although I am not a Rabbi, a Tzedakah question was asked of me in traditional Jewish format — a She'aylah. I answered in similar traditional fashion because it was obvious that the questioner would have wanted it that way.

She'aylah — A Question:

As a rabbi, I have the Zechut (privilege)(or the 'Ol - yoke) to engage in the Mitzvah of Tzedakah. While I thank God that I serve as His vehicle to do Tikun Olam (Repairing the World) in my small way, and while I am able to say, "How happy is my portion and lot", that my life is filled with the opportunity to do Mitzvot, I am troubled by a manifestation of my work.

Time and time again, in doing Tzedakah work, I find it a most unpleasant experience. I am lied to, deceived, and demeaned by those who have *come to me* for help.

Case in point: A woman calls me at home at 4:00 p.m. "Rabbi, I need to see you. My name is _____." She's not a congregant. I say, "I can be at the shul anytime you say." She replies, "It'll take me about 15 minutes to get there." I say, "I'll see you in 15 minutes."

I go to shul. A half hour later a cab pulls up. A woman in her early 50's, with her daughter, who is in her mid-20's. They proceed to tell me a long story, the essence of which is this: She has recently been divorced; there has been no settlement because her lawyer has tied it up in court and has stolen from her. (A lawsuit is now pending against *him*.) Her daughter is suffering from M.S., and needs treatment in Maryland. Can I help?

I ask a few pertinent questions. *(Who is the doctor? What about the girl's father? How did you come to call me?)* (They went through the phone book.) I'm told, "Don't call the doctor; it'll be too embarrassing." *Where have you been living?* ("Hotels.")

I pull out my checkbook. I write a check for $150. The woman, reading upside down, watches me write. First she starts *yelling* at me, "What good is $15 going to do!" I calmly tell her to read again. She quickly apologizes.

Then she tells me: A check is no good. It has to be cash. It's now 5:00 p.m. I have no cash. Even if I wanted to go to the bank and cash it, I can't. She keeps pushing and pushing, "What good is a check?" I'm getting upset. I tell her. Take it or leave it. Good-bye.

Then she starts yelling, "Take us to the bank." They have no car. There is no public transportation here.

I get our caretaker to drive her to the Howard Johnson's down the street (which I pay him $5 to do). She and the daughter stay overnight there (rooms are $75 a night).

Next morning I get a call from the bank — the woman and her daughter

are there making a scene demanding to have the check cashed. I vouch
that I wrote it. It's against bank policy to do so, but the manager cashes
it — he doesn't want a scene.

I've had this experience a number of times — and others like it on
occasions too numerous and too painful to recount.

More often than not, I find doing Tzedakah leaves me angry, hurt, and
depressed.

I have no intention of stopping. But . . . .

What can you tell me to make it easier for me? Maybe the problem
is that we have a myth of good-deed doing leaving you exhilarated. But
even when the person is honest and pleasant and appreciative, it's not *joy*
I feel, but only heartbreak and pity. (Though there are few of *these* types,
and more of the former.)

Your insight would mean a great deal to me.

Teshuvah — Answer:

Rabbi _____,

Your question is so filled with frustration, anger, and pain. The un-
satisfactory personal feelings that often result from Tzedakah work is a sen-
timent often expressed by congregational rabbis who frequently confront
individuals and families such as you describe. Though my personal experience is different — being often one step removed from day-to-day
Tzedakah work in such immediate situations, I shall attempt to present some
insights from the Talmud and later sources, and then some practical ideas.
For the sake of clarity, I shall list the items numberwise:

1. The Talmud and Midrashim are replete with examples of the problem of individual feelings of the person requesting Tzedakah from another.
In some instances, it is obvious that the one in need summons great courage
when going to ask. Some, indeed, would rather suffer, though their families
might also suffer (see Ketubot 67b). The extreme case is a more Hollywood-
type phrase, "I would rather die than take charity", though I do not doubt
that there are many people off the Big Screen who think that way, and act
accordingly. We should be grateful that Tzedakah encourages people to
ask when in need, and that if both the giver and the recipient are educated
in Jewish texts, they will know that the utmost care must be taken to
preserve the dignity of the recipient. You are aware of these many texts,
I am sure.

2. You are aware, also, of the constant, gnawing danger, "What if they
are not deceiving me, not stretching the truth so much?" The most prominent Talmudic tale on this issue is, of course, the story of Nahum Ish Gamzu (Ta'anit 21a), who, because of a moment's hesitation — not realizing
the extreme precariousness of the poor person's condition — found the
man lifeless, in an ever-so-brief moment. I have also discovered a similar
tale of Rabbi Yochanan and Resh Lakish (Leviticus Rabba 34:10, Margoliot
4:793; Yalkut Shimoni Behar 665). Numerous other texts stress how much
Tzedakah is a life-and-death situation, either physically, as in the two
abovementioned stories, or psychologically and spiritually, where the refusal

to give by the giver causes an ever-growing spiral of depression and despair in the person in need.

The Rabbis chose to play it safe, urging Tzedakah-doers to give, even if the one asking is deceiving the giver, or is not in such desperate need as might be apparent. Furthermore, besides the welfare of the recipient, the Rabbis consider the welfare of the giver in such situations. In Ketubot 68a, one may interpret that giving, even in ostensibly suspect situations, keeps the issue of Tzedakah, its life-giving force, its assuredly cosmic implications constantly in mind, sensitizing the giver, even in painful, frustrating situations, to the ever-changingly complex human situation.

Thus, since Tzedakah is defined Talmudically as giving of your own resources to a recipient, it is obvious that from a practical standpoint you are performing the Mitzvah appropriately.

3. There is a moderating principle to be considered: One may ask questions concerning a need for clothing, but not concerning a need for food. (Bava Batra 9a, the exception being for Purim meals, because of the extreme joyousness of the occasion, Maimonides, Mishnah Torah, Laws of Megillah 2:16-17.) Your inquiries in this case, and in other cases, are entirely appropriate, in that you are known as being an individual extraordinarily concerned to perserve the one-in-need's dignity. You would never overstep your bounds and humiliate that person, in anger, in frustration, in a state of helplessness in the presence of overwhelming human suffering, or whatever other circumstances might present themselves. Inquiry is certainly permitted in "clothing-type" cases where the ultimate welfare of the recipient is at stake — perhaps allowing you to tie that person to other resources, a physician, lawyer, clothing store owner, who could be of additional assistance.

4. As to the motivations of people who appear to be taking advantage of the giver — It would not be fair to say the Rabbis would not consider that the giver's concern. In a number of sources, notably Ketubot 68a, they maintain the belief that whoever might unjustifiably request Tzedakah by means of deception will, in the end, indeed be in need of some of that Tzedakah. That is a matter of faith, and I would sense that this does not square with your particular experiences. Rather, you no doubt sense that they will continue to do so, Tzedakah con-artists, as it were, and there is no way you or I could speak empirically to the statistics based on the Rabbis' principle. Again, that is not our issue. Our issue is performing the Mitzvah of Tzedakah.

5. I believe I have given more than sufficient attention to the unsettling feeling of deception. I would turn now to the frustration that you feel, a lack of good feelings, satisfaction, uplift from the act . . . . no "joy" to use your term. I am certain that after you wrote me the question, you understood your off-center use of joy ("Simcha"), since, as a congregational Rabbi you have had many, many occasions for visiting the deathly ill, burying the dead, and comforting mourners. All these Mitzvot have to be done with "Simcha". — which I would translate as "A Life Affirming Sensitivity". They are hardly happy occasions, as would be implied by the

word "joy" And yet, all Mitzvot must be done with Simcha. Despite your disappointing feelings, your dismay, you must agree that, having performed the Mitzvah of Tzedakah, you continue to affirm Life, God's goodness in the world, the many wonders of which our teacher, the late Rabbi Abraham Joshua Heschel, spoke in his writings — the awesomeness, glory, and amazing aspects of being alive as one of God's creations. That, I would say is "joy", as Simcha is meant to be. At this juncture I mention the tale of Binyamin HaTzaddik, another of the Righteous Ones (Bava Batra 11a), who, confronted with a starving woman with seven children, and finding insufficient funds in the communal Tzedakah account, fed them with his own money. He hardly felt this worthy of wild, abandoned dancing, and yet, I sense his Simcha at being chosen an agent for such important work in his own life, a privilege. (Which is why, I believe, the word ZChH, Zocheh, Zechut are used in the Midrashim to express the idea of Tzedakah — meaning "to be privileged to do the Mitzvah of Tzedakah". And bending the root further, perhaps to mean "be purified by performing the act". Refer back to the story in Leviticus Rabba 34:10 for an example of use of the term.) Ultimately, we must always keep in mind (Pesachim 54b) that no one ever really knows whet is in another's heart, and we cannot always fathom what the one-in-need's motivations are for asking.

6. And still, there is this feeling of frustration you express. The Midrash indicates in the name of Rabbi Yehoshua (who, like Nahum Ish Gamzu was one of Rabbi Akiva's teachers — something to consider when we review the life of that unique individual) that the poor person does more for the Mitzvah-doer than the Mitzvah-doer does for the poor person (Leviticus Rabba 34:8). On a high, spiritual level, we are both aware of how doing Tzedakah enlightens us, sensitizes us, gives us opportunities to express our humanity and Menschlichkeit, *and* ought to enliven us. This last phrase is what is missing from your letter and inquiry. I would recall one other text (Shulchan Aruch, Yoreh De'ah 249:1): How much is one required to give? If one can afford it, enough to satisfy the needs of all those in need. If one cannot cover all those costs, then up to 20% is considered doing the Mitzvah to an extraordinary degree, 10% is considered average, ...

Since your personal resources are limited, and even considering the funds available in your Rabbi's Discretionary Fund, there is still a limit as to how much you can do, we should understand that the Rabbis knew that rarely, if ever, could an individual solve all the problems of those in need. Impoverishing oneself is not a Jewish approach (causing you to be in need, yourself) (Maimonides, Mishnah Torah, Hilchot Arachin V'Charamin 8:13), and the reality is very real: there is too much to be done, and too little resources financial and otherwise to do it all. It would thus appear that, in order for you to regain your sense of benefit, personal benefit, from doing the Mitzvah of Tzedakah, you might wish to adopt the following practice: set aside a certain amount of the available Tzedakah money for Tzedakah-acts which are immediately and definitely beneficial to an individual, and simultaneously satisfying and uplifting to yourself. You might purchase a Telecommunications Device for the Deaf for the synagogue, purchase some piece of medical equipment for an organization such as Yad Sara, which will lend it free of charge to someone who needs it, go to a grocery store and buy $100.00 worth of food and deliver it personally to a food bank, or some similar act. Otherwise there is a danger to you, and obviously to your beneficiaries: a cynicism, a disappointment, a doubting of the glories of Tzedakah's power to heal, uplift, and revivify. After all, the Halachah, the Law, does not prescribe exactly how much is to be given in each situation — that is up to your discretion. I am convinced, after an examination of the ritual of Hatavat Chalom ("Making Dreams Better") found in complete editions of the Prayerbook, that despair and dysfunctionality — yours, in this situation — go against the basic grain of Jewish tradition which urges us to pursue Mitzvah work aggressively, with vigor and affirmation. So choose an immediate Tzedakah-situation to solve that is to your particular liking, one that is close to your own particular soul's make-up.

It would also be well to recall (Bava Batra 10a, Proverbs 10:2) that "Tzedakah saves from death" also applies to the Tzedakah-doer, keeping us from discouragement, cynicism, and despair, moving us to more of the grand and sublime in Life.

My books are scattered on my desk and the adjacent table, my mind still swims, and yet, I am most grateful to you for having approached me with this question. I have spent a number of weeks considering it and am generally at peace with the comments I have outlined above — though it is often difficult for words to assuage the anguish of the past's painful situations, and the anxiety over the approaching encounters you may expect.

I would welcome further discussion with you on this matter. It is a privilege to be turned to, though the issues you raise reach to the very touchiest and deepest aspects of Life and Life as a Jew. I hope the Teshuvah has been of some comfort — and practical use — to you.

AN UNPLEASANT DAYDREAM

I am finishing my morning walk near the shopping center, gazing through the windows at the banjos and sheet music, the new Baskin-Robbins flavors, the marquee for Congressional Five, the big movie theatre. It's an ideal morning. Washington is gorgeous today, not too humid, reverberating with bird-voices of at least a half dozen varieties. Because of the day, I feel poetry in my bones. I will set aside errand-work so I can windowshop, lie on the grass, and watch the sky, and consider new poems.

I buy a paper, saying to myself, "Don't read it yet, because you'll break the mood. Central American *tzuriss* and the state of the economy and other newsworthy items will bring you down." So I just scan the front page.

Too much. The mood is gone. It's not that I am shocked — just saddened. Page One at the bottom, there is a big picture, not uncommon in the late Spring: two cars smashed head-on, wrapped around each other, with the descriptive caption of seven dead, one barely alive, and a case of D.U.I. — driving under the influence — someone drinking, someone driving. Seven (almost eight) dead.

I daydream myself into the next day, when the names of the dead are listed . . . . a few of whom are Jewish, half of them teen-agers, and the D.U.I. alcoholic driver is both — Jewish, teen-ager, plus the cause of the deadly accident.

Such is a daydream I have, daydreamed some dozen times in the last few months.

TOTALLED CARS, OBSCENELY SHATTERED BODIES, AND JEWISH EDUCATION

I wonder in my daydreams (continued) about the driver, so I ask (in my daydream) who he was, where he went to school, and begin to investigate with teachers, principals, friends. Nine years of Jewish Day School in the kid's head, and Dead On Arrival at Georgetown Hospital.

Wrecked lives.

Now it's not so much a daydream, wrecked lives.

May 22, 1983, The Washington Post: Eric Breindel, age 27, is arrested for allegedly buying five packets of heroin from an undercover agent at a Holiday Inn in Washington. Eric is a graduate, Phi Beta Kappa, magna cum laude, from Harvard, Harvard law graduate, staff member for Daniel Patrick Moynihan's work on the Select Committee on Intelligence — privy to Top Secret information.

There is other background material: Breindel had been taking prescription painkillers for years because of an old wrestling injury, child of Holocaust survivors, etc . . . each item's relevance remaining clouded to me as I re-read the article. Names of Jewish intelligentsia who thought the world of him were granting interviews, expressing sadness, and still the ultimate relevance of the details remained beyond me.

He was arrested with a Winston B. Prude, a former Justice Department lawyer, who also allegedly purchased some drugs.

My sum-total reaction is curiosity mixed with pain: I want to know what his Jewish education was, this Eric Breindel of Harvard and wrestling and Holocaust and Moynihan background. I am sad, yes, for a career and a life gone to hell. But more than that, I see some secular values of our culture — some devastating values — blaring through the words, and the sound of an incredible vacuum, which is the Jewish education he (or the D.U.I.) might have had to withstand the flood.

NO ANGER

There was a time in the Sixties when we fought for Relevance in our course curricula: Vietnam, the bombing of Cambodia, civil rights. Those were good days, I believe. Then we pulled back as things settled down and job markets got tight and the economy demanded good grades. We concentrated on the narrower aspects of Jewish education, and bar and bat mitzvah training and the craving to teach modern Hebrew returned to their positions of primacy — weaknesses and shortcomings we well recognized from the earlier years.

Kids from Jewish day schools and Jewish camps and afternoon schools still didn't know the terms *Bushah*-humiliation (and its relevance to hiring and firing practices, and self-image, and God's image), nor *Hin Tzedek*-honest weights and measures (and its relation to the marketplace of gauges and calibrations and faulty parts in airplanes and automobiles), *Ona'at Mammon*-deceit and overpricing in business (and its relation to mark-ups and discounts in the stores in our neighborhoods), *Bal Tashchit*-wanton destruction of property (chemical dumps wasting the genes of the yet-to-be-born, the waste of national budgets, the waste of human beings' potential to be human), *Genayvah/Gezaylah*-stealing in many ways ($700,000,000 a year in pirated movies and videotapes), *Lo Tachmod* and *Lo Tit'aveh*-not to crave and not to covet the property of others (killing ourselves and our families to buy the fancy-too fancy things in life in order to keep up with the neighbors), *Devarim HaAsurim Mishum Sakkanah*-things which are forbidden because they are dangerous (Valium, heroin, daredevilry for the sake of teen-agerhood), and, of course, *Tzedakah,* to name a few.

Relevance has been back-shuffled into second place, and we shall most certainly pay the consequences — this coming from a student who was trained in both schools, for I have been in schools with both kinds of curricula. I can use all of the scholarly tools of Judaism needed to study almost any Jewish text in Hebrew, Aramaic, or Yiddish (except Kabbalistic material), both relevant and Pure-Scholarly. And I do, indeed, love to take one of my more obscure books off of the shelf and examine some far-fetched piece, tracking down words in Greek, checking an Akkadian phrase now and again, seeking out different manuscript variations of a particular passage. It is — in my world of jet-setting and whirlwinds of long-distance phonecalls and piles of letters — a glorious pleasure.

But, as a popular speaker for kids and post-kids (people up into their thirties and later), what I hear from the audiences is frightening. On the one hand, I am elated when I am at a Federation young leadership retreat and I sense an immense thirst for Torah and Talmudic texts, for human-values material, but on the other hand, there is an undertone of sadness — they know it and I know it — for every one of them, there are three, five, eight, ten, twenty others who haven't got the least remote knowledge or interest in the material. And for every day school or afternoon school or Jewish camp I visit where there is some swing to this type of material, there are five, eight, ten, fifteen other schools and camps that plod right along giving "The Usual", for whatever reasons.

I know there's going to be a screech of brakes, a crash, a crumpling of cars.

I just know it.

I know that upstanding graduates of yeshivahs and Ramah and NFTY camps and Solomon Schechter Day Schools and Hebrew and Judaica schools in Seattle and Chicago and Atlanta will spend some of their days unnecessarily in hospitals or jails or in other miseries.

I just know it.

I know that our children will not be bank robbers, not in the classical sense at least, but I wonder which ones will appear in the papers in computer robberies of banks and other white collar crimes. I feel it in my bones. The names will be in the papers sooner or later, for sure.

A PROPOSAL FOR A SURVEY

Though I think it is unnecessary, it would perhaps be useful shock treatment to the powers-that-be that a sophisticated survey be conducted of Jews and the general population up to age forty. Since I do not know the mechanics of such studies, I can only give a raw outline of what ought to be covered:

Let a comparison be done between Jewish and non-Jewish samples to see if the alcoholism rate, drug-abuse rate, suicide rate, and conviction rate for white collar crimes is significantly different between the two groups. Jewish educational background should be recorded in detail, in order to assess whether or not there are any cause-and-effect relationships. Baldly put: is there any connection whatsoever between the content of their Jewish studies and their later character development.

While I personally believe that the time is *now* for re-arranging the content of the curriculum of Jewish education, for some people it might be necessary to wait until statistics prove the theory. Then, while it will be too late for many of the interim students, at least there will be some remaining purpose for their joining in the struggle.

CONFRONTING TWO ASPECTS OF THE ISSUE

It is redundant to state that the Jewish family is in disarray. Studies, articles, books, lectures, and videotapes abound with proof of this fact.

For that reason alone we should enter the fray full force now, and begin to attempt to compensate *in loco parentis* to whatever extent possible, to offer values-of-value for a full, meaningful life, unencumbered by the trappings that destroyed the career of Eric Breindel (and that will surely kill our developing teen-agers in cars or back rooms with drugs, alcohol, and whatever else is a killer.) That is the first confrontation.

Second, some schools will claim that it is not their posture to teach values, but rather simply to transmit the content of the texts at hand. I think that is is essential for every school to state clearly whether or not they are a Value School or not a Value School, whether they have a critical interest in the welfare, humanity, and ethical stature of their students (their Menschlichkeit) or whether they do not. This declaration of purpose — one way or the other — should be included not only for afternoon and Sunday schools, but also for day schools, Jewish colleges (Hebrew College in Boston, Baltimore, Spertus, Cleveland, all of them), and , not least of all, the seminaries: Reconstructionist, Yeshiva University, Hebrew Union College, The Jewish Theological Seminary, and all other institutions of higher Jewish learning.

For those that say, "No, that is not our primary purpose" — then an asterisk will be placed by their names in a catalogue of places to study. Non-asterisked schools and institutions will indicate places pursuing not only scholarship and knowledge-*per-se,* but also wisdom and significant Jewish values to live by.

Do not misunderstand: I am not so naive as to believe that the study of Relevant Jewish Texts on Menschlichkeit will automatically produce Menschen. But I am stating that without the pursuit of this material, our future hopes grow considerably dimmer. At least Menschlichkeit will be an issue, a focal point, a purpose-in-life of central importance, a meaningful struggle. Menschlichkeit comes easy only for a Select Few, but we wish to present and give dignity to the struggle for all those who would wish to accept the challenge, the larger numbers.

"Value Schools" will be sought out by some and "Non-Value Schools" by others. But, at the least, there will be no deception or confusion — students, parents, family, and friends will know which is which and what is to be expected.

Ideally, I cannot believe that principals, faculty, deans and chancellors are apathetic to this issue. They would prefer that their students emerge from their schools as tending-towards-decency-and-integrity. Still, there is this hole, this gap. I cannot recall any one person telling me that in his or her Jewish schooling — day school, camp, Jewish university — that "sleaze", "life in the fast lane", "shrewdness", or similar material was a central topic of study, and only occasionally do I hear of the positive aspects of Menschlichkeit as course material they had studied. I do not even recall (during any season of graduations) any highschool student telling me his Jewish school showed those famous, gory films of car wrecks, DUI's, prom night horrors, graduation night deaths.

I believe the time is ripe.

IN CONCLUSION

Tzedakah has been a favorite topic of mine for the past few years. I can muster many stories from the Yeshiva in Harrisburg to the afternoon school at Holy Blossom Temple in Toronto to a retreat week-end for a class in a reform synagogue in Kansas City to Ventnor, New Jersey's, USY group . . . all uplifting, encouraging stories about giving, caring, rising above the day-to-day to encounter some more grand view of life and its blessing and obligations. I have a file drawer full of these items, and a new story comes to my attention every week.

But I see that Tzedakah is not enough, though it is, I believe, the most critical curriculum point of departure.

If every school would ask itself a question such as this — "What is to prevent any of my students from becoming a biochemist working for a drug company from falsifying data from research of a specific medicine?" —then we could begin re-orienting our teaching content and methods. Because for now, there is very little to prevent reading a name like Greenberg or Rabinowitz or Ben-Ami from appearing in the papers in the midst of such a story . . . . Grants. GRANTS! You can't afford to lose your grant. Pressures from the boss. Overwork. Need to make a living . . . . All of those on one side of the balance, and, on the other side, only — in theory — an unethical act, and — in practice — potentially lethal consequences for thousands of people taking the drug.

I share the anguish of parents who pour out their hearts to me and my friends. The stories of the bad *chevra* their kids seek out — other kids who are wasting their lives, kids who wallow in alcohol, drugs, irresponsibility, dangerous games, cheating, many plagues. I share their pain as the mothers and fathers watch them wander aimlessly, unable to grasp even the least shred of meaning in their lives, grabbing hold tightly to too many of the secular values swirling around thier daily existence.

There's just too much pain and heartache around to let this slip by us now. Perhaps the starting point is parents storming the schools and saying, (carcrash newspaper clipping in hand), "What are the odds of this happening to my child?"

POSTSCRIPT: THREE YEARS LATER, HAPPY AND SAD NEWS

A professor of an institution of higher Jewish learning explains, "This year I'm trying something new which is only tangentially connected to my academic work. I'm giving an experimental course to a small group of rabbinical students in which we read Hebrew texts that possess personal, spiritual, and religious value. What I'm trying to do is to help them discover personal values in classical texts." Good to read, sad . . . . something new, experimental. So late, so little.

13 THINGS KIDS DON'T KNOW ABOUT TZEDAKAH

I confess: about a year ago I had decided I wanted to devote all my lecture and teaching time to adults. I believe it was largely for selfish reasons — the adults could offer me more insights from their own life stories and varied fields of expertise, and I could therefore conclude a talk having been that much more personally enriched by their ideas. A store owner could tell me "the true real-life story of making a living," a doctor could bring me into the intimate realms of Life and Death, a lawyer could share his exhilaration in overseeing an estate where $100,000 was left for the Jewish deaf or a day school . . . all wonderful material for my mind and writing, rich with the strong rhythms of People and Dreams, Dignity and Hope.

On the other hand, the younger generation's frame of reference was narrower: school, grades, achievement, first love and unlove, junkfood, decisions for college and graduate school. There was more, of course, but generally I demanded *still* more, a broader vision of life, a deeper understanding of joy and *tzuriss,* loss and redemption of the people, more than the kids could give.

Much of my material is still addressed to adults, but I have just reviewed the recent few years' discussions with the "kids" — seventh graders through college students — and I see that I have learned things I could never have discovered from the parents and grandparents. This article is only a summary of some of the negatives, the holes in one area of Jewish education: Tzedakah-Gemillut Chassadim, how Jews give away their money, their time, their energies in acts of gentle kindness. What often happens is that I take ideas from a talk with the kids, and bring the results to the parents some other time — the questions and answers of some of the new generation, a generous, but responsibility-laden gift for the adults.

The results of my review are recorded, besides, in the hope that what I have learned from the young will bring about a distinct shift in the direction of Jewish education. A good scream now and again at the Education Establishment is healthy for the community, though frankly, the past has shown that educators and teachers react disappointingly slowly. The frustrations are well-known and on a grand scale.

Then let us begin this one last *Geschrei,* a simple non-scientific review of what I have learned from the "kids" about Tzedakah.

1. *They Do Not Know about the People for Whom They Were Named*

I ask them, "How many of you know your Jewish name? About 85-90% of the hands go up.

I ask, "How many of you know for whom you are named?" About 50% of the hands go up.

And I ask, "How many of you know anything about the person for

201

whom you were named, how they lived, what their personalities were?"
No more than one out of five responds . . . many of these indicating that
all they know is that it was "some great-aunt," "a grandfather."

I believe — as an exasperated educator — that the children are being
deprived of models. If they knew the grandeur of the lives of those who
played a part in their lives before they were born — the kindnesses of a
beloved aunt, the openheartedness of an uncle lost in the War, the
generosities of a grandmother whose only legacy might otherwise be one
single photograph from the Old Country — if only the knew, they might
wish to assimilate those Menschlich qualities into their own lives.

> Susan is named "Chaya Sara", for some great aunt who used to bake
> challah for the poor and leave the loaves on their doorsteps before
> Shabbas.

> Mose Ber from Detroit (whose American name I forgot) is named for
> a great uncle whose two brothers died. Each of the three brothers had
> three or four children — ten in all, and this Moshe Ber chose to raise
> all ten. So Moshe Ber told me, his face showing pride, his words com-
> ing in a rush of joy and admiration.

2. *They Do Not Know What Jews Do with Unclaimed Bodies*

New Jersey. A dozen kids, two doctors' children. The topic is "Introduction to Jewish Medical Ethics." We stray to the topic of the need
for bodies for medical school anatomy classes. The near-unanimous opinion is that an unclaimed body should automatically be given to a medical
school.

> The Talmud indicates that a Met Mitzvah — an unclaimed body —
> is a particularly sensitive category of Mitzvah, one to be handled with
> specific care. Even the High Priest is obligated to handle the burial
> if necessary (though Kohanim are generally forbidden to come into
> contact with the dead — except their own close relatives). Even if he
> is on the way to performing the Passover sacrifice, he must delay that
> and bury the unclaimed body. And the body is considered so precious
> — so important is the dignity of a person, alive or dead — that he
> may be buried even in the immediate area where he is found, if that
> is necessary. Jewish tradition, rather than take advantage of the
> vulnerability of one who has died without friends or relatives, demands
> the utmost concern and accommodation.

I ask, "What is a Chessed Shel Emet Society?" No response.

A Chessed Shel Emet Society buries people, occupying itself with the
dead to such a degree that it insures any Jew — no matter how poor,
no matter how anonymous — a proper burial, with dignity, with a
marker. No Jew, without his expressed consent, should be sent to an
anatomy table, or a potter's field, a poorman's grave. Shirley works

the switchboard at the Jewish Theological Seminary. For forty years her mother was the president of the Chessed Shel Emes Society of Yonkers, New York, collecting money from members and other people of the community, to insure a proper burial for everyone. They were notified by hospitals and other agencies of a death, and if there was no one to bury the deceased, they would make all the arrangements. Shirley remembers sitting with her mother at the cemetary before the High Holidays, with a pushka, collecting coins and dollars for this Mitzvah.

3. *They Do No Know Where Their Keren Ami Hebrew School Tzedakah Money Went.*

I ask, "Where did your Keren Ami money go?" Half say, "Israel," — maybe 65%. Some say, "Trees."

I ask, "Where — besides for trees — in Israel?" Most say nothing.

I think that some think that Keren Ami is really Karen Ami, some lady who has been supported in High Style through their contributions and who will some day visit their school and say, "Thank you for the Gelt."

A friend in Israel tells me that a director of a certain charitable institution bought a car from the institution's budget which is used minimally for the institution, mostly for private use.

I ask, "Would you have wanted your money to go there?" Silence.

4. *They Do Not Know Jewish Tzedakot*

I ask, "Could you name for me some places, where you could give your money?" "The American Cancer Society," "The Red Cross," "United Way," "Goodwill," "The Salvation Army," "Federation." At one point, eight non-Jewish charities had been named, and only one Jewish Tzedakah. All of them, at that one study session, major organizations.

There is a group of people in Israel — ten or fifteen paratroopers whose friends were killed in the Yom Kippur War — who collect money for their friends' orphaned children, for summer camp, for bar mitzvahs, for whatever. They have no name or printed publicity for their organization, except, I suppose, "The Chevra," and word of mouth.

There is a couple in Jerusalem that collects old wedding dresses that they lend to poor brides.

There is a Tzaddik in Pittsburgh who goes to mental institutions in a wide area, providing for the Jewish retarded and mental patients who need Pesach and Purim and Chanukkah.

There is a man in Jerusalem — a former Clevelander — on the lookout for Mitzvot to do.

5. *They Do Not Now What a Jewish Free-Loan Society Is*

I ask, "What is a Jewish free-loan society?" thinking that the name itself will tell them. One out of forty or fifty has heard of one or knows of one in the local community. Once a Gemillut Chessed — Free-Loan — Society is explained, some show skepticism that anyone would do anything for anyone for free.

> *The Jewish Catalogue,* Volume II, pages 424-25 (the Yellow Pages) lists a few of the free-loan, free-shelter, and free-clothes organizations in the American and Canadian Jewish communities.

> Dr. David Weiss, renowned Jerusalem immunologist and lecturer, informed me that there are 250-300 Gemillut Chessed Societies in Jerusalem alone. The one he works with has not had a single default in eighteen years.

I say, "Speak with your parents and grandparents. They have heard of these things."

6. *They Do Not Know Where to Find the Jewish Poor in Their Community.*

I ask, "Suppose you wanted to make sure some Jew living in poverty had a decent Pesach or Sukkot meal — where would you go?" Except in New York (most of the young Jews know of the 200,000 or so poor Jews on the Lower East Side, in Queens, in Brooklyn), the answer is occasionally, "In the old Jewish section of town. Such-and-such a street." But usually the answer is no hands raised, no words.

> In the Providence, Rhode Island, area there was a minimal response. I found a map, through a friend who works with the Jewish elderly, with red dots for every house where an elderly person lives who receives a government-subsidized meal (either at home or at designated centers). Not everyone lives at or below the poverty line, but that is the map with which to start.

7. *They Do Not Know Jewish Retarded Adults*

I ask, "How many of you have retarded relatives?" Five out of sixty hands go up; one is unsure.

I ask, "How many of you might find others, if you asked your parents about the family tree?" A couple of more hands go up as the students begin to recall stories. One raises his hand, but is confused: he is thinking of senility, an old aunt or grandmother in a convalescent home.

"How many of you have met a retarded Jewish adult, enough to have had a conversation with him or her?" (A Jewish Day School:) Ten out of forty-five hands go up, eighth and ninth graders.

> The Irene Gaster Hostel for Retarded Adults in Jerusalem had a long struggle to find a new location. The neighbors were forcing them out. They look around and the new neighbors say, "No." Neighborhoods

in the States say the same, "Property values. Zoning laws. Danger." The usual. [They found a new location in 1985.]

"Best Boy," a film by Ira Wohl became a "sleeper" and an "event" at a Toronto film festival. A documentary of Ira's over-fifty retarded cousin, Phillip, it was shown again and again at the festival and then began to move to the commercial theaters. There were staggering reviews, despite the most primitive movie equipment, including crude hand-held microphones. It won an Oscar in 1980.

"Go see it when it comes to town," I suggest.

(The shock of the day school is that it is in Toronto, a place where much has been done for retarded adults by Rabbi Joseph Kelman. I was in Israel one summer and met a group of them on tour.)

8. They Do Not Know the Nature and Extent of Exorbitant Overheads, Waste, and Fraud

I ask the students, "What percentage of your dollar goes to what the publicity say? Would you give if you knew that only 43¢ was used for what it was supposed to be used for?" An absolute "No" from everyone.

UJA fundraising expenses and overhead are usually below 15%, an astoundingly low figure.

Some smaller, volunteer organizations (such as the paratroopers) can function with no overhead or minimal expense.

The December 19, 1979, New York Times, reporting an investigation of fund-raising tactics of New York police associations, stated that as much as 90% of the money was kept by the professional fund-raisers hired to solicit funds. The Metropolitan Police Conference of Eastern New York (comprising some eighty patrolman's associations) collected $676,000 in 1978, of which $436,000 — 64% — went to a private fund-raiser. TV newscasts at Christmastime remind people to beware.

I say to the kids, and to the adults, "Any place that doesn't send you a copy of its budget when you ask for one should not get your money. It is *your* money." And specifically to the kids, "Particularly because you may have so little to give — be careful."

Charity USA (NY Times Books, 1979,) by Carl Bakal is a lengthy, detailed account of just why we must be careful.

9. They Do No Know How Much They Are Supposed to Give

I ask, "How much should Jews give to Tzedakah?" three answers: (1)"Ten percent." (2) "As much as is necessary." (3) "As much as you want."

The Schulchan Aruch states, "One shold give up a fifth of one's possessions—that is the Mitzvah to an extraordinary degree. One tenth is considered an average percentage, and less is considered weak eyesight.''

Passionate discussion follows, sensitive insights, honest concern.

10. They Do Not Know What a Righteous Person Is, Nor Have They Met One

I ask, ''How many of you have ever met a righteous person?'' A group in Florida responds: three out of twenty-eight, two of whom described a person who always davvined and was always at shul. In another place, another teen-ager asks, ''What does 'righteous' mean'' — not asking for the connotations, but merely the dictionary definition. But they had all met brilliant people, people with straight A's on their report cards. Larger percentages had met great athletes than had met Tzaddikim.

In Utica there are Tzaddikim, I am told. In Toronto. In Sacramento, Atlanta, Chicago, Boston, New Haven, St. Louis. This is what people tell me.

11. They Do Not Know the Difference Between Tzedakah and Fund Raising

I ask, ''What Tzedakah projects have you been involved in?'' ''Walkaton,'' ''Jogathon,'' ''knocking on people's doors,'' ''people knocking at our door for Girl Scouts or The Heart Fund.'' Often there are broader aspects to their work, youth-group projects such as entertaining at the local old age home for Purim and Chanukkah or a local clothes drive, but more often than not, they describe organization or school projects: a car wash, raffle, and the like. The funds are usually turned over to some central office for distribution.

I describe friends with two separate checking accounts, one for Tzedakah and one for daily expenses.

I mention homes with pushkas where the family sits together to decide where the money should go.

And Tzedakah collectives: people pooling their Tzedakah money and meeting to decide where to give.

People who make it a day-to-day activity, their Tzedakah work.

12. They Were Not Informed That Bar or Bat Mitzvah Time Was the Time to Begin Full-Fledged Sophisticated Tzedakah Giving

I ask, ''How many of you were told that you should have taken 10-20% of your bar or bat mitzvah money and given it away to Tzedakah?'' One hand in twenty, two out of fifty.

Suspecting a particular reason, I ask, ''How many of you were told to put your money away for college?'' Always more than half, usually more than three-quarters.

I do some Tzedakah-mathematics with them. ''Let's take an exceptional, fancy case." I say, "Let's assume the child goes to Brown or Princeton or Brandeis or Harvard. At $35,000 for this college education — and this is a conservative figure nowadays — if you take away 10% of $1,000 of the Bar Mitzvah gifts, that leaves $100/$35,000, or .28 of one per cent.

I ask, "Why do you think the Talmud and Shulchan Aruch say that even a poor person must give Tzedakah?" They answer, "So that they will be reminded that no matter how poor they might be, there is always someone in a worse condition." And some answer, "Giving is a sign of a Jew's self-dignity, a privilege. Everyone should have that privilege."

I ask, "Why didn't they — parents, teachers, rabbis — tell you that?" No reasonable answer other than saving for college, an Israel trip, and similar very expensive projects.

Sometimes I become Hellfire and Brimstony: "You were cheated. *I* was cheated. Raise hell." Often I let it pass.

13. *They Do Not Discuss Tzedakah at Home, Nor Do They Know Why It Is Not a Topic of Discussion With Their Parents*

I ask, "How many of you discuss Tzedakah at home with your parents? Where or how they give or how much or why?" Perhaps three out of forty-five raise their hands.

"Why Not?" I ask, unsure myself, surprized that my home was an exception. The answers are hazy, halting, unsure.

"Money is my parents' own business." (Justifiably so to a great extent.)

"We don't talk abut anything." (Exaggerated, said humorously, typically by a teen-ager.)

"My parents are cheap." (I am astounded, and assure the student that this was assuredly not the case, and that she should search for other possible reasons. Later, I am more astounded when the local Jewish professionals tell me the child was right.)

By now, it is clear I should provide some summary of this backlogue of informal statistic-taking. It is obvious that the topics of Tzedakah and Gemillut Chassadim are generally mentioned only on the most primitive levels in our Jewish schools — including the day schools and yeshivot. Rarely (except Boston, Miami, and some scattered locales) is Tzedakah taught as a course. There is no listing for it in the catalogue of the Jewish Theological Seminary, and I am certain that this is true of other institutions for advanced Jewish study. It is almost never made a prominent part of the rabbis' speeches to the bar or bat mitzvah child. The children emerge into Jewish adulthood with a Siddur or Kiddush cup or Shabbat candlesticks, but no nicely-designed pushka, no list of Tzedakot to commit themselves to. (The exception I know of — though there are more, I am sure — was a rabbi-friend who gave a pushka to each bar mitzvah or bat mitzvah kid.)

A threatening, discouraging gap is created between the Hebrew School and Keren Ami days and the young Jew's emergence into the Big World where the preponderant number of young adults find themselves unaware of the privilege of giving. They do not know the most basic rules, the mechanics of Tzedakah, nor do they have many human precedents or models. They are grossly and embarrassingly ignorant of its wonders and joys.

There is a saving grace, though — a critical one. It can be explained by the old joke, "What is the difference between ignorance and apathy?" "I don't know and I don't care." While the former may be true of the next generation, I do not believe the latter to be the case. They are definitely not apathetic to the tradition and insights of Tzedakah. Indeed, the response, with the proper, sensitive presentation of the material, is nearly universally enthusiastic. This generation is much more involved in volunteer work, infinitely more bound to the destiny of the State of Israel, distinctly more committed to the rescue of Soviet Jews and other Jews in danger than I was at their age. If you raise the issue of Iranian Jews, they are sympathetic and willing to commit time, and more, to a solution. Mention the loneliness of the Jewish elderly in their community, the alienation of the Jewish deaf (whose intermarriage rate is very high) the needs of the Jewish retarded, and they are responsive. Extraordinarily responsive.

Now all that we need is a sweeping, revolutionary, never-done-before re-ordering of our Jewish educational priorities: the badgering of teachers and principals and rabbis, the hell-raising with synagogues and JCC's, the battering down of old, seamy doors of the Establishment to get them to see that the alternative is a generation of bright, well-degreed, well-to-do egocentric Jews. A generation where brains mean everything, acfhievement per se is rewarded with high honors, and the heart is left to atrophy. The demonstrations and manifestoes, placards and marches, and sit-downs and strikes — the whole Megillah of tactics we learned in the '60's can now be put to full use LeShaym Shamayim — for the sake of heaven and for the Jews' own integrity and preservation.

The Customary Talmudic Conclusion

The Talmud says that all the organs of a person's body depend on the heart, and the heart depends on the pocket. In one sense it means, no doubt, that, without financial security, we cannot function in a stable, reliable fashion. But surely it also means that only through sincere, careful, and care-full giving can the Jew fulfill his meaning as a member of the People of Israel.

KIDS WILL BE KIDS

How much is hormones and how much is culture?

How come the Talmud never had a word for "teen-ager"?

I'm not about to say sixteen-year-olds don't drool naturally over some hunk, but is so much rebellion-and-moods in their make-up and genes?

Come now, someone has to believe a Good Life of Mitzvahs can ease those years of growing up without so much craziness.

I am not a certified expert by the Board of Teen-Age Understanders, but it appears to me from loose but vigilant observation that a good afternoon once a week at the hospital, or packaging and cooking food for the forgotten can eliminate anywhere from 27% to 93% of the muck and tension in a kid's mind.

I've said it in my lectures again and again: the more Mitzvahs, the less teen-age suicides. And certainly the more Mitzvahs, the less depression and confusion and downright, bald unhappiness.

I would sincerely invite those skilled in studies and statistics to find control groups of our kinderlach to watch them at their Mitzvah work. I would predict the findings: more and more kids you just want to hug, more and more of them less obsessed with the Idolatry of Good Grades, less alcoholism, less drugs, less joy rides and break-ins, and even a lowered rate of sibling screaming and tears, and less visits to psychologists and counsellors.

Here is the challenge:

Follow a youth group in a year's span that's learning sign language and drawing the Jewish hearing-impaired closer to the synagogue, Jewish study, and Shabbat.

Observe a bunch of teen-agers who work with the local meals-on-wheels.

Check out the seventeen-and-eighteen-year-olds who perform the Mitzvah of *Shemirat HaMet,* sitting up at night with dead bodies for the local *Chevra Kaddisha*-Burial Society the night before a funeral.

Make pilot programs and write articles. Publish results. Give us graphs and formal findings, bell curves and stats.

You'll see — Kids aren't just kids.

MITN TOCHISS OFN TISCH:
THE CASE OF THE WHIRLING CHICKENS

WHAT I NEVER SAW AS A CHILD

Throughout my childhood I was surrounded by Europeans. Not classy Parisians or stuffy-accented Londoners like I used to watch in the movies. No, these were mostly Polish-Russian Jews, *Poilische Yiddn, Litvaks, Galitzianers,* and the like, all kinds of refugees from the regimes of Czars and other tyrants, bringing with them their Yiddish sounds and smells and gesticulations. I could expect to gain entreé into these inner circles every Rosh HaShana and Yom Kippur when my family would escape with my grandparents to New Jersey, to Asbury Park or Lakewood or Atlantic City or Bradley Beach. I am sure that I looked like a *goy* to them — I was American through and through, a little *shaygetz,* child of parents born in unromantic-sounding towns like Highlands and Keansburg, New Jersey. My parents were of the Americanization Generation, picking and choosing, keeping or casting away whatever was appropriate in their own eyes for growing up in The Golden Land. I didn't have that problem: I was an Arlingtonian, a Virginian, child of Americans whose accent (to this day) includes nothing more serious than an occasional "dat" instead of "that" and "dese" in place of "these"now and again.

I was not raised bi-lingually. What Yiddish I did learn I picked up since high school, and even that is not enough to understand the many punchlines to jokes people will tell me after one of my lectures. They hear my talk peppered with phrases from *The* Mother Tongue, my tossed-in words here and there, and afterwards ask, "Where did you learn Yiddish?" I have to confess to them that they have heard 80% of my mastery of the language during that single talk.

Oh, I was filled with Eastern Europe as a child!

But there is one thing I never saw, even though we arrived at the hotels hours and hours before Yom Kippur would actually begin. For some reason I was never taken to witness The Great Chicken Whirling. You know, *kappores.* You take a chicken (live) and whirl it around your head, reciting lines like, "May this chicken be an expiation for my sins." Then *(nebech)* (or so I was told) the poor chicken would go the way of all *kappores*-chickens — slaughtered. Some people, I am told, even laid the guts out on the rooftops, though I've never found a good explanation for this specific practice.

I knew they were doing it, somewhere, perhaps no more than a hundred yards from where I was dressing in scratchy suits, grumbling, "How long will the *chozzen* keep us in shul this year with his wailing?"

Nowadays, as an adult, I have become unsettled by the thought of those unfortunate chickens, the birds that might have been able to carry away my childhood and childish sins, with their souls flying directly to the

Heavenly Throne. I even wonder now if there might not be a mammoth coop in the sky, somewhere in God's backyard, where the revivified hens and roosters receive their daily feed from His Divine Hand. Others before me — including some very great rabbis — looked askance at this practice, and even forbade it in their towns, but I know for a fact that people still did it, thousands of Jews, casting away their sins in blood and feathers and ungodly cluckings.

SOME PERSONAL NOTES FROM THE AUTHOR

Me — I was fortunate. I was sent away to college in the early Sixties to learn not only mathematics, literature, and a smattering of geology, psychology, and philosophy, but also to enter a full-degree program in Torah study: Bible, Talmud, Hebrew language and literature, Jewish thought, history — all kinds of Torah. I didn't have too much of a chance earlier on because the only Jewish day-school in Washington was quite a distance away, and it wasn't yet such a popular idea to go to such a school, at least not in my home. We were not yet ready for day-school education.

I left for New York, for the Combined Program at Columbia and the Jewish Theological Seminary with a "typical Conservative afternoon school and Hebrew High School education". I had some supplementary study with my rabbi (even two pages of Talmud uncertainly under my belt) by the time I arrived on Morningside Heights. What happened during the many years up there was, simply stated, an opportunity to study Jewish texts first hand, from the original. Bible: the terrifying Job, lyrical Psalms, Chumash, thundering Jeremiah, the wailing of the Book of Lamentations. Talmud: court practices, divorce settlements, blessings, holidays, oaths — all from the big books, the giant books of Talmud. (Even now I tend to lean to the right, a slight sag in my bone structure from carrying the Big Books to class.)

I can see now my friend Joel's trunk hanging low, from the day we loaded $400.00 worth of Big Books after a carnival-day in the Jewish book stores on the Lower East Side.

I can also see rearranging the shelves, placing the ten awesome volumes of the Shulchan Aruch law code in a place of honor.

They were all so heavy, printed on magnificent paper with fine bindings, filled, page on page, with words waiting to be read.

Any and all of my Talmud professors will tell you that I was not the shining light of the class. I loved Talmud, but could not manage the logic of the arguments. I think it was my reaction to failed dreams of being a mathematician. Still, I loved Talmud, and all of Rabbinic literature — particularly the stories, certain unusual laws tucked away in unexplored places, and sayings that held out to me some direction for my energies. So, even after I left, I kept on with the words of Rabbi Shimon ben Elazar, Choni the Circlemaker, Rav and Shmuel, Maimonides, and the genius of Tzefat,

Joseph Caro. By then I had begun to discover that there was an ever-growing array of Jewish values stored in those pages.

I became a teacher and lecturer. And even after I had become a poet and writer (quite by mistake), I remained a teacher and lecturer. The last few years I have taken to distributing xeroxes at some of my talks, selections from the Talmud, Midrash, and law codes: uncomfortable texts, passionate texts, eerie texts. Then the class or audience and I work our minds back into the unique way of thinking, and living, of the Rabbis. Mothers, fathers, fancy-named people like gastroenterologists and software configuration specialists, high-status *yiddn* and just plain so-called run of the mill Jews join me for face-to-face confrontations with the ancient words. We dig, we search, we scratch deeper and deeper into the echoes of things past, working towards consolation, exhilaration, insight, or a moment's soaring rise above the daily *shlep* we all experience too many days in our lives.

I love it.

THE SILENT DEATH OF THE CHICKS

So much for the background and nostalgia. I have called this article, "Mitn Tochis Ofn Tisch" — a wonderful Yiddish way of saying, "Let's put our cards on the table." It is time to get more serious.

While I am not much of a courageous person, I think we ought to state a case quite baldly: the majority of Jews living in America today are living adult Jewish lives with child-quantity-and-quality Jewish educations. For all the new day schools and yeshivas; for all of the new Judaic studies courses at universities and seminaries; for all of the admirable and successful attempts of many UJA and Federation sponsored adult study groups.

For the masses Out There, the Big Numbers, they are living on kiddies' knowledge of Yiddishkeit.

As I explained before, I was fortunate, as were many of my friends, the teachers. Now it is time to share the good fortune.

The situation is indeed devastating. One illustrative example: on a recent Shabbat in shul, the rabbi explained that he had mentioned to a group of adults that there is reason to believe (among historical scholars) that the miracle of the extended burning of the Chanukkah candles may not really have occurred. Some contend that it was a pious legend created hundreds of years after the Maccabees. The rabbi then told the congregation that many of the adults seemed shattered, dumfounded.

Channukah is, of course, a holiday of victory and security, and even more so the story of the fight against assimilation. Candles are nice. Miracles are wonderful, but the hard part of the holiday theme is this staying Jewish in the midst of the pulls and urges of pagan values. I think the rabbi agrees that the adults would have rather had a more comfortable tale to recite (one which, to be sure, could be re-interpreted and loved and honored with adult-thinking) — than to hear a sermon on staying *really* Jewish, *living* Jewish, making life-decisions on the basis of Jewish values.

The devastation is obvious: when there is a bar or bat mitzvah in synagogue, one need only scan the congregation to see how many do not have the vaguest notion of what is happening. (The cynic would say, "It's hard to tell the Jews from the non- Jews.")

But that last scene isn't even the focus of the devastation. It is, rather, the upshot of the Channukah-and-candles-question: what we in Jewish education should be primarily concerned with is how many people have acquired a knowledge of Jewish values, sufficient exposure to allow them to integrate these *Values-for-Living* into their everyday lives. Inside the synagogue, outside the synagogue, in the day-to-day, do the Ancient, Big Books hold sway in their decisions on business moves, hiring and firing practices, relations with their mates, their children, their parents, their community, relations with their own selves? There I think (using a Talmudic phrase), *Layt Man De-Palig* — none of my teacher-friends would disagree: the awesome majority is not even aware of the options and availability.

And I do not wish to imply that education automatically leads to the integration of these values; but without the exposure to the texts, there is not even the choice. All there is to choose from is America's secular offerings.

And I do not wish to imply that I and the teacher-friends have achieved the Glories of Jewish Living. Rather, the implication is, we choose now to *attempt* to live out some of these values, with no more or less human failings than anyone else. That must be clearly stated. This is not an arrogant piece of flaming criticism; it is somewhat of a cry.

WHO SLAUGHTERED THE CHICKENS?

We can't lay all of the blame on one factor. Certainly not. But I keep thinking of those chickens. I think it is true that the majority of the adult generation decided that they would "do it for the kids." We have heard that beaten-dead-horse story again and again. If *they* couldn't read Hebrew, at least *their kids* would. If *they* didn't have this or that, at least *their kids* would.

The problem is that since the parents had little sense of the extent and breadth and depth and height of what Jewish values offer, they were willing to settle (though they did not know it was "settling") for what was being offered locally by the shul, the schools, the whole panoply of communal educational services. If that much. And that was, as we see, sometimes not enough. What of the adults?

The results: we see the results daily, at an adult education lecture when the audience's eyes light up when they hear the most elementary exposition of Jewish values.

In Canada, things are different. Students of Jewish demography know that most Canadian Jewish communities have a much closer connection to the European experience: there are higher percentages of refugees and survivors, more Jewish values being handed down, as my grandparents did for my parents. After a recent talk in Ottawa, one woman spoke with me, telling me how obvious so much of what I said had been. Of course. She was right. She had much more Yiddishkeit in her mind and bones than most of the American audiences I address, and I hadn't shifted into a different, higher gear. They were waiting for Advanced Torah, and I was still explaining the elementary stories.

In the United States, in the midst of the millions of success stories, we still hear the wheezing of the *kappores*-chickens, the children who were to become the beneficiaries — the expiation for the parents' shortcomings. We see it in their personal unhappinesses and worries and woes, their failures, and their total lack of ability to deal with these critical events within a Jewish framework.

Educators, Jewish educators, believe that in the realm of human problems — dealing with deceit, depression, friendship, financial crisis, love, caring and uncaring — The Books have much to offer. They are meant to be called into use not only for crisis (though that, too), but essentially for establishing living patterns which will yield a good life, a fulfilling life, a happy life.

If I did not believe that the Talmud, Maimonides, Shulchan Aruch and other texts offered some real insight into happy family life, communal life, and the welfare of the Jews and humankind everywhere, I would probably change vocations. And yet, other than pockets here and there, we still hear the roaring gasp of the emerging adult Jew over all the hurrahs of our successes. The children's generation — still children or growing into adulthood — did not expiate for the sins. They are not yet prepared to assume Jewish adulthood with Jewish values in their guts. And the adults did not have their Jewish educational shortcomings repaired. All parties have come up short.

I would imagine that if you put the educators in a room alone and asked them to spill it all out, they would tell you the same thing, even the best of them, the ones who have been in it for thirty years or more and who have indeed achieved great things. Ask them to survey the broad span of the community and ask them whether involvement, commitment and active Jewish living predominate, or whether the prevalent flow is apathy, lack of knowledge, and the pagan "Look Out for #1" philosophy blared over the air waves and shimmering on the popular book stands.

They will tell you.

The Big Them is winning

And one main reason is "The kids will get what I didn't get."

MAKING PLANS (Based, In Part, on the Talmud, Maimonides and Shulchan Aruch)

The Talmud says that adult education is more important than the education of the children. (Kiddushin 29b) On the same page we have a historically recorded case of a parent who pulled his child out of school because he was not as capable a student as the parent — and the parent went to study in his place.

The giant, Maimonides, rules similarly. (Hilchot Talmud Torah 1:4)

The giant, Joseph Caro, rules similarly in his law code, the Shulchan Aruch. (Yoreh De'ah, 245:2)

Some remedial efforts for this unfortunate situation might include:

1. In every reasonably-sized town, make certain that at least one person on the communal payroll is a Visionary. The little plaque on the door should read, "Michael Pomerantz, Visionary," "Marcie Kahn, Visionary," "Jeffrey Susskind, Visionary." Picture windows with a view might also be helpful. They should be left alone to visionize, and they should be given the resources to do the same caliber of projects that Henrietta Szold had, Herzl had, Eliezer be Yehuda had.

2. A certain percentage of the reasonably administratively competent should be kept on to assist in carrying out the new plans. Those who are pedagogically incapable in this structure should be eased out, perhaps with the assistance of Jewish family service agencies, helping them to find other jobs where they can function better within the Jewish community. Competence and incompetence can both be harmful, and it would appear that the former would serve well, only if the real power lies with the visionary — who is, as is well known, often incapable of structuring and realizing programs in a practical manner.

3. In every reasonably-sized town, at least one full-time adult education teacher should be hired, with no students under adult age, and *with absolutely no administrative responsibilities.* A teacher to teach — at a salary at least equal to that of the highest paid Jewish professional in that town. The salary will draw these superb teachers from other fields, into the classroom where many of them would much prefer spending their time and efforts.

4. Restructure budgets in order to make this — Adult Jewish Education — The No. 1 Priority in Jewish education. One example: Camps Ramah and the UAHC camps, I am sure, would be pleased to have summer-long institutes for adults, an extension of the week-end retreat concept. Were massive scholarship funds available, I am certain they would welcome such an opportunity. Locally, the costs of bringing in high-powered, text-oriented lecturers and scholars-in-residence would be prohibitive, unless the budget were restructured in a radical fashion.

5. Prepare and disseminate reams of curriculum material, based on Talmudic and other sources, that would deal with (my favorite word) *gutsy* Jewish values and human behavior. (If necessary set up a research institute in some city called the National Jewish Institute for the Research of Gutsy Jewish Values in Talmudic and Post-Talmudic Literature for the Teaching and Enjoyment of Adults.) Some of the courses that might be offered would possibly include:

    A. Laughter
    B. Dreamers
    C. The Changeability of People
    D. Infinities and Eternals
    E. Loneliness, Intimacy, and Suicide

    F. Life's meaning
    G. Fear, Breakdown, and Crisis
    H. Integrity and Prostitution
     I. Craving and Envy
     J. Cynicism and Paganism *(Avoda Zara)*
    K. Failure and Self-Image
    L. Money
    M. Sensitization and Desensitization
         1. For doctors, lawyers, social workers,
            and other professionals
         2. For non-professionals
    N. Limits
    O. Tears and Sadness
     P. Defects, Blemishes, and Cancer
    Q. Anger
    R. Hope and Despair
     S. Dignity and Humiliation
    T. Arrogance
    U. Choosing
    V. Will and Ethical Will Writing
    W. Commitment
    X. Life and Death, Killing and Saving
    Y. Lyricism in Day-to-Day Living
     Z. Righteousness and Self-Righteousness
    Aleph: Psychiatry and Torah
    Bet: Profession Vs. Family
    Gimel: Bitterness
    Dalet: Joy
    Hay: The Body
    Vav: Helloes and Good-byes
    Zayin: Evanescence
    Chet: Making a Living and Living
    Tet: Stealing, Theft, and Robbery
    Yod: Repetition and Boredom
    Yod-Aleph: Gutsy Mitzvahs
    Yod-Bet: Easy Mitzvahs
    Yod-Gimel: Passion
    Yod-Delet: Passionate Torah
    Tet-Vav: Swans and Cheetahs — A Day at the Zoo
    Tet-Zayin: Kindness
    Yod-Zayin: Origins and Beginnings
    Yod-Chet: Endings
    Yod-Tet: Simple People
    Kaf: Aphorisms, Maxims, Truths and Half-Truths
    Kaf-Alef: Making a Difference
    Kaf-Bet: Oi, Wow, and Other Half-Words
That's for starters. Forty-eight courses.

IN CONCLUSION: MYRIAM MENDILOW AND THE CHINESE PROVERB

It's an old Chinese proverb: Give a man a fish, and he will have something to eat that day. Teach him how to fish, and he will never go hungry.

So why do I quote a Chinese proverb after a long article on Jewish values and Jewish texts and Jewish living?

I did not learn this Ancient Chinese Proverb from a Charlie Chan movie, nor at Schmulka Bernstein's, Kosher Chinese Restaurant on New York's Lower East Side, rolled up in a fortune cookie at the end of an overpowering meal. I heard it first, and hear it frequently, from Myriam Mendilow, founder, and director of Life Line for the Old in Jerusalem. She's the lunatic who took beggars off the Jerusalem streets, and old people who were sitting alone and lonely in rooms waiting for the Angel of Death—and put them to work. Twenty five years ago.

A Class-A Lunatic and Visionary.

She tells the visitors who come to Life Line that work is the road to dignity, and throws in the Oriental aphorism as a little dessert-touch to her talk. I don't think she started this vast revolution in the lives of the Elders of the Holy City on the basis of some fish tale, though. When you hear her shout, plead, and scream, her words begin with Maimonides' Rule #1 of Tzedakah: the greatest act of Tzedakah is assisting a personn to find employment, to regain self-sufficiency helping him or her regain his or her self-dignity.

There are hundreds and hundreds of people who know that that is indeed #1 on Maimonides' Tzedakah list (and thousands and thousands more who never heard of it, or Maimonides.) But even among the hundreds, who took the awesome step to make it happen?

There ought to be a song written about Myriam Mendilow, something called "My Kind of Woman". Maestra-Teacher of Jewish Values in Jewish Life.

But it would be unfair and impractical to bring her over here for some raging, foaming lectures around the United States. (Oh, when she screams, she screams loud!) She'd raise all kinds of hell. And they need her over there, working with the Elders of Jersusalem.

That leaves us practically alone over here. Not entirely alone: there are people here, including many of my generation who are looking for revolutions, now that the War in Vietnam is over.

The invitation is open. Let all who would take part, come into the power structure and take the initiative; all who are hungry for different nouishment, let them come and make plans.

AGEISTS:
CHILDREN'S PREJUDICE AGAINST THE ELDERLY

The problem is freaks. Outcasts, pariahs. Jewish education, and, specifically, Tzedakah education ought to be centralizing this problem in the curriculum.

Racial, ethnic, sex prejudices and the Jewish reactions to such phenomena are being dealt with in many places, though it is hard for someone my age, 42, to try to describe to a 15-year-old what the first days of desegregating schools in Virginia was like. I can still picture the spotlights all around a junior high school near my home, and the presence of police cars, the night before it all began. The younger people can more easily understand the good fight that is being fought on behalf of women's rights and rights for individuals with disabilities. It is happening all around them — in the re-striping of the their parking lots, for example, to accommodate people who use wheelchairs. They know words like "racist" and "sexist" — it is common vocabulary.

And yet, though they might intuitively fell that many of the elderly in our society are neglected or lonely or feel unwanted or useless, they don't know the word 'ageist' nor have they such a clear course of action to correct the situation. This goes for adults, too. There is still a groping, and wandering for specifics, hard facts, solid suggestions.

Because of my eleven years of visits to Life Line for the Old in Jerusalem with nearly 6,000 teen-agers from United Synagogue Youth, I have been reminded of the problem over and over again. There, in the workshops of Life Line, we see active, creative, inspiring elderly people at work, making gorgeous products, rebinding school textbooks, and engaging in normal activities. I find it hard to remind the kids that Life Line is not an old age home, nor an activities center, but a workplace. It is where old people, even some with extreme physical disabilities, come to work five days a week.

In the last year or so, however, I was most fortunate to discover that a friend of mine, Dr. Leora W. Isaacs of Bridgewater, NJ, had done her doctoral dissertation on the topic of prejudice towards the elderly among children. (The actual title is *The Development of Children's Attitudes Towards the Aged*, 1983, City University of New York Graduate Center.) I have discussed the dissertation with Dr. Isaacs on a number of occasions, and have had a chance to review two articles drawn from that work: one, for a secular journal, and the other, published in the Fall of 1986, for the journal *Aging and Judaism*, entitled "With Our Young and With Our Old". With her kind permission, I would like to summarize some of the contents of this work.

Most important of all, her conclusions (from this, and previous research): ageist thinking, i.e., prejudices and other negative attitudes towards the elderly begins *by the time children reach preschool age!* Quite simply put, this ought to scare us all. Dr. Isaacs did a number of tests with 144 children, one of which particularly fascinated me: a child was ushered into a room where an adult was sitting at a table, with puzzles on the table. The child was told they were going to work the puzzles, and would the child please bring over a chair? There was a measuring scale, a ruler-chart of some sort, to note the distances the child placed the chair from the adult. The results: if the adult was an elderly person, the child would place the chair farther away than if it were a younger person.

Other distinctions she noted:

1. The children initiated eye contact less often with the aged individual, in comparison with younger ones.
2. They spoke fewer words with the aged individual, in comparison with the younger ones.
3. They initiated conversation less frequently with the aged individual, in comparison with the younger ones.
4. And, they asked for assistance less frequently from the aged individual that from the younger ones.

Now, since this was a dissertation, Dr. Weinstein did a number of other tests, applied all the requisite statistical methods, accounted for a variety of factors in each child's background — all the tools of modern research in this field of endeavor. It's a Kosher, substantial, fascinating, and troubling piece of work.

One line is very powerful (in the article for *Aging and Judaism):*

"Six-year-olds expressed significant levels of prejudice against aged individuals on the attitude scale in addition to behavioral indices."

So it is by age six that the problems begin, both attitudinally and behaviorally. The prejudices include perceiving the elderly as "socially, psychologically, and physically deteriorated, restricted, and isolated". So Dr. Weinstein reports — the latter phrase summarizing six other journal articles authored by respected researchers.

Dr. Isaacs seeks out the sources of the prejudices, besides the general prejudices swirling around children from society in general, the media, and other factors. One of her phrases is most apropos, "Lack of familiarity breeds contempt." Otherwise known as the "frequency of contact hypothesis", it is clear that children do not have a great deal of regular day-to-day contact with elderly people. If they did, the hypothesis goes, it would help build more positive attitudes towards the aged, and prevent or remove some of the negative attitudes. But that isn't sufficient — there is the "quality of contact hypothesis". More positive attitudes will develop if the child sees the aged person in a context where they "show that they possess useful knowledge or exert control over their environment". And she adds, " . . . positive beliefs about the effectiveness and capabilities of old people are not related as much to frequency of children's contact with old people *as to the role in which they are preceived."* (My italics.) This is where visiting the elderly in old age homes, great Mitzvah that it is, is not sufficient, because the children learn to view the elderly as weak, dependent, recipients and not givers, dynamic, creative. Indeed, Dr. Isaacs believes this "would rather emphasize the debilitating effects of the aging process and strengthen existing negative stereotypes." She is *not* saying they shouldn't do the visits, entertain, sit and talk with the elderly in the old age homes, but the says more should be done.

And now, the juicy part, for the Jews, for programming, for education, starting with the youngest of children — Dr. Isaacs' five practical suggestions:

1. The children should be exposed to the aged where they can interact with them when they are in "respected and prominent roles. In religious schools, nursery schools, Jewish day-care facilities, synagogue libraries, tutorial programs, and JCCs, older adults can serve as paraprofessionals, or volunteers, as tutors, aides, guest lecturers, or skill teachers, story-tellers or oral historians. They can apply their skills, knowledge, and experience, deriving the dual benefits of achieving self-esteem and providing a vital role model for the youth."

2. There is a greater need to integrate Jewish texts and insights into all aspects of the school curriculum: Bible, Siddur, holidays, Talmud text studies. All of these lend themselves to greater sensitivities to the uniquely Jewish mode of interaction with elderly individuals.

3. Authors and publishers of Jewish texts and materials should re-orient their emphases from the aged as peripheral and secondary in society, moving much more towards portraying them as vital individuals, important in the life of individuals and society in general. (I hear this time and again when I ask the teen-agers I see at Life Line to describe to me some commercials about the elderly. They rattle off: laxatives, insurance, arthritis, all kinds of medications, all the way down the line, one after another. The aged as weak, as in need of help, as almost-in-the-grave.)

4. Outside of the class, in our life as Jews, we should be fostering the distinctly Jewish views of the aged and aging. Dr. Isaacs refers to a "realistic" description and approach — which to her, and hopefully to us, means stressing the strengths and abilities, not only their incapacities.

5. Intergenerational programs are critical: intergenerational choirs, a model Seder where both young and old are active participants, activities where both elements are hard at work, being their greater selves, lively, alive, giving as well as taking. (Joint Yarmulka making, Tallis making, Challah cover making, Tzedakah box making, etc., could be added to the list.)

To summarize — the shock of Dr. Isaacs' findings still sits terribly uncomfortably with me. I have been obsessed with the dissertation and articles since I first learned about them, and have referred to them in many of my talks. Imagine: by elementary school age, children have already devalued old people, they believe they can't do things, they are weak, essentially helpless and needy. It is a long haul to build on that, beginning with Dr. Isaacs' practical suggestions, a long haul to set things right.

I used to joke that every review of some academic work or piece of research was called "seminal" . . . not just good, not just thorough, but a seed-planter for future generations. I now think that this is an entirely appropriate term for Dr. Isaacs' work. We should hope it will guide us in a course of action that will reverse the trends that have caused so much pain and unhappiness, and move us all into grander, more glorious relationships with the aged.

NECESSITIES OR LUXURIES?

A Tzedakah teaching exercise for teen-agers and adults from Rabbi Joseph Braver, Director of Professional Services and Continuing Education of the Board of Jewish Education, Baltimore, MD.

The following is a list of 25 items that most people in the United States take for granted, as part of their lifestyle. How do they fit into your lifestyle and income level?

Next to each item that you consider a necessity, write the letter N; if you believe it to be a luxury item, write L next to it.

1. A credit card
2. Life insurance policy
3. New clothes every year
4. Dining out once a month (or more frequently
5. An annual vacation
6. A savings account
7. Food and water
8. Health insurance
9. A car
10. A telephone
11. Daily newspaper or news magazine
12. Going to the movies once or twice a month
13. Color television
14. Cable TV
15. Home computer
16. An annual salary increase
17. A place to live
18. Air conditioning
19. Cosmetics, grooming supplies
20. Wristwatch
21. "To be in style" in terms of clothes, books, the arts
22. Four or five hours a week for your own time to spend it as you choose
23. At least two-three hours a week to help other people
24. Percentage of your income for charity and community programs
25. An equal amount (see #24) for recreation and vacation purposes

Pretend that you lost your job and have no regular income. Now, go over the list again. What N items would you now change to L?

How do you think a poor person would answer the questions?

Which of your N items would you consider doing without in order to help the less fortunate?

I can see that my Tzedakah studies have made my investigations too lopsided. I have been neglecting the broader issues of money—not only what it can do for others, but what it does to people in general, what it can and cannot buy outside the Tzedakah realm, what joys and sorrows it might bring, how difficult it is to get hold of in hard times, and what people will do (legally and illegally) to get it. Some critics might think that, since I am a poet, I am not sufficiently connected to some simple realities that are tied closely and tightly to money . . . . So I began to explore some Rabbinic material on money itself, hoping to round out the picture on the basis of the sources. As with Tzedakah, it is clear that the Rabbis also had a profound grasp of Money-in-General, as will be explored in the following pages.

For example:

We are taught:
Three things can drive people insane and can cause them to overstep God's bounds — the hardships of poverty . . . .

(Eruvin 41b)

By quickly scanning the newspapers, we can see the desperate look on the faces of the newly-unemployed, read the statistics of climbing suicide rates among similar samples of the population, hear tales of discouragement and depression from the miners, factory workers, bankrupts throughout the land — the New Poor — to understand this passage. I do not believe the words at all imply that people may be driven beyond their limits of sanity because they are money-grubbers. To the contrary, I think the Talmud says that for many honest, hard-working people, the loss of employment and income may well be the first step to unthinkable crises in the Being of Human Beings. Awesome, terrifying.

For another example, the Midrash, after a fine folk-tale of a king and a weasel, propounds the following principle:

It is not the weasel that steals, but rather the hole
[where the weasel stores the stolen goods] . . . .

(Leviticus Rabba 6:2)

Again, we need only scan the papers or listen to the news to see and hear the following statistics:

(1) One out of two Cartier watches sold today is a fake.
(2) One out of five records and tapes is a pirated product.
(3) One out of ten pairs of designer jeans is a fake.

Though it is sometimes too obvious to mention, the Midrash is saying, "If there were no people buying stolen goods, there would be no reason for the thieves to steal." Three sources of interest come to mind:

(1) As a writer, I am uniquely aware of a certain vulnerability that comes with my professional choice — I can be plagiarized hundreds of miles away, lose royalties, and never know what has happened. Fortunately, I am not such a best-selling author that anyone would want to pirate one of my books and sell the phony copies on the open market, but it is clear from studies of the publishing and entertainment industries that fraud and theft are rampant.

(2) I think of an old "Hawaii 5-0" program where the Honolulu police department not only arrests a man who stole blank airline tickets from a travel agency, but also the person sitting at the bar who bought an outrageously discounted ticket back to the mainland. The charge was, naturally, possession of stolen property. To plead innocent, claiming that he was unaware that the ticket was stolen, was much too shaky ground for the bar-fly to manage.

(3) The Talmud, again, observes:

> In Rabbi Shela's academy they said, "Whoever keeps away from wrongdoing is made fun of by others."(Sanhedrin 97a)
> Rashi comments: "Everyone says he is a fool."

This is the peer-pressure principle. "Everyone is doing it." Hot items are easily obtainable; high school students can get hold of them with little difficulty. An old friend who used to teach in the New York public schools once jokingly asked if I wanted a bicycle or typewriter. He could get them for me at *very* cut rates.

As a summary of these texts, the Shulchan Aruch rules as follows:

> It is prohibited to buy a stolen item, and it is equally prohibited to assist in the process of transfer and change.
> By doing such things we only strengthen the hands of the law-breakers and transgress the principles of "You should not put a stumbling block in front of the blind." (Leviticus 19:14)
> It is further forbidden to derive benefit from stolen goods . . . .
> For example, it is forbidden to ride on or to plow with a stolen animal.

> (Choshen HaMishpat 369:1-2)

I would pause for a moment at this stage of the article, to allow for a little perspective. What has become clear in the last years of delivering talks on Tzedakah is this: the Tzedakah-involved are uplifted by the tremendous impact-for-good that Tzedakah-work can do. On the other hand, they are depressed by the devastating effect that all manner of stealing (open or subtle) has on the Common Person. It undercuts our sense of trust. Whether we are wandering in a store at Christmas time and see sales galore (only to discover that there was a radical mark-up before the mark-down), or whether it is the EPA rules of automobile gas mileage ratings, or whether it is the used car dealers' lobby that prevents Congress from passing stricter laws for honesty in their trade....whatever the case may be, we are inundated by one event after another that says, "That's the way people are. That's business."

I see it in kids, even fifth graders and younger, a certain cynicism: You can't trust people. People are out there to cheat you. People will take advantage of you any chance they get. As it is so succinctly put by the false Wise Ones of generations past and present, "It's a jungle out there, son. A real jungle."

I don't buy that line. Still, the everpresence of the pressures of the marketplace beat away at the consumer, the Person in the Street, which is why it is that much more important to examine carefully what Judaism has to say about The Jungle. The recurrent phrase we would seek is, "The Talmud says . . . The Midrash says . . . Our law codes says . . ."

The Talmud says:

Rabbi Yochanan says,
One who steals from another even the value of a penny —
it is as if he took away his soul [killed him]. . . .and as
if he took away the souls of his children.

(Bava Kamma 119a)

And the Midrash says:

Rabbi Aibo said:
This is the way money rules people — as Rabbi Yudan said in the name of Rabbi Aibo, "A person dies before even half his cravings are satisfied. . . .If the person has one hundred [coins], he wants two hundred. If he has two hundred, he wants four hundred."

(Ecclesiastes Rabba 3:12)

And the Rabbis further teach:

One who steals from the public must make restitution to the public. It is a more serious crime to steal from the public than from an individual, because with an individual, one can go and make direct, individual restitution and apology, but with public funds, one cannot restore the loss and apologize to each individual in the community.

(Tosefta, Bava Kamma 10:8)

A student of the Talmud would know — long before it became

fashionable to rip-off A.T.&.T. with false and stolen credit cards or put phony claims in for car insurance — a student of the Rabbis would know that this is hardly to be written off as, "Well, what do they care? They have plenty of money anyway." I think we have all come to learn that it is we, ourselves, the consumers, who eventually pay for the ones who steal fromt he electric company by tampering with the meters, or any one of the thousands of rip-off variations that are perpetuated daily. And whether or not — from a pragmatic standpoint — we end up paying. It undercuts socie-ty's ability to function, to provide to assist, to make life liveable. If we wish to rail against high utility bills and to fight with legal action, that is our right and privilege. But the Talmud says that the way of stealing is not the way.

I regreat the sermonic tone. Just recently, though, I saw on the news a report with a sad statistic that went something like this. "Beefed-up security in stores, and shoplifting losses, will cost the consumer $500.00 this year." Let's even say the that the figure is overblown. Let's say it is only $250.00. What we all could do with that extra $250.00!

Here is another variant on the topic of misplaced money values:

Better to give less to Tzedakah from money which is your own, than to give more from stolen or unfairly-acquired means. As the popular say-ing goes, 'She prostitutes herself for apples, then gives them to the sick.'

(Ecclesiastes Rabba 4:9)

This is the end-justifies-the means principle. The stance of the rabbis is clear, though. In another passage, the Midrash points out the paradox of some types generosity:

Who represents the principle of "being gracious to the poor"?
(Proverbs 28:8)
The Evil Esau [the Roman government]
But was not Esau-the-Evil-One an oppressor of the poor?
We are speaking here of people like the Roman officials who go
into the villages and plunder the farmers, then come into the
city and say "Bring us the poor. We want to do the Mitzvah
[Tzedakah] with them."

(Pesikta deRav Kahana 10:1)

Many more sources could be mentioned concerning the strong-arm tactics, near illegalities, and blatant breaking of the law of some abusive money makers. Jewish tradition has rules for selling cattle and fruit and land, for pricee-setting, consumer protection, restoration of lost articles, grievance suits, and compensation for damages. Three of the largest volumes of the Talmud — *Bava Kamma, Bava Metzia, and Bava Batra* — deal with these topics in extensive detail. Guardians, liens, oaths in court and out of court, extortion, bribery.

I leave these subjects for more extensive study — about four hundred double-sided pages as a beginning. Many of the topics can only be pass-ingly mentioned here.

Making a living is one of those aspects of money-and-life that is prominently represented in Talmudic and Midrashic texts. Very succinctly we are told:

> Rabbi Yehuda says, "Whoever does not teach his child a trade, teaches him robbery."
>
> (Tosefta Kiddushin 1:11)

Rabbi Yishmael takes this even farther, stating:

> "Choose life" (Deuteronomy 30:19) — this refers to teaching your child a trade.
>
> (Jerusalem Talmud, Kiddushin 1:7)

On many campuses around the country today these guidelines have become warped. Many universitites are pervaded with an atmosphere of students *studying-and-studying-hard,* which is commendable. But, as we hear from professors, administrators, and fellow students, their studies are often too-highly concentrated, excluding many broader subjects in the humanities. Furthermore, and more serious, I believe, they are studying almost exclusively for the sake of landing an all-important (All-Holy?) job. Hillel directors and parents are expressing concern about this narrowing of vision. It is encouraging to note, though, that at Yale, there are at least a thousand students, Jewish and non-Jewish, involved in volunteer community projects — despite the normal study-and-work load. And at the University of Pennsylvania, Project Chaver is doing well: many students are doing regular Mitzvah-work within the community. And the L.A. Hillel Council's Mitzvah Project on many campuses is dazzling. These are commendable efforts in light of the many negative pressures.

No one denies — and certainly not the Talmud and Midrash — that the job of making a living is difficult:

> "By means of hard labor shall you eat." (Genesis 3:17)
> Rabbi Ammi said,: "Making a living is twice as difficult as giving birth."
> Rabbi Elazar said, ..."Just as the Final Redemption will be
> miraculous, so, too, is there an element of the miraculous
> in making a living. . . .and making a living is greater than
> Redemption, because Redemption may be achieved through an
> Angel, whereas making a living is under God's Own aegis."
> Rabbi Yehoshua ben Levi says, "Making a living is greater
> than splitting the Red Sea."
>
> (Bereshit Rabba 20:22)

I recall taking a ride with my mother a number of years ago. You know how it is at certain times, how you think your parents are ancient, creatures from some prehistoric age. I tested the theory with Mom, asking her if she knew how to sing, "Brother Can You Spare A Dime?" — the famous song from the Depression. She did, indeed, know the song, and told me stories of what it was being a child of the Depression. *There* was a chunk of the real world crashing into my wandering, idealistic imagination.

And how did my parents characterize my Grandpa Bill, proprietor of a small dry goods store in Keansburg, New Jersey? What they wanted me to remember about him was that, even in the Depression, he could still give credit on a dime pair of work gloves — in a time when credit wasn't worth a damn, when there was less than half a hope to be paid back. Even in those days, my Grandfather did not sell away his trust in people.

Those are realities I needed to hear. Since then I have been stunned over and over again by variations on that theme, from one extreme to the other: the kindnesses and utter brutalities involved in making a living. Here is one from the Talmud:

> Rabbi Natan bar Abba said,
>
> The wealthy of Babylonia deserve to go to Hell!
> See, for example, when Shabbetai bar Maraynus came to Babylonia.
> He looked for help in setting up a business, but they did not
> help. And even when he asked for help for food, they did not
> give him any.
>
> (Betzah 32b)

This is the opposite, a travesty of makin a living: those who were comfortable and could have helped, did not. The student of Talmud is not accustomed to hearing such strong exclamations from the teachers. But Rabbi Natan Abba was outraged. Hundreds of years later, Chassidic tales would abound with the stories of rich, cheap *yiddn* whom the Rebbi tries to instruct in the ways of generosity. One Rebbi reported that he had given a sermon explaining how the rich should be ready to give and the poor ready to receive. He commented sadly that he was only half successful in his appeal.

The Talmud, Midrash, and Law Codes note:

(1) Give away a tenth, so that you may become wealthy. (Shabbat 119a)
(2) No one ever becomes poor from doing Tzedakah. (Maimonides, Hilchot Mat'not Ani'im 10:2)
(3) We are taught: Rabbi Shimon Ben Elazar says, "Do [the Mitzvah] while you can still find it [the means], and it is still available to you, and still in your power to do it." (Shabbat 151a)
(4) If one does not do Tzedakah and acts of lovingkindness from his possessions, they will become an obstacle to him. (Midrash Zuta, Song of Songs 15)

Very nice, comforting words. But you would have expected words like those from people who teach about Tzedakah. And you would expect them to add:

> (5) Rabbi Yehoushua ben Levi says, "Whoever accustoms himself to doing Tzedakah will have children who are wise, wealthy, and fine storytellers.
>
> (Baba Batra 9b)

Wealth is the issue, wealth and well-being. Wealth, richness-of-life, using money-riches to enrich one's own life and the lives of others. Here is a classic source in the Talmud concerning wealth, one of my favorite passages:

> We are taught:
> Who is truly wealthy?
> Whoever gains peace of mind from his wealth. This is Rabbi Meir's opinion. [A lovely opinion, but one we would have anticipated.]
> Rabbi Tarfon says, "Whoever has a hundred vineyards and a hundred fields and a hundred workers working in them. [A very *real* realistic definition from a very wealthy man.]
> Rabbi Akiva says, "Whoever has a spouse who does exquisite deeds." [Akiva was married to the Woman of His Dreams, Rachel.]
> Rabbi Yossi says, "'Whoever has a bathroom near his dining room table." [What can we say about Rabbi Yossi's cook?]
>
> (Shabbat 25b)

Four wide-ranging opinions. Some to be expected, some rather astounding. We would all like to complete this article with a warm feeling: yes, the Rabbis understood the power of money to make or break a human being. Yes, they know that the road to dignity is to take whatever resources are available and to share some portion with others who are living in more precarious life situations.

And yet, I feel the Talmud, Midrash, and Codes are often meant to trouble us — even more than to soothe us. It would seem that, since the Work of the World is unfinished, we, as Jews, should have some feeling of being unsettled, ill-at-ease until things are set more right than when we were born. Because of this, I present three more texts:

(1) Rav Pappa said, "Paying your debts is a Mitzvah. (Arachin 22a) Sadness. The newspapers are filled with articles about repossessions of some very nice cars — from people who have kept up their car payments, but who have failed to pay back their student loans.

(2) One of Rabbi Shimon's students left Israel and returned very wealthy. The other sutdents saw this and wanted also to leave Israel. Rabbi Shimon took note of this and took them to a huge valley near Meron,

and then prayed to God. The valley filled with gold dinars.

Rabbi Shimon said to his students, "Whoever wants to take from this money may do so, but be aware of the fact that whoever takes now is taking some of his portion in the World to Come."

(Tanchuma, Pekuday 7)

I am not writing this as a diatribe against those who leave Israel nowadays to make a living here or in Europe or in other parts of the world. Other than living in Jerusalem for one year a long time ago, I have never had to struggle with the daily problems of inflation and job-search over there. However, I do think that the broad meaning of this passage is — what were the students ready to surrender (and what are *we* willing to surrender), of our dreams, our hopes, our higher life-meanings — for the sake of wealth? Wealth and depth-of-character are not contradictory terms in the Talmud. All wealthy people are not *Momzerim*. (Indeed, Rabbi Akiva and Rabbi Yehuda HaNassi showed great respect for the wealthy.) Neither are all poor people portrayed as Righteous Ones. That would be too naïve a mind-frame for the Talmud. Still, the Talmud recognizes that pull, the danger that the pursuit of wealth — without a larger perspective of what life is for — that for wealth we will surrender our better selves for the sake of coins and video games, fast cars and all other manner of Things.

Finally, a true story about two Talmudic figures. It is the best kind of Talmudic story because it proves that the rabbis did not just preach, but lived out — with all their human shortcomings — what principles they felt were important in life:

(3) It was said that Rabbi Tarfon was an extremely wealthy person, but would not give sufficiently to the poor. Once Rabbi Akiva found him and said, "Would you like me to buy you a city or two?"

Rabbi Tarfon said, "Yes, I would." He then gave him four thousand gold dinars.

Rabbi Akiva took them and gave them to the poor. After a while, Rabbi Tarfon ran into Rabbi Akiva and said, "Where are the cities that you purchased for me?"

Rabbi Akiva took him by the hand and brought him into the House of Torah-study, and put a copy of the Scroll of Psalms in front of the student. They read and read until they came to the verse, "One who gives generously to the poor — his righteousness shall stand him in good stead forever." (112:9)

Rabbi Akiva said, "This is the city I have purchased for you."

Rabbi Tarfon arose and kissed him and said, "My teacher, my hero. My teacher in wisdom, and my hero in Menschlich living!"

He then gave him more money to give away on his behalf.

(Massechet Kallah, towards the end)

It's a nice "And they lived happily ever after" ending, but I promised I would not deal with unrealistic matters. Of course I love the story, its good ending, the benefits of giving Tzedakah. But nowadays I concentrate on a different aspect of this tale: how could it be that Rabbi Tarfon, great teacher of his generation, surrounded daily by the likes of Rabbi Meir, Rabbi Yehoshua, and Rabbi Akiva — how could it be that he lived years and years without giving sufficiently? What was it in his personality that loved money so much that he was keeping almost all of it for himself?

That is a new starting point for me now: what money does *to* people. From that point of departure I will continue to explore what it does *for* people.

SUGGESTED TITLES
FOR SPEECHES AND SEMINARS
ON TZEDAKAH

1. What Do Paul Newman, Bruce Springsteen, and Kenny Rogers Know About Tzedakah We Don't Know?
2. The Almighty's Dollar
3. Where Heaven and Earth Touch
4. Mitzvahs: A Piece of the Action
5. Investing in Futures
6. Everyday Miracles
7. Gym Shoes and Irises: Personalized Tzedakah
8. The Magic Touch: Menschlichkeit and Tzedakah
9. Real Live Tzedakah
10. Mitzvah Heroes — Everyday People
11. Mutual Fund Investment (title appropriated from Jason Kaplan, B'nai Israel USY, Rockville, MD)
12. Looking Out for #1 — The Holy One
13. Getting A's and/or Being a Mensch: Tzedakah, Status, and Achievement
14. Giving from the Heart (from the Knee, From the Elbow, Anywhere) — Giving Till It Hurts (Till it Doesn't Hurt)

IN CONCLUSION: PART OF A POEM
FROM MY BOOK, *THE GARDEN*

Then along came Tzedakah
on a snorting white steed, rearing high on its legs.
All of a sudden people bought food,
wrote checks, sat at hotlines, and shopped for the shut-ins.
They drove the lonely to synagogue.
They took in children wandering the streets.
They counselled and pushed
and made shiny wrapped packages called Dignity and Hope
and delivered them to Old Age Homes
complete with a choir of youth group kids,
every age unafraid of wrinkles and bends.

(Tzedakah saves from despair
and death.)

The kids brought their pets to the sick
and sick at heart to be petted
and played with, smiled at, cooed over,
and you would be hard pressed, you would,
to tell just who exactly was saved from death:
the pettor or the pettee or the kid with the puppy
who missed a little homework because
he was too busy at the Home for the Lonely
which is located in All Neighborhoods in Every Town
in America
day, night, snow, sleet, rain and sun times,
shooing away death with a gentle bark and a purr and touch.

(Tzedakah saves.)

Whole troops of them!
The infinite team of salvation makers
and life restorers:
The teacher, the real estate broker, his daughter,
the toy maker, towel dealer, and mechanic,
the academic by day and spoon feeder by night,
regiments of the fat and short and average,
Cary Grant bodies and nerd faces,
PhD's and twelve-year-olds

(saving Tzedakah from death.)

Yes. Indeed.
There's a battalion an army or two out there,
in jeans, and sweatshirts, slacks, blouses,
loafers, scarves and gloves—
just your run-of-the-mill normal people—
squeezing into The
Great Crowded Group Photograph in the Sky.

(The Tzedakah Photograph.)

Appendices

Appendix A

A Master List of All Tzedakah Projects
Mentioned In This Book

1. Air Life Line Association, 1722 'J' St., #14, Sacramento, CA 95814, 916-442-5165.
2. ALYN Orthopaedic Hospital, POB 9117, Kiryat HaYovel, Jerusalem, 412-251 (Corner Olsvenger and Shmaryahu Levin Streets). (American Friends of ALYN: 19 W. 44th St., Suite 1418, NY, NY 10036, 212-869-0369.)
3. American Friends of Life Line for the Old — See "Life Line for the Old".
4. American Friends of Yad Sara — see "Yad Sara".
5. American Jewish Joint Distribution Committee ("The Joint"), 711 3rd Ave., NY, NY 10017, 212-687-6200.
6. American Jewish World Service, 29 Commonwealth Ave., # 101, Boston, MA 02116, 617-267-6656.
7. The Ark, 2341 W. Devon Ave., Chicago, Il 60659, 312-973-1000.
8. Arnson, Curt, c/o AKIM-Jerusalem, 42 Gaza St., Jerusalem, 631-728.
9. Association of Ethiopian Immigrants, c/o Mekonen Tekele, POB 44921, Haifa.
10. Association of Hebrew Free Loan Societies, c/o Julius Blackman, 703 Market St., # 445, San Francisco, CA 94103, 415-982-3177.

11. Battered Women's Shelter, Jerusalem: Beit Tzipporah Battered Women's Shelter - Isha L'Isha, POB 10403, Jerusalem, Contact, Joan Hooper, 639-740.
12. Beged Kefet, c/o Les Bronstein, 80 Cranberry St., # 9G, Brooklyn, NY 11201, 718-624-2925.
13. Bet Tzedek, 145 S. Fairfax Ave., # 200, Los Angeles, CA 90036, 213-939-0506.
14. B'nai B'rith Project Hope, 1640 Rhode Island Ave., NW, Washington, DC 20036, 202-857-6600. Washington area: c/o Len Elenowitz, 8801 Post Oak Rd., Potomac, MD 20854, 301-983-1345.
15. Bread for the City, 1305 14th St., NW, Washington, DC 20005, 202-332-0440.

16. Cantorial School, Jewish Theological Seminary, 3080 Broadway, NY, NY 10027, 212-678-8000.
17. CHAI = Concern for Helping Animals in Israel, c/o Nina Natalson, POB 3341, Alexandria, VA 22302, 703-820-1742.
18. Chazon F'taya, c/o Simcha Ovadia-F'taya, POB 6070, 6 Shimon Chacham St., Jerusalem, 814-454.
19. Christian Service Project, c/o Sister Margaret McCaffrey, POB 21, Shreveport, LA 71161, 318-221-4539.

20. City Harvest, 11 John St., #503, NY, NY 10038, 212-349-4004.

21. Coalition for the Homeless, 105 E. 22nd St., NY, NY
212-460-8110

22. Colleges — Mitzvah Projects:

B'nai Brith Hillel Foundations, 1640 Rhode Island Ave., NW
Washington, DC, 20036, 202-857-6560.

Los Angeles Hillel Council Mitzvah Project, 900 Hilgard Ave., Los
Angeles, CA 90024, 213-208-6639.

23. CSS/RSVP/NYC (Community Service Society/Retired Senior
Volunteer Program/New York City, 36 E. 22nd St., NY, NY
212-614-5485.

24. Conference (and Coalition) for Alternatives in Jewish Education, 468 Park Ave. S., # 904, NY, NY 10016, 212-696-0740.

25. Cook for a Friend, c/o Judy Schwartz, The Neuman Center,
6600 Bustleton Ave, Philadelphia, PA 19149, 215-338-9800.

26. Council of Jewish Federations Task Force on Jewish Individuals with Disabilities, 730 Broadway, NY, NY 10003,
212-475-5000.

27. Daddy Bruce's Barbecue, 1629 E. Bruce Randolph Ave.,
Denver, CO 80205, 303-295-9115.

28. Debra Friedmann - see "Panda the Clown".

29. Dorot, 262 W. 91st St., NY, NY 10024, 212-769-2850.

30. Dumpster Dipping: write Suzanne Gladney, c/o The Temple,
712 E. 69th St., Kansas City, MO 64131, 816-483-1885.

31. Dysautonomia Foundation, 370 Lexington Ave., NY, NY
10017, 212-889-5222.

32. ECHO (Ezrat Cholim Organization, National Jewish Institute
for Health), 32 Alturas Rd., Spring Valley, NY 10977, 914-425-9750.

33. Encyclopaedia Judaica, c/o Shaare Zedek Hospital, 49 W. 45th
St., NY NY 10036, 212-354-8801.

34. Ezrat Avot, 7 Tarmav St., POB 5063, Jerusalem, 287-894,
ATTN: Naomi Sharabi.

35. Foundation to Sustain Righteous Christians, c/o Rabbi Harold
Schulweis, Valley Beth Shalom, 15739 Ventura Blvd., Encino, CA
91436, 818-788-6000.

36. Gay Men's Health Crisis, 254 W. 18th St., NY, NY,
212-807-6572.

37. Gomel L'ish Chessed Interest Free Loan Society, c/o Dr. David
Weiss, 56 Ben Maimon St., Jerusalem, 669-363.

38. Hatzilu, c/o Al Cohen, 38 Gainsville Dr., Plainview, NY 11803,
516-349-7063 or 536-0290.

39. Heber, Rabbi Leib, c/o Western Pennsylvania Auxiliary for Exceptional People, 281 Sharon Dr., Pittsburgh, PA 15221, 412-421-1757.

40. Helping Hands, c/o Dr. M.J. Willard, Dept. of Rehabilitative Medicine, University Hospital, 75 E. Newton St., Boston, MA 02118.

41. Interpreters for the Deaf and Sound Systems for Hearing Impaired Individuals:
Interpreters:
Rabbi Dan Grossman, c/o Temple Sinai, Dillon Rd. and Limekiln Pike, Dresher, PA 19025, 215-643-6510.
Toby Marx, 6 Makatom Dr., Cranford, NJ 07016, 201-272-2549.
Laura Rubin, 40 Hurning Ave., Cranford, NJ 07016, 201-276-2649.

Sound systems for synagogues for hearing impaired individuals:
Rabbi Richard Hammerman, Congregation Bnai Israel, 1488 Old Freehold Rd., Tom's River, NJ 08753, 201-349-1244.
Rabbi Sheldon Lewis, Congregation Kol Emeth, 4175 Manuela, Palo Alto, CA 94306, 415-948-7498.
42. Irene Gaster Hostel for Retarded Adults, c/o Curt Arnson, AKIM-Jerusalem, 42 Gaza St., Jerusalem, 631-728.
43. Israel Levin Senior Center, 201 Ocean Front Walk, Venice, CA 90291, 213-392-3362.

44. Jewish Alcoholics, Chemically Dependent Persons, and Significant Others Foundation, Inc. (JACS), 10 E. 73rd St., NY, NY 10021, 212-879-8415.
45. Jewish Braille Institute of America (JBI), 110 E. 20th St., NY, NY 10016, 212-889-2525.
46. Jewish Center for Special Education, 4312 15th Ave., Brooklyn, NY 11219, 718-782-0064.
47. Jewish Chaplain, UJA-Federation, 7900 Wisconsin Ave., Bethesda, MD 20814, 301-652-6480 (for locating Jewish elderly in non-Jewish old age homes).
48. Jewish Community Center, 6701 Hoover Rd., Indianapolis, IN 46260, 317-251-9467 (for making use of JCC for unemployed people seeking jobs).
49. Jewish Education Service of North America (JESNA), 730 Broadway, NY, NY 10003, 212-260-0006.
50. Jewish Foundation for Group Homes, 11710 Hunters Lane, Rockville, MD, 20852, 301-984-3839.
51. Jewish Fund for Justice, 1334 G St., NW, Washington, DC, 20005, 202-638-0550.
52. Jewish Guild for the Blind, 15 W. 65th St., NY, NY, 212-595-2000.
53. Jewish National Fund, 42 E. 69th St., NY, NY 10021, 212-879-9300.
54. Jewish Welfare Board Jewish Book Council, 15 E. 26th St., NY, NY 10010, 212-Le-2-4949.
55. Joint Distribution Committee (JDC, Joint), see #5.

56. King, Rabbi Bernard, c/o Shir Ha Ma'alot-Harbor Reform Temple, 2100-A Mar Vista, Newport Beach, CA 92660, 714-644-7203.

57. Life Line for the Old, c/o Myriam Mendilow, 14 Shivtei Yisrael St., Jerusalem, 287-829. American Friends of Life Line for the Old, c/o Linda Kantor, 52 Wellington Dr., Orange, CT 06477, 203-795-4580.

58. Linda Feldman Rape Crisis Center, POB 158, Jerusalem, 245-554.

59. Literacy Volunteers of New York, 666 Broadway, NY, NY, 212-475-5757.

60. Lord's Place Family Shelter, c/o Brother Joe Ranieri, POB 7117, W. Palm Beach, FL 33405, 305-736-7006.

61. Marlboro, NJ, Jewish Center Tzedakah Committee, POB 98, School Road West, Marlboro, NJ 07746, 201-536-2300. Chairperson: Anita Bogus, 201-536-3358.

62. Martha's Table, 2124 14th St., NW, Washington, DC 20009, 202-328-6608.

63. Ma'on LaTinok, c/o Hadassah Levi, 45 Rambam St., Givata'im, Israel, 03-324-080. Hadassah's beeper: 291-251, Beeper # 963.

64. Mattel Toys, 800-421-2887 (for Hal's Pal's dolls).

65. MAZON, c/o Irving Cramer, 2228 Westwood Blvd., #200, Los Angeles, CA 90064, 213-470-7769.

66. Melabev, POB 293, Jerusalem, 285-661, ATTN: Phyllis Jesselson.

67. Metropolitan Council on Jewish Poverty, 9 Murray St., 4th Floor East, NY, NY 10007, 212-267-9500.

68. MITZVAH-The League for Family Rights, c/o Lynn Sharon, POB 3186, 6 Shatz St., Jerusalem, 226-339 (for divorce mediation).

69. N Street Village of Luther Place Memorial Church, 1226 Vermont Ave., NW, Washington, DC 20005, 202-667-1377, ATTN: Rev. John Steinbruck.

70. National Association for the Jewish Poor, 1163 Manor Ave., Bronx, NY 10472, 212-378-5865, ATTN: Gary Moskowitz.

72. National Institute for Jewish Hospice, 6363 Wilshire Blvd., #126, Los Angeles, CA 90048, 213-653-0795.

73. National Jewish Welfare Board, see No.54.

74. National Organization on Disabilities, 2100 Pennsylvania Ave., NW, Washington, DC 20037, 202-293-5960.

75. National Yiddish Book Center, c/o Aaron Lansky, POB 969, Old East Street School, Amherst, MA 01004, 413-256-1241.

76. New Israel Fund, 111 W. 40th St., #2600, NY, NY 10018, 212-302-0066.

77. ORT (= American ORT Federation), 817 Broadway, NY, NY 10003, 212-667-4400.

78. Panda the Clown = Debra Friedmann. 4615 Verplanck St., NW, Washington, DC 20016, 202-364-1505.

79. Pearlstein, Chuck, 22522 N. Bellwood, Southfield, MI 48034, 313-352-0482.

80. PEF-Israel Endowment Funds, 342 Madison Ave., #1010, NY, NY 10173, 212-599-1260, ATTN: Sidney Musher.

81. Prisoners' Projects:

See: Pearlstein, Chuck, #77.

Rabbi Michael Swarttz, c/o Board of Rabbis of Greater Philadelphia, 117 S. 17th St., #1000, Phila., PA 19103, 215-563-1463.

82. Project Ezra, c/o Misha Avramoff, 197 E. Broadway, Room U-3, NY, NY 10002, 212-982-4124.

83. Rape Crisis Center, See #58.

84. Rocky Mountain News, 303-892-5381.

85. ROFEH — Reaching Out Furnishing Emergency Healthcare, 1710 Beacon St. Brookline, MA 02146, 617-728-0521.

86. Sanctuary: See #30.

Rabbi Charles Feinberg, 1406 Mound St., Madison, WI, 53711, 608-256-7763.

87. Shema V'Ezer, 11710 Hunters Lane, Rockville, MD 20852, 301-984-4455.

88. Singing in Hospitals, see #16.

89. SOVA (Kosher food pantry), 3007 Santa Monica Blvd., Santa Monica, CA 90404, 213-453-4606, or c/o JCC, 2601 Santa Monica Blvd., Santa Monica, Ca 90404, 213-870-8883.

Other Kosher food banks:

See #7.

Also, The Neuman Center, 6600 Bustleton Ave., Philadelphia, PA 19149, 215-338-9800.

90. Synagogue Council of America Task Force on Jewish Hospice, 327 Lexington Ave., NY, NY 10016, 212-686-8670.

91. Synagogue Food Pantry:

Congregation Tifereth Israel, 3219 Sheridan Blvd., Lincloln, NE 68502, 402-423-8569.

92. Synagogue Shelters for the Homeless:

Shearith Israel, 1180 University Drive, NE, Atlanta, GA 30306, 404-873-3147.

Temple Israel, 1014 Dilworth Rd., Charlotte, NC 28203, 704-376-2796.

93. Trevor's Campaign for the Homeless, c/o Trevor or Frank Ferrell, 120 W. Lancaster Ave., Ardmore, PA 19003, 215-649-6400.

94. Tzedakah Boxes for Bar/Bat Mitzvahs Kids Made by the Elderly: The Temple-Congregation B'nai Jehudah, c/o Rabbi Michael Zedek, 712 E. 69th St., Kansas City, MO 64131, 816-363-1050.

95. Tzedakah Habit, c/o Harriet Hoffman, Jewish Federation of Greater Dallas, 7800 Northhaven Rd., Suite A, Dallas, TX 75230, 214-369-3313.

96. United Jewish Appeal, 99 Park Ave., NY, NY 10016, 212-818-9100.

97. United Jewish Appeal-Federation, Washington, DC, 7900 Wisconsin Ave., Bethesda, MD 20814, 301-652-6480.

98. United Jewish Federation of Pittsburgh, c/o Jane Berkey, 234 McKee Place, Pittsburgh, PA 15213, 412-681-8000.

99. Wedding Dresses for Those Unable to Purchase Their Own: The Rabbanit Bracha Kapach, 12 Lod St., Jerusalem, 249-296. Daniel and Charlotte Kuttler, 7 Keren HaYesod St., Jerusalem, 233-991.

100. Yad Ezra, 15 HaRav Sorotzkin St., POB 7199, Jerusalem, 526-133, Attn: Shmuel Katz

101. Yad LaKashish-Life Line for the Old, see #57.

102. Yad Sara, 43 HaNevi'im St, Jerusalem, 244-047. American Friends of Yad Sara, 1 Parker Plaza, Ft. Lee, N.J. 07024, 201-944-6020, Attn: Charles Bendheim.

103. Zahavi — Jerusalem Association for Rights of Large Families, c/o Dr. Eliezer Jaffe, 1 Metudela St., Jerusalem, 690-744. Jaffe's home: 637-450.

104. Ziv Tzedakah Foundation (Canada), c/o Merle Gould, 31 Glen Rush Blvd., Toronto, Ontario, Canada M5N 2T4, 416-486-7425.

105. Ziv Tzedakah Fund, 263 Congressional Lane, #708, Rockville, MD 20852, 301-468-0060.

A Few Tzedakah Collectives and Small Tzedakah Funds:

Arizona: Tzedakah Fund, Inc., c/o Stan Mayersohn, 7726 E. Sheridan St., Scotsdale, AZ 85257, 602-945-5354.

Connecticut: Chavurah Tzedakah, c/o Ellen Donen, 10 Maher Dr., Norwalk, Ct 06850, 203-847-5667.

District of Columbia: Chevrat Tzedakah, c/o Erica Raphael, 8519 Milford Ave., Silver Spring, MD 20910, 301-585-9170.

Illinois: Egalitarian Minyan Tzedakah Collective, c/o Rich Moline, 180 N. Michigan Ave., #1710, Chicago, IL 60601, 312-726-1802.

Massachusetts:

Brandeis University Tzedakah Collective, c/o Hillel, Brandeis U., Waltham, MA 02254, 617-647-2177.

Brookline: Ohel Chesed, c/o Bob Housman, 46 Columbia St., Brookline, MA 02146, 617-738-8449.

Sudbury: Tzedakah Hevra, c/o Brenda Rosenbaum, 19 Pine Needle Rd., Wayland, MA 01778, 617-653-7515.

New Jersey: Ma Tov Tzedakah Collective, c/o Temple Shalom-Anne Schwartz, 215 S. Hillside Ave., Succasunna, NJ 07876, 201-584-5666.

Appendix B

Making the Synagogue Accessible
to Individuals with Disabilities

1981 was declared "The International Year of Disabled Person." For religious institutions that meant becoming conscious of the accessibility of their buildings. It was hoped that this would spur new efforts to make needed changes so that every house of worship could display the following "Certificate of Occupancy":

OCCUPANCY
IN THIS BUILDING
IS
LIMITED TO EVERYONE

There are no barriers
to belonging
that
God's people
cannot
overcome

Think of your synagogue. Just how accessible is it? Perhaps the following check-list* will prove helpful in your evaluation.

An accessible congregation is one which has overcome three barriers:

1. The physical or architectural barriers which make it difficult for persons with handicaps to enter.

2. The communication barriers in sight, sound and understanding which impede the communication of the message and inhibit the participation.

3. The attitudinal barriers which make persons with handicaps feel unwelcome.

Put a check-mark next to each item the synagogue has; work toward having a check-mark for the entire list.

---

*Based on Rev. Harold Wilke, "What is an Accessible Church?" THE HEALING COMMUNITY (White Plains, New York), and CHURCH AND SOCIETY (New York: Jan-Feb, 1979).
Appendix B is taken from United Synagogue Youth's Sourcebook *Meshane HaBriot. . . .Who Makes People Different* (Carl Astor, 1985.)
For further information, contact the Council of Jewish Federations Commission on Individuals with Disabilities, 730 Broadway, NY, NY 10003, 212-475-5000.

Approaches

1. Parking spaces marked "Reserved for the Disabled." Spaces should be 12 feet wide to open door; no loose gravel... _____
2. Level approach to the synagogue; sidewalk to curb or curb ramps to street.................................... _____
3. Ramps where there is a change in grade level and/or steps at some entrances:
   Ramps into building................................ _____
   Ramps into sanctuary.............................. _____
   Ramps up to Bima................................. _____
   Ramps where steps are unavoidable................. _____
   Multi-level buildings are barricades for some disabled unless modifications are made............................ _____
   Non-slip surface material, not heavy carpet............ _____
   Minimum ramp width of 32 inches.................... _____
   Rise of no more than one foot for 12 feet of ramp...... _____

4. Handrails 32-38 inches wide, 30-32 inches high:
   Handrails at inside/outside ramps.................... _____
   Handrails at inside/outside steps, including steps to Bima. _____
   Handrails in traffic halls.......................... _____
   Handrails in washrooms and toilets.................. _____

Doors

1. Entry doors 36-38 inches wide (at least one door)....... _____
2. Inside doors 30-32 inches clear opening................ _____
3. Doors swing without conflict with wheelchairs. It is easier to open a door inward............................... _____
4. Vertical door handles or horizontal door bars, rather than slippery round knobs................................ _____
5. Blunt doorsills .... _____
6. Sliding doors with recessed lower channel. These are even better for wheelchairs than some swinging doors............ _____

Corridors

1. Corridors at least 36 inches wide. It takes at least 54 inches to turn a wheelchair................................ _____
2. Non-slip floors.................................. _____

Sanctuary

1. Accommodations for those on crutches or with walkers. One or two rows of seats or pews 32 inches apart......... _____
2. Accommodations for wheelchairs by removing a few rows of seats near the front, allowing space to maneuver comfortably _____
3. Non-slip, non-glare floors .... _____
4. Padded seats for some pews, or seat pads that can be handed out _____

Rest Rooms

1. Rest room entries 30-32 inches wide..................... _____
2. At least one stall 5 feet deep in the Men's and Women's Rooms, wide enough for a wheelchair 38 inches wide, and slide curtain or door that swings out........................ _____
3. Grab bars in the toilet seat stall, 30 inches high, extending 24 inches from midway of the commode; in the urinal stall, the bar fixed vertically to stabilize one on crutches......... _____
4. One washbasin 30 inches high for wheelchairs........... _____
5. Faucets easily handled with one hand.................. _____

Water Fountains

1. Water fountain spouts with controls up front .... _____
2. Placement not in alcove .... _____
3. Hand or Foot operated. Conventional water coolers can be improved by mounting a small fountain on the side, 30 inches from the floor................................... _____

Transportation Barriers

1. Synagogue near a bus stop.......................... _____
2. Parking near entrance of building..................... _____
3. Volunteer drivers and cars for synagogue activities........ _____
4. Volunteer drivers with vans with wheelchair ramps....... _____
5. Van with power lift for wheelchairs. This is necessary for people unable to transfer from chair to car with dignity. Lack of manageable transportation is a severe limit to participation in synagogue activities for many.................... _____

Lighting

1. Adequate light at book levels in all pews................ _____
2. Light from below the speaker's face to enliven and facilitate speech reading..................................... _____
3. Sight lines to speaker's face without glaring, bothersome lights _____
4. Sight lines to speaker's face without glaring window light. Flickering, scintillating light causes increased fatique for many visual or hearing impaired people.................... _____
5. Braille Siddurim, Chumashim, Machzorim, and Megillot.... _____
6. Large-print Siddurim, Chumashim, Machzorim, and Magillot for the partially sighted................................ _____

Amplification

1. A good sound system, without dead spots.............. _____
2. Earphones in some pews for hearing impaired........... _____
3. Possibility of an interpreter in sign language............. _____

June, 1986 MAZON Grant Allocations

1. SOVA

A kosher kitchen operating in the Los Angeles area. On June 11, 1986, they will open their third operation in the predominantly Jewish Beverly-Fairfax area, serving the needs of a rather elderly community. We have granted $1,250 to them to stock the shelves of their new center as it will give them a significant boost in their ability to feed the hungry of that specific community.

2. WEST PRESBYTERIAN CHURCH SENIOR CENTER

A center looking to improve the quality of life for the low income elderly of St. Louis. Helping them to remain in their homes as long as possible and providing them with at least one hot, nutritious meal per day as well as some important social inter-action.

They presently have 35 frail and disabled senior citizens on their waiting list for home-delivered meals. As of July 1, 1986, their federal funding will be cut 9.5%. Our grant of $1,250. would provide one home delivered meal per day, 5 days per week for those 35 elderly people for a period of 5 weeks. This gives them that short span of time to expand their efforts to get more funding from different elements of the community in order to replace the lost federal dollars.

3. MARYLAND FOOD COMMITTEE, Baltimore, MD.

A Grant of $1,250 will be earmarked for a "Tight Food Budget Poster Project". This is an educational outreach program to the very low income community in the state of Maryland that instructs these people as to how to stretch their meager food dollars in terms of types of foods that are most nutritious, quantities and sizes that are most economically purchased and other related information that will make these people more sophisticated in the process of their food buying.

The Maryland Food Committee is an educational and advocacy organization that does this and many other worthy projects for the betterment of the hungry community in Maryland and this country.

4. WILKINSON EMERGENCY SERVICE CENTER OF EAST DALLAS

Our grant of $1,250 will help this center feed a largely recent immigrant Asian population. This is a community that has not yet been able to integrate themselves socially and economically into the American society and live on a bare subsistence level. Our funds will be used directly to purchase food for their pantry to serve the growing numbers that are coming in each day to this very vital center.

5. FOUNDATION TO SUSTAIN RIGHTEOUS CHRISTIANS, Los Angeles, California

We have made a grant of $2,500 to support feeding programs of this foundation that has been organized in the Jewish community in the United

States to deal with the fact that there are numbers of "righteous Christians" in this country, in Europe and in Israel who, in 1986, find themselves destitute. The years since the Holocaust have not proved to be kind to these now-elderly people and it is felt that the American Jewish community is certainly obliged to sustain them in these, the last years of their lives. This program is headed by Rabbi Harold Schulweis, a member of the Mazon Board of Directors.

6. AMERICAN JEWISH WORLD SERVICE, Boston, Massachusetts

We have granted $10,000. for a small farmer agricultural development project in the country of Sri Lanka. This program will train local volunteers to work in their own country from an economic, social and agricultural level to develop projects viable for that area that can sustain 25 local communities. We find in this program innovation of method as well as the development of a program that will teach the local people to be self-sustaining.

7. WEEKEND MEALS FOR THE HOMEBOUND, New York City, NY

We have granted $2,500. to this exceptional program which supplements programs such as "Meals on Wheels" that occur on Monday through Friday, dealing with the homebound on the East side of New York City. It is vital that a supplemental week-end program serve these people as their level of subsistence is already very marginal.

BIBLIOGRAPHY

(A personal, non-exhaustive list)

I. BOOKS

1. *Annie's Coming Out,* Rosemary Crossley and Anne McDonald, Penguin books, 1982. (A *must.* An Ann Sullivan-Helen Keller type of story.)
2. *The Assisi Underground,* Alexander Ramati, Stein and Day, 1978. (Priests who rescued Jews in Italy during the Shoah.)
3. *The City of Joy,* Dominique Lapierre, Doubleday, 1985. (The author spends a number of month's in the slums of Calcutta.)
4. *Ethical Wills,* Rabbi Jack Riemer, Dr. Nathaniel Stampfer, Schocken, 1983.
5. *From Generation to Generation,* Arthur Kurzweil, William Morrow, 1980.
6. *Givers and Spenders - The Politics of Charity in Israel,* Eliezer Jaffe, Printiv, 1985.
7. *Hidden Survivors - Portraits of Poor Jews in America,* Thomas J. Cottle, Prentice-Hall, 1980. (Conversations with elderly poor Jews. Devastating.)
8. *The Kid Next Door (My Best Friend),* Robin Zimmerman, Robinell Publishing, Denver, 1983. (A young woman in Denver tells of her relationship to a friend who uses a wheelchair. Powerful for children and adults.)
9. *Lest Innocent Blood Be Shed,* Philip Mallie, Harper Colophon Books, 1980. (The village of Le Chambon in France protects its Jews during the Shoah)
10. *Minamata,* W. Eugene Smith, Holt, Rinehart and Winston, 1975. (Photo essay on victims of an industrial disaster.)
11. *The Moses of Rovno,* Douglas K. Huneke, Dodd, Mead, 1985. (Fritz Graebe, Righteous Christian, saves hundreds of Jews during the Shoah.)
12. *My Generations,* Arthur Kurzweil, Behrman House, 1983. (This, and 5, 59 help people discover the heroes in their families.)
13. *My Special Friend,* Floreva G. Cohen, Board of Jewish Education, NY, 1986, (Photo essay of a young Jewish child and his Jewish friend who has Down's Syndrome.)
14. *The Plague,* Albert Camus.
15. *The Quality of Mercy.* William Shawcross, Simon and Schuster, 1984. (Shawcross, son of one of the British prosecutors at Nuremberg, examines international relief efforts to Cambodia in 1979, in the context of other, larger issues.)

16. *Raoul Wallenberg, Angel of Rescue,* Harvey Rosenfeld, Prometheus Books, 1983
17. *Schindler's List,* Thomas Keneally, Penguin Books, 1983. A *must,* Oskar Schindler, Righteous Christian, saves many hundreds of Jews during the Shoah.)
18. *Summoned to Jerusalem, The Life of Henrietta Szold,* Joan Dash, Harper & Row, 1979.
19. *Trevor's Place, The Story of the Boy Who Brings Hope to the Homeless,* Frank and Janet Ferrell, Harper & Row, 1985.
20. *Wallenberg, The Man in the Iron Web,* Elenore Lester, Prentice-Hall, 1982.
21. *With Raoul Wallenberg in Budapest,* Per Anger, Holocaust Library, 1981.

II. STUDIES, MAGAZINES, ETC.

1. Caring for the Elderly: A Guide for Jewish Families, Diane Perry, Jewish Family and Children's Service, Baltimore.
2. Doing Good, New York Magazine, October 13, 1986.
3. Donors and Non-Donors for the United Jewish Appeal-Federation, Report on Surveys of, Penn & Schoen Associates, September, 1985.
4. Hunger in America, the Growing Epidemic, Physician's Task Force on Hunger in America, Harvard University School of Public Health, 1985.
5. Judaism and the Urban Poor, an Exploration of the Issues of Urban Poverty in the Light of Jewish Tradition, a Mini-Course, Rabbi Robert Goodman, Steven Moss, et al., Board of Jewish Education, Chicago and the Jewish Council on Urban Affairs, 1982.
6. The Maaser Form, Guide to, Rabbi Yechezkel Feldberger, Empire Press, 1985. (Like a tax form, but all about Tzedakah-giving.)
7. Products for People with Vision Problems, 26th Edition, 1980-1981, American Foundation for the Blind, 1980.
8. The Richest People in America, The *Forbes* Four Hundred, *Forbes Magazine,* 1986.
9. The Synagogue as a Caring Community, Union of American Hebrew Congregations.
10. Tips for Tabs (Temporarily Able Bodied), George Alderson, GHA Publications, Altoona, PA, 1985. (Guidelines for vocabulary concerning individuals with disabilities.)

III. MOVIES AND VIDEOTAPES

1. "Annie's Coming Out" (Also called "A Test of Love"), see I:1.
2. "Number Our Days", about the Israel Levin Center for elderly people in Venice, CA. (Oscar award winner.). Book available under same title.

3. Sally Fox on Tzedakah. Sally role plays five different Tzedakah situations. Excellent material for discussion (3-6 minute sketches). (Order: POB 3606 OSU Station, Columbus, OH 43210, 614-299-7320.)

4. "Where I want To Be", 30 minute video of residents of group home for retarded Jewish adults in Washington area. (Order: Jewish Foundation for Group Homes, 11710 Hunters Lane, Rockville, MD 20852, 301-984-3839.)

5. "Yad Sara", 12-minute tape of Yad Sara's activities in Israel. (Available through American Friends of Yad Sara, 1 Parker Plaza, Ft. Lee, NJ 07024, 201-944-6020, ATTN: Charles Bendheim.)

IV. GENERAL OVERALL RESOURCES FOR TZEDAKAH EDUCATIONAL MATERIALS

1. A.R.E. (Alternatives in Religious Education), 4505 S. Yosemite, #365, Denver, CO 80237, 303-770-2020.

2. CAJE (Coalition for Alternatives in Jewish Education) Program Bank, 486 Park Avenue S., Room 904, NY, NY 10016, 212-696-0740.

3. JESNA (Jewish Education Service of North America)-National Education Resource Center (NERC), 730 Broadway, NY, NY 10003, 212-260-0006.

4. Torah Aura Productions, 4423 Fruitland Ave., Los Angeles, CA 90058, 800-BE-TORAH.

5. USY (United Synagogue Youth) Tikkun Olam Publications, 155 5th Ave., NY, NY 10010, 212-533-7800.

V. MATERIAL FROM JEWISH EDUCATION AGENCIES

1. Baltimore - Board of Jewish Education, 5800 Park Heights Ave., Baltimore, MD 21215, various materials on the aged, hospitality, etc.

2. Boston - Bureau of Jewish Education, 333 Nahanton St., Newton Centre, MA 02159,, 617-965-7350, *Why Be Good? Sensitivities and Ethics in Rabbinic Literature.*

3. Houston - Commission for Jewish Education, 5603 S. Braeswood, Houston, Tx 77096, 713-729-7000, *Tzedakah is . . . Caring Through Sharing.*

4. New York - Board of Jewish Education, 426 W. 58th St., NY, NY 10019, 212-245-8200, various materials.

VI. THREE ADDITIONAL EXCELLENT TEACHING MATERIALS

1. *The Jewish Elderly: From Generation to Generation, An Experiential Approach,* Dorothy Herman, Central Agency for Jewish Education, 4200 Biscayne Blvd., Miami, Fl 33137.

2. *Tzedakah, Gemilut Chasadim and Ahavah, a Manual for World Repair,* Joel Grishaver and Beth Huppin, A.R.E., 4505 S. Yosemite, #365, Denver, CO 80237. (Marvellous for the classroom.)

3. . . . *Who Makes People Different: Jewish Perspectives on the Disabled*, Carl Astor, United Synagogue of America, Dept. of Youth Activities, 155 5th Ave., NY, NY 10010.

VII. ADDITIONAL FILMS (Suggested by my friend, Judy Kupchan, of the Teacher Center of the Board of Jewish Education of Greater Washington)

1. "Hundred and Two: Mature: The Art of Harry Lieberman", 28 minutes, 1980, Light-Saraf Films (16 mm), 131 Concord St., San Francisco, CA 94112. Harry Lieberman, accomplished primitif artist, who began painting at 86, and whose subjects are Jewish life in the Eastern European Shtetl-village, Biblical themes, and Hassidim.
2. "A Rock in the Road", 6 minutes, BFA Educational Media (16 mm), 13-A Jules Lane, New Brunswick, NJ 08901. An amusing, metaphorical trigger film on the issue of social responsibility.
3. "The Shopping Bag Lady", 21 minutes, Learning Corporation of America, 1350 Avenue of the Americas, NY, NY 10019 (16 mm). The story of a teen-ager's discovery of the human being "behind the bag lady", and the beginning of her sensitivity towards others.

VIII. ONE MORE FROM THE AUTHOR

"A Smile in Their Eyes" (video), American Friends of ALYN, 19 W. 44th St., #1418, NY, NY 10036. A glimpse inside ALYN Orthopaedic Hospital in Jersusalem, the life of those who live there, the greatness of Mitzvah work.

GLOSSARY

(H = Hebrew, Y = Yiddish)

Afikoman (H, from Greek): a piece of Matza hidden during the ritual of the Passover Seder. It is hidden early on during the evening's activities, and at the end, when a child finds it, he or she receives a reward.

Alef (H): first letter of the Hebrew alphabet.
Alef-Bayt (H): the Hebrew alphabet.

Aliyah (H): literally "going up." Either moving to Israel or going up to read from the Torah during religious services.

Aluf (H): in modern Hebrew — a champion or general. In some ancient texts it means a hero, mentor, instructor.

Avoda Zara (H): worshipping other gods, paganism.

Bal Tashchit (H): Literally, "do not destroy." Biblical injuction against willfully destroying anything. Applies also to wasting food.

Bar Mitzvah (H; fem.-Bat Mitzvah; fem. pl.-B'not Mitzvah): young Jew's ritual ceremony of entering Jewish adulthood, usually at age 13. Nowadays adults are also become bar/bat mitzvah, if they did not have such a ceremony when they were younger.

Bascherrt (Y): destined, something fated to happen.

Bat Mitzvah (H): see "Bar Mitzvah."

Bava Kamma, Bava Metzia, Bava Batra (Aramaic): sections of the Talmud dealing with civil law.

Bikkur Cholim (H): visiting the sick.

Bima (H): pulpit or reader's platform in the synagogue.

Bina (H): wisdom, insight.

Bushah (H): humiliation, embarrassment, shame.

Challah (H): loaves of bread made from twisted dough, baked specifically for the Sabbath and Jewish holidays.

Chametz (H): Literally "leavening." On Passover, all leavened bread, and products made with leaven are prohibited. The chametz is removed from the house before Passover begins.

Chanukah (H): Jewish holiday commemorating the victory of the Maccabees over the Greek-Syrian overlords, 2nd Century B.C.E. An anti-asssmilationist holiday, festival of religious freedom. (Also spelled Channukah, Hanukkah.)

Chanukat HaBayit (H): ceremony of dedication of a new home."Chanukah" means "dedication." One part of the ritual is the hanging of a Mezuza (see 'Mezuza').

Chassid (H): literally "righteous person, saint." Later, in the 18th century, it came to mean members of an Eastern European movement begun by the Baal Shem Tov. Chassidism is known for its sense of joy and ecstasy, particularly manifested in prayer, song, and dance. (Pl., Chassidim)

Chassiday Ummot HaOlam (H): Literally, "the righteous ones of the nations of the world", referring to non-Jews who risked their own lives to save Jews during the Shoah-Holocaust.

Chaver (H): friend, colleague.

Chavurah (H): a group of individuals who gather for religious purposes of praying or study, communal meals, or other Jewish activities.

Chessed Shel Emes (H-Y): a burial society. Literally, "the true act of love",because those who perform the preparation of the body and the burial can have no expectation of compensation from the deceased.

Chevra (H): a group, society, group of friends.

Chevra Kaddisha (H, Aramaic): The Holy Society; a burial society.

Chozzen (H-Y, also Chazzan): the cantor for religious services.

Chumash (H): the Five Books of Moses, Genesis-Deuteronomy.

Davvin (Y): to pray.

Edel (Y): noble, gentle, genteel.

Ehrlich (Y): honest, having integrity.

Emmes (Y-H; also Emet): the truth.

Falasha (Ethiopic): term formerly used for Ethiopian Jews, but since it is a negative, outcasting term used by non-Jewish Ethiopians, it is no longer acceptable.

Farsi: the language of Iran, Iranian.

Fein (Y): fine.

Frailach (Y): happy, joyous.

Galitzianers (Y): Jews who came from the part of Poland known as Galicia.

Gemillut Chassadim (H): acts of caring, loving kindness.

Genayvah/Gezaylah (H): types of stealing and robbery.

Geschrei (Y): a cry, an outcry.

Grob (Y): coarse.

Hachnassat Orchim (H): the Mitzvah of hospitality.

Haftorah (H): a selection of readings from the Prophets, read at synagogue services. A bar/bat mitzvah celebrant usually reads the Haftorah if there is a bar/bat mitzvah occasion that week.

Haggadah (H): the book containing the liturgy for the Passover-night rituals (Seder-ritual).

Halachah (H): Jewish law.

Halbashat Arumim (H): the Mitzvah of providing clothes for those who need them.

Hashavat Avaydah (H): the Mitzvah of returning lost objects.

Hatavat Chalom (H): the ceremony of "Making Dreams Better" for people who have had bad dreams.

Hin Tzedek (H): "A just measure", referring to the Mitzvah of having honest weights and measures.

Ish Kasher (H): "a Kosher person", a Mensch, a decent human being.

Kappara (H): expiation, atonement, forgiveness.

Kavod (H): dignity, self-respect, honor.

Kaylim (H): instruments, utensils, tools, vehicles.

Keren Ami (H): the Tzedakah fund of many religious schools.

Kiddush (H): the blessing over wine. (Literally "sanctification")

Kinderlach (Y, sing -kind): affectionate diminutive term for children.

Kohen (H, pl. Kohanim): a priest.

Kol Nidray (H-Aramaic): a prayer recited the evening of Yom Kippur as the Holy Day begins.

Ladino: the language of Sefardi Jews, Jews who came from Oriental countries originally from Spain — Turkey, Greece, the Island of Rhodes, etc. A combination of Spanish, Hebrew, and other local words.

LeShaym Shamayim (H): for the sake of Heaven.

Litvak (Y): a Jew from Lithuania.

Ma'asim Tovim (H): good deeds.

Machzor (H): prayerbook for the High Holidays.

Magen David Adom (H): The Red Star of David, comparable to the Red Cross in other countries.

Malach (H, pl.-Malachim): an angel.

Massechet (H): a section of the Talmud; e.g., Chagiga, Kallah.

Matza (H): unleavened bread eaten on Passover.

Mazal (H; Y = Mazel): luck.

Mazon (H): food.

Megilla (H, pl.-Megillot): literally "a scroll", often referring to the Biblical books of Esther, Ecclesiastes, Song of Songs, Lamentations, and Ruth. Copies of the 5 Scrolls together are often kept in synagogues with the prayerbooks, as they are read at various times of the year.

Mensch (Y; adj.-Menschlich; abstract-Menschlichkeit): an upright, responsible, decent, caring, compassionate person.

Meshuggah (Y, var.-Meshuggeh): crazy.

Mezuza (H, pl.-Mezuzot): a small container holding an inscription from the Torah that is hung on the doorposts of Jewish houses, according to instructions in Deuteronomy chapter 6.

Midrash (H): Jewish literature from the first 7 or 8 centuries of the Common Era containing stories, aphorisms, and other narratives. Any non-legal portion of Rabbinic Literature. Also used for a specific story or tale.

Minyan (H): a quorum of ten needed for congregational prayer.

Mishigoss (Y): craziness.

Mitn Tochiss Ofn Tisch (Y): literally, "with the rear end on the table", figuratively, with your cards on the table, speaking frankly.

Mitzvah (H): literally "commandment" or "instruction"— good deeds done by people according to the prescriptions of traditional Jewish texts, such as visiting the sick, comforting mourners, and giving Tzedakah. Used frequently in this book as a synonym for Tzedakah.

Momzer (H-Y, pl.-Momzerim): a bastard. Pejorative term for someone you really don't like.

Nachas (Y): satisfaction.　To "shep nachas" is to get satisfaction from something — often used in relation to one's children.

Oleh (H, pl.-Olim): someone who moves to Israel.
Oneg (H): delight. "Oneg Shabbat" means the "delight of the Sabbath" and often refers to the cookies and cake and coffee after Friday night services.

Pesach (H): Passover.
Poilische Yiddn (Y): Jews from Poland.
Prost (Y): crude, peasantlike, coarse.
Purim (H): Jewish holiday celebrating the victory of the Jews of Persia over the wicked Haman. The holiday is celebrated with great joy, dancing, parades, masks, and merrymaking.
Pushka (Y): a Tzedakah box.

Rachmoniss (Y): compassion.
Rambam (H): Maimonides, the great Jewish philosopher and legal giant of the 12th Century.
Rav (H): Rabbi.
Refusenik: a Soviet Jew who has been refused on his request to emigrate.
Rosh HaShanah (H): the Jewish New Year.

Schmooze (Y): to chat.
Schvitz (Y): to sweat, also, a sauna.
Seder (H): Passover-night ritual of reciting the tale of the Exodus from Egypt. (Pl.-Sedarim)
Sefardi (H): a Jew from Oriental countries; non-European Jews. Originally Jews who were expelled from Spain in 1492.
Sefer Torah (H): the scroll of the Torah, handwritten text, in scroll form of the Five Books of Moses.
Shabbat (H., also Shabbas): the Sabbath.
Shaliach (H, fem.-Shelichah): messenger, agent.
Shayn (Y, abstract-Shaynkeit): beautiful, having a beautiful soul.
Shemirat HaMet (H): the Mitzvah of watching a body from the time of death until the time of burial.
Shiva (H): literally 'seven'. The seven days of mourning when the mourners remain at home. Religious services are conducted there and comforters come to express their words of consolation.
Shlep (Y): to drag.
Shoah (H): The Holocaust.
Shul (Y): a synagogue.
Shulchan Aruch (H): major code of Jewish Law.
Siddur (H): prayerbook.

Simcha (H): joy, a joyous occasion.

Sincha Shel Mitzvah (H): the joy of performing a Mitzvah.

Sinchat Torah (H): the holiday celebrating having completed, and having started again, the reading of the Torah.

Siyyum (H): ceremony celebrating the completion of section of study of the Talmud.

Sukkot (H): holiday in the Fall celebrating God's protecting care Jews while they wandered in the wilderness for 40 years.

Ta'anit Chalòm (H): a fast to counteract the effects of a bad dream.

Tallis (H, also-Tallit): a shawl-like garment with ritual fringes (Tzitzit) on the four corners, worn by Jews during morning prayers.

Talmid (H): student.

Talmud (H): immense compendium of discussions, tales, aphorisms, legal give-and-take, and insights about Judaism, developed in Jewish academies (Yeshivot) during the first five centuries of the Common Era.

Tchatchkas (Y): toys.

Teshuvah (H): (1) a legal reply to an inquiry about Jewish law. (2) repentance.

Tikkun Olam (H): fixing up the world.

Tikvah (H): hope, also the name for a program at Camps Ramah for special children.

Tochiss (Y): rear-end. See 'Mitn Tochiss . . . '

Torah (H): literally "teaching". Originally meaning the Five Books of Moses, expanded to include the entirety of Jewish study and learning.

Tzaddik (H, pl.-Tzaddikim, fem.-Tzadeket): a righteous person.

Tzedek (H): justice.

Tzuriss (Y): woes, worries, troubles.

Yad VaShem (H): the main memorial to the Holocaust in Jerusalem.

Yarmulka (Y): a head covering.

Yasher Koach (H): literally, "May you be strong." A statement of well-wishing, recited to someone who has just done a Mitzvah.

Yerushalayim (H): Jerusalem.

Yeshiva (H): a school for Jewish study, academy.

Yiddn (Y, sing.-Yid): Jews.

Yom Kippur (H): the Day of Repentance. Most solemn day of the Jewish calendar.

Zamler (Y): literally, 'Gatherer'. People who gather books for the National Yiddish Book Center.

Zechut (H) : a privilege.

Ziess (Y, abstract-Ziesskeit): sweet.

DANNY SIEGEL is a free-lance author, poet, and lecturer who resides in Rockville, Maryland, when not on his speaking tours or in Israel distributing Tzedakah monies. He is the author of five books of poetry, four of which are now out of print, as well as two anthologies of his selected writings.

Danny is the author of a book of essays and three anthologies on the subject of Midrash and Halachah. He is also co-author with Allan Gould of a book of Jewish humor, and tapes of his poetry readings and humor presentations have been produced.

Siegel is a popular lecturer at synagogues, Jewish federations, community centers, conventions, and retreats, where he teaches Tzedakah and Jewish values and recites from his works. His books and talks have received considerable acclaim throughout the entire North American Jewish community.

The publication of *Gym Shoes and Irises, Book Two,* rounds out Danny's devotion to the "how-to" of personalized Tzedakah begun many years before the issuance of the first *Gym Shoes and Irises,* in 1982.

TZEDAKAH NOTES

TZEDAKAH NOTES

TZEDAKAH NOTES

TZEDAKAH NOTES